To my favorite niece —
Knowing your interest in
sailing —

with all my love
Uncle Gene

Atlantic

The Last Great Race of Princes

Scott Cookman

John Wiley & Sons, Inc.

For my parents, Jane and Leon Cookman,
who showed me that reading and sailing
made fine passages to wonderful places.

This book is printed on acid-free paper ∞

Copyright © 2002 by Scott Cookman. All rights reserved

Published by John Wiley & Sons, Inc.
Published simultaneously in Canada

Design and production by Navta Associates, Inc.

This publication is designed to provide accurate and authoritative information in regard to the subject matter covered. It is sold with the under-
standing that the publisher is not engaged in rendering professional
services. If professional advice or other expert assistance is required, the
services of a competent professional person should be sought.

ISBN 0-471-41076-4

Printed in the United States of America

10 9 8 7 6 5 4 3 2 1

Contents

Acknowledgments

This book would have been impossible without the gracious assistance of the New York Yacht Club (NYYC). I'm especially indebted to NYYC members Dick Thursby and Rich von Doenhoff, who opened the club's library and archives to me and also helped open doors at Britain's Royal Yacht Squadron. The expert, selfless assistance of the club's librarian, Bill Watson, was simply invaluable.

On the other side of the Atlantic, I'm indebted to Major Robin Rising of the Royal Yacht Squadron (RYS) for access to its holdings on the 1905 race. Diana Harding, RYS archivist, deserves special thanks for copies of original logs, charts, and much more. Accredited Public Record Office (PRO) military and naval researcher Bob O'Hara was instrumental in spearheading the RYS effort (during Cowes Week, no less).

Thanks is also due to the professionals at Mystic Seaport, the Museum of America and the Sea: Wendy Schnur, reference assistant at Mystic's G. W. Blunt White Library; Victoria Sharps, cataloger Rosenfeld Collection; Philip Budlong, associate curator; and Peggy Tate Smith, rights and reproductions coordinator.

For the book's superlative illustrations, charts, and tables, the conceptual and technical expertise of artist-yachtsman John Lane is fully and gratefully acknowledged.

Special thanks go to my assistant, Margaret Martin, for biographical and photo research and administrative and manuscript production assistance.

The encouragement and direction provided by my editor at John Wiley & Sons, Hana Umlauf Lane, was of inestimable value.

I must also recognize my sole, constant companion during the writing of this book: a stray alleycat named Mooglie, who adopted me when the manuscript was begun and remained largely draped atop the computer monitor until it was finished.

CHAPTER 1

The Great Ocean Race

It was the final, privileged tournament of a gilded age: the last great race of princes, whether titled by birth in the Old World or minted by money in the New.

It pitted the emperor of Germany, two British lords, and eight American millionaires against one another in a winner-take-all yacht race, without handicaps or time allowances, across the breadth of the North Atlantic—considered by mariners as "the vilest ocean for weather on the planet." Money was no obstacle or incentive. Prestige—winning the solid gold German Kaiser's Cup for nautical supremacy on the high seas—was all that mattered.

Eleven of the fastest, most opulent yachts ever built participated—including masterpieces by legendary yacht designers such as George Lennox Watson, William Fife Jr., Edward Burgess, and John Beavor Webb. Outfitted without regard to expense, their owners included Kaiser Wilhelm II, perhaps the wealthiest monarch in Europe; the twenty-sixth earl of Crawford, among the richest peers in the British Empire; Allison Armour, heir to the vast Armour meat-packing fortune; American steel heir Edward Coleman Esq., prodigal son of Andrew Carnegie's business partner; Wall Street banking heir Edmond Randolph; and Broadway stagecoach heir Wilson Marshall, to name a few. The vessels were skippered by perhaps the single greatest assemblage of professional yacht racing captains in history. They included *three-time* America's Cup winner Charlie Barr; transatlantic yachting record-holder James Loesch; legendary Gloucester fishing skipper Tommie Bohlin; and Lemuel Miller, winner of the 1904 Cape May, Brenton's Reef, and Astor Cups, something of the Triple Crown of ocean racing at the time. They crossed the starting line off Sandy Hook, New Jersey, at 12:15 P.M. on May 18, 1905.

Before them yawned the North Atlantic, a trackless, largely islandless expanse of 10,588,000 square miles of open ocean—an area three times the size of the United States. By the most direct, great circle course, the finish line at the Lizard, a rocky headland in Cornwall at the westernmost tip of Britain, lay 2,875 nautical miles (3,305 statute miles) away—roughly the distance from Moscow to Beijing. In between lurked the Nantucket Shoals; Georges Bank; Cape Cod; Sable Island's notorious "graveyard of ships"; the Eastern Shoals, 100 miles off Cape Race; near-perpetual fog and foul weather on the Grand Banks; icebergs in hundreds adrift from Greenland; man-killing water temperatures; gales; monstrous mid-ocean seas; and sudden, almost unbelievably violent cyclonic storms. For the yachts contesting for the Kaiser's Cup—completely under sail, without benefit of modern-day weather forecasts or ice reports, without radio or any means of communication beyond signal flags and lamps, and without radar or global positioning systems, wholly dependent upon sun or star sights to fix their position—it was a very hazardous proposition. For twelve days in the spring of 1905, the world watched—horrified and enthralled.

Incredibly, when it was over, the winner had set a monohull transatlantic racing record that has yet to be beaten.

After the race itself, however, all its participants—winners and losers—were caught up and swept away by unforeseen events. Some in the so-called Great War. Others by the Great Depression. All of them in the end of an age that had seemed timeless.

Before the world turned upside down, however, there were no wealthier, more powerful, or more daring men than those who raced across the Atlantic in 1905 for the Kaiser's Cup. This is their story.

The World of 1905

Man has not reached the North or the South Poles.

There is no Panama Canal.

By steamship, it takes a week to cross the Atlantic. By express train, it takes more than three days to cross the United States.

The British Empire, largest in history, rules a fifth of the earth's landmass and 375 million subjects—a quarter of its population. London is the globe's economic, military, and diplomatic capital.

The United States is a second-rate power.

Three out of five Americans still live on farms, without plumbing, electricity, or telephones. Outside major cities, virtually no roads are paved. Few Americans have ever seen an automobile. According to the 1900 census, fewer than 5,000 are produced annually (1,681 coal-powered steamers, 1,575 battery-powered electrics, and but 936 newfangled gas-powered models).

The average American laborer earns $12.98 per week (for 59 hours of work), or about $675 a year. It does not go far. Annually the *New York Times* estimates it costs an average American family $200 in rent (homeownership is out of reach for all but the well-to-do), $200 for food, and $150 for clothing. There are no vaccines for measles, mumps, chicken pox, typhus, diphtheria, influenza, or polio. Life expectancy is 47.3 years.

For rich Americans, however, it is wonderful time to be alive.

There is no Federal income tax. No inheritance tax. No Federal Reserve Bank. No Securities and Exchange Commission, no Commodities Trading Commission, no Federal Trade Commission. There are no unions to speak of. No labor laws. No minimum wage. A handful of imperially wealthy American capitalists either own or control production of an estimated 90 percent of the world's oil, 37 percent of its steel, 34 percent of its iron, and 32 percent of its coal. Family dynasties run the nation's railroads (Vanderbilts, Harrimans, Goulds), banks (Morgans, Belmonts), and its commodities (Armours, Swifts, Morrises, Cudahys), shipbuilding (Cramps), and tobacco industries (Dukes, Lorillards).

The U.S. map looks starkly different. The Philippines are a colony. Arizona, New Mexico, Oklahoma, Alaska, and Hawaii are territories, not states. Buffalo, New York, is the nation's up-and-coming city—with four times the population of little-known Los Angeles.

America's national pastime looks different, too. In baseball's National League, the New York Highlanders (ancestors of the Yankees) confront the Boston Pilgrims (ancestors of the Red Sox). In the American League, the Brooklyn Superbas (father of the Brooklyn Dodgers and grandfather of the Los Angeles Dodgers) face off against the New York Giants (ancestors of the San Francisco Giants).

Paper clips, picture postcards, safety razors, ice-cream cones, and the Yellow Pages are among the latest fads.

Internationally, Russia and Japan are at war.

An unknown Swiss patent worker named Einstein has just published three arcane theories on physics. The one concerning relativity excites the least interest.

Puccini's opera *Madame Butterfly* opens at La Scala—a public failure.

Kaiser Wilhelm II of Germany, who will precipitate the bloodbath of the First World War nine years later, issues a challenge for an international, transatlantic yacht race, the first ever. It will be run boat against boat, with no handicaps or time allowances. The prize is a fantastic, solid gold trophy cup.

Like the race, it is of his own design—intended for his own special purpose.

Land Fading in the West

Was the thing sensible anyhow? It was the North Atlantic.
That the month was May and not far removed from summer
was true. But it was the North Atlantic . . . *the vilest ocean*
for weather on the planet.

—Paul Eve Stevenson,
yawl *Ailsa*

*N*inety-eight miles offshore, Paul Stevenson, special correspondent
for the yachting magazine Rudder assigned to cover the 1905 German Emperor's Cup transatlantic race, awoke bewildered. A westerly wind stripped away the early morning rain and mist, revealing
a stark 360-degree expanse of empty, lead-colored ocean. There was
no sign of the other ten "grand yachts" that had crossed the starting line with Ailsa eighteen hours before. The fleet of spectator boats
that had blackened the waters around Sandy Hook, New Jersey, had
vanished. The only thing that remained was little Ailsa, second-
smallest yacht in the race, rolling beneath his feet. She was all that
was left between him and the immensity of the North Atlantic.

The noon sight showed they'd logged fewer than 100 miles since
the start. Despite all Captain Lem Miller had done, Ailsa had averaged a dismal speed of only 4 knots (fewer than 5 miles per hour,
the pace of a brisk walk). That left almost 3,000 nautical miles of

angry, open ocean to the finish line at the Lizard, the treacherous headland off England's southwestern coast.

Miller hove the lead to sound the depth. It showed 32 fathoms (192 feet), the sea bottom black-speckled sand and gravel—a sign they were still over the long, downward-sloping continental shelf, not quit of America, not yet over the abyssal depths of the North Atlantic. The skipper took the water temperature, too. It registered 50 degrees Fahrenheit—cold enough to kill a man overboard in an hour.

It was a discouraging beginning to what Rudder had for weeks been calling the "Great Ocean Race." The start had been postponed a day because of blinding fog that had made a shambles of everything. With less than a quarter-mile visibility, some competing yachts had anchored in the protective Horseshoe Bay behind Sandy Hook, others in New York's Lower Bay, others back near Staten Island. At about dawn, a tugboat towing a long line of garbage barges in from sea had materialized out of the gloom on top of the anchored American yacht Fleur de Lys—the smallest boat in the race. Veering to avoid a collision, the last barge in the tug's towline swung out and struck her squarely amidships. It tore away 40 feet of her rail and bulwarks.

Behind Sandy Hook, the big, new British Cunard luxury liner Caronia, carrying spectators, lost her bearings. She grounded on the East Knolls Bank, her fine bow buried 10 feet deep in sand and mud. It would take two days for tugboats to drag her off. The chartered passenger steamer Sirius, crammed with Atlantic and Indian Harbor Yacht Club members to see the start of the race, blundered out of the main shipping channel in the fog and grounded as well. The tugboat Vigilant, carrying the racing committee, caught fire when an overheated smokestack ignited the roof of her deckhouse. While battling the blaze, she ran afoul of the fishing pounds off Sandy Hook and grounded on a sandbank. The fleet of steamers, ferries, and launches come to watch the start of the race muddled around, narrowly missing one another in the pea soup fog. When they learned of the postponement, they beat a retreat back to New York.

The next day had dawned no better. There was more fog, rain, and a dead calm. By midmorning, however, a very light breeze of *about 6 knots whisked away the fog. But it was a headwind out of the east, blowing directly in from the sea, the worst possible wind for starting the race. None of the competing yachts could reach the starting line under sail. All eleven were ignominiously towed out to the line between the race committee boat and the Sandy Hook lightship.*

Two of the biggest—the British square-rigger Valhalla *(245 feet long) and the American three-masted schooner* Utowana *(198 feet)—fouled the starting line and had to return and start again.* Ailsa, *by virtue of her small size (127 feet long overall, 90 feet at the waterline) and racing yawl rig, made the most of the gentle headwind. To Stevenson's delight, she was first over the line.*

But five seconds behind her charged the American two-masted schooner Hildegarde *(134 feet), followed twenty-five seconds later by the big American three-masted schooner* Atlantic *(184 feet). Thirty seconds afterward came the American schooner* Endymion

The William Fife Jr.-designed racing yawl *Ailsa* was first of eleven wickedly fast yachts over the starting line in the 3,000-mile Kasier's Cup transatlantic race.

(136 feet) and thirty seconds after that German kaiser Wilhelm II's black-hulled schooner Hamburg *(158 feet). Less than a half hour later, the fog rolled in again—thick and white—and all the yachts were lost to view. Stevenson, reporter's notebook in hand, could see nothing to report.*

For the rest of the day Ailsa *tacked ghostlike into a blur. At nightfall, the wind hauled around from east to west and freshened. By midnight it was blowing hard, with driving rain. Stevenson didn't sleep much. The crew made six sail changes during the night, but he understood none of the deck orders. Though she flew the American flag and the burgee of the New York Yacht Club, Stevenson and two other "guests" were the sole Americans aboard.*

Her owner, millionaire Wall Street investment banker Henry S. Redmond, had remained ashore. He told the press he was too busy with work to accompany his vessel in a race that might take weeks; the newspapers acidly hinted he was the only owner too busy—or too frightened—to do so. He would follow her progress from the New York Yacht Club's palatial new headquarters on West Forty-fourth Street. He was represented on board by his friend Grenville Kane, an amateur yachtsman who fancied himself an accomplished navigator, and Henry Reuterdahl, a maritime artist. Stevenson had accepted Kane's last-minute invitation to chronicle Ailsa's *quest for the cup. All three Americans were strangers to one another.* Ailsa's *crew was stranger still.*

Captain Miller, as Stevenson recorded, was "a hardy native of North Germany with a small springy body" and fierce handlebar mustache. He spoke English with a heavy German accent, but most of the time, out of necessity, he spoke German, Swedish, or Norwegian. The first mate, Christian Olstadt, was a Swede. Stevenson judged him "evidently a good seaman" but could not be certain. The man spoke "entirely unintelligible English with stunning rapidity." Second Mate Jonathan Svensen was Norwegian, "compact, agile, vigilant and muscular—the right bower [turn-of-the-twentieth-century jargon for anchor] in a close call or mistake at sea" who spoke little English whatsoever.

The ship's cook spoke no English at all. He was a Dane who Stevenson noted was "a sample of the majesty buried in Den-

mark." Whether this meant he was a majestic cook, royally laconic, or a good cheese gone bad, Stevenson didn't say. The ship's steward, on the other hand, was a gaunt Englishman "with astonishing powers of sustained monologue." He was "constantly congratulating Great Britain for having given him birth." The instant they'd crossed the starting line, he pronounced, "We're 'eaded for Gawd's country now," a phrase he never tired of repeating. Stevenson, staring at the maw of the North Atlantic, didn't see God's country.

The rest of Ailsa's crew numbered eighteen, all of them Norwegians. Through Miller, Stevenson was assured to learn that some were "big, deep-water men, just in from Cape Horn or the Spice Islands of the East after a half a year at sea." Others were "from the steel meshes of our great buildings—for the spiders that weave the metal webs twenty-five stories above our heads and the men who bride our greatest rivers are recruited from the sailor lads, the boys who whistle at the tempest on the yardarm."

That is, at least, what Captain Miller told him. Ailsa had been the last boat out of the yards before the race and the last to fill out her crew. Her men certainly weren't the best available, they were the best Miller could scrape together before setting sail. Most had never raced before. None had worked together. None had had more than a few days to get to know Ailsa.

Miller himself was a paradox. Ships' captains usually are. But Miller (formerly Mueller) was a sublime paradox. He was a German driving an all-Scandinavian crew to win a trophy—offered by his sovereign—for a millionaire American yacht owner he barely knew. More than that, he was racing against an old friend and mentor, the legendary Captain Charles Barr, who—somewhere on the empty ocean all around—was at the helm of Miller's pride and joy and previous command, Atlantic.

If Stevenson had been writing fiction, he couldn't have invented the irony of it. Miller had been Barr's first mate in three America's Cup winners: Columbia (1899 and 1901) and Reliance (1903). As such Miller had acted, quite literally, as Barr's eyes. At the helm, Barr controlled the all-important mainsail, but in his position at the wheel he couldn't see the almost equally important headsails. These were under the immediate charge of Miller, the first mate. As yachting journalist William E. Simmons wrote at the time, "This officer must be a man of good judgement, for if the headsails are not properly trimmed the yacht will not make her best speed." (1) Miller had helped Barr make speeds fast enough to win three America's Cup challenges, sweeping Shamrock I *by as much as ten minutes in 1899 and edging* Shamrock II *by thirty-five seconds in 1901. In* Reliance *in 1903 he and Barr beat* Shamrock III *by a bit over a minute. In these latter close races, the trim and draught of Miller's headsails probably contributed as much to victory as Barr's flawless helmsmanship. They had been a perfect team, an unbeatable duo.*

Following those victories, like most professional racing skippers of the time, each man had gone on to richer, full-time employment skippering rich men's yachts. Barr went to work for American railroad millionaire Morton Plant, skippering his schooner Ingomar *to an unprecedented string of racing victories in Europe at the Cowes and Kiel Regattas in 1904. Miller took a similar job with American millionaire Wilson Marshall, heir to his father's stagecoach fortune, racing his steel-hulled, state-of-the-art schooner* Atlantic. *Miller worked for Marshall for two years, taking him on cruises to the West Indies, making the outside races and squadron runs of the New York Yacht Club. In 1904, Miller had won for Marshall the Cape May, Brenton's Reef, and Astor Cups, all of them relatively long ocean races at the time.*

But early in 1905, as soon as Marshall entered Atlantic *in the Kaiser's Cup race, Miller was fired. He was given virtually no notice. He was undoubtedly shocked to discover that his replacement was Barr. Marshall had wanted a "name" skipper for the big race, and Lem Miller wasn't a big enough name.*

The whole thing went down hard with the proud Miller. Suddenly unemployed, he was forced to take the only job

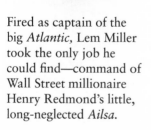

Fired as captain of the big *Atlantic*, Lem Miller took the only job he could find—command of Wall Street millionaire Henry Redmond's little, long-neglected *Ailsa*.

offered him. Worse, he had to haggle about salary to get it. It wasn't much: command of Henry Redmond's long-neglected yawl Ailsa, *a pip-squeak in size and speed to his beloved* Atlantic. *Nonetheless, it was a job and, more importantly, a crack at the Kaiser's Cup. His orders from Redmond were unequivocal: win the race "with safety and despatch [sic]." From the moment he took the job, Miller focused relentlessly on Redmond's powerful accent on dispatch, not showing much interest in the safety part.*

It was the forgotten safety part that haunted Stevenson that first snail-gray morning at sea. Indeed, Ailsa's *participation in a transatlantic race had been universally questioned before the start. Of all the yachts entered, she was the only one not designed for ocean work. She was a racer—pure Whippet—designed by Scotsman William Fife Jr. of the fabulous yacht-designing "Fifes of Fairlie," whose creations "were a guarantee of their speed." But she was what today would be called an inshore racer, built to race in relatively protected European waters at Clyde, Cowes, or Kiel, or in America's Cape May or Brenton's Reef offshore races. She was never intended for open ocean racing.*

She was light- and low-built for speed. To reduce weight, the dimensions of her beams and frames were finer and more delicate than those of oceangoing yachts. In a sense, her skeleton was fish-boned when it ought to have been whale-boned to weather an Atlantic crossing. Likewise, she was thin-skinned, her planking less than 1 inch thick. The seams between planks were caulked with a patent "stopping mixture," which never set hard enough to crack when the seams worked in a seaway, meaning that in rough water, the planking contracted, expanded, and flexed like skin. What's more, she had only 5 feet of freeboard to keep the monstrous waves of the Atlantic from climbing her sides. How her light, elastic hull, standing only 60 inches above the water, would survive the pounding mid-Atlantic, where storms whip seas white to the point of invisibility and raise waves 45 feet high, was unknowable.

That was scarcely the only unknowable weighing heavily on Stevenson's mind. The boat's tenuous rig concerned him more. Originally designed by Fife as a cutter (a single mainmast), she had been rerigged as a yawl (mainmast and much smaller mizzenmast or jiggermast, stepped behind her helm) to increase her speed. This modification won her many inshore races on both sides of the Atlantic. She had won the 1902 Astor Cup racing against legendary American designer Nathaniel Herreshoff's America's Cup defender Vigilant, *which was testament in volumes to Ailsa's speed. But in a race* across *the Atlantic, her racing yawl rig was thought to be far too delicate and frail.*

She was, pointedly, the only yawl entered in the race. Yachtsman *magazine had been blunt in its criticism: "How this rig will fare in mid-Atlantic is a question." Stevenson's employer,* Rudder *magazine, had been even blunter, calling* Ailsa *"a most unsuitable type of vessel for ocean racing and it is most surprising that she was allowed to enter."*

Redmond bought her in the spring of 1901, raced her for two years, and—growing bored with the sport or the expense—had put her away like a spoiled child's plaything. She'd been out of commission for two years—hauled out of the water and sitting in a cradle at City Island—when Redmond hurriedly entered her in the race. A survey revealed her fastenings badly eaten away and most of her planking rotten. Though she received a complete refit (some said rebuilding) at the yacht yards of Tams, Lemoine, & Crane in New York, nobody knew if the repairs would hold up in heavy winds off Long Island, much less in mid-Atlantic.

There had been no opportunity for a real sea trial under sail before the race: just day sails on Long Island Sound and one or two brief jogs outside New York's Lower Bay. No time to really test her new mainmast (which was 5 feet taller), new topmast, spinnaker boom, or her new rigging (both standing and running) or new sails. No time to test her new rudder post or rudder. No time really for Captain Miller to learn anything about her or the stresses she could stand. Even with trials, there was no telling if she could weather mid-Atlantic storms blowing 48 to 55 knots. In violent winds of up to 60 knots, she could come apart.

Stevenson knew all this in the pit of his stomach. He was no neophyte to yachting or racing. Writing about both was his stock-in-trade. He himself described Ailsa *as "a fragile, composite [wood planking on steel frames], little ninety-foot [LWL] racer, with a single mast, if you didn't count the sapling [mizzenmast] in the stern." In fact, his assessment was generous.* Ailsa *was but 89 feet long at the waterline. Only the American entry* Fleur de Lys, *with a waterline length of 86 feet, was smaller. But* Fleur de Lys *was a staunch-rigged two-masted schooner, designed "chiefly for ocean work," with the "reputation of being the strongest built boat ever turned out" of Bath, Maine, a shipbuilding town famous for stoutly-built, seagoing vessels. In comparison, Stevenson called* Ailsa *"a spoon-faced racer as frail as an egg."*

Even more worrisome was her captain. The New York Times *disturbingly reported that "with Lem Miller, mate to Capt. Barr on* Columbia *and* Reliance, *and former sitting master of* Atlantic, *an acknowledged dare-devil, in charge there are those who say they would not want to sail on her." Part of this fear stemmed from the fact that* Ailsa *wasn't an oceangoing or particularly seaworthy boat in the first place. The fact that she'd practically been rebuilt was another. But a good part of it was due to Captain Miller himself. He was a man out to prove he could do what nobody—Marshall, Barr, or the press—thought he could do: win the Kaiser's Cup in* Ailsa. *As the* Times *cannily observed, he was prepared to do anything to prove it. In an open ocean race, that made a very dangerous combination.*

Despite misgivings, Stevenson jumped at the invitation to sail in her. It promised to make his career. He would be the only journalist to cover the ocean race firsthand, start to finish, from aboard one of the competing yachts. His bylined story would be trumpeted in Rudder, *the preeminent American yachting magazine of its time, whose stern-faced editor, Thomas Fleming Day, a pioneer of ocean yacht racing, had no tolerance for failure. And Stevenson had signed a handsome book contract to write about the race afterward. All that promised notoriety and quite a lot of money.*

Prior to the start, he dismissed the dangers of sailing in Ailsa: *"Wouldn't that be just the spice of it all," he wrote, "this three-thousand mile dash across rough water in a ninety-footer?"*

It would be—if he survived. In the first transatlantic yacht race, six men hadn't.

CHAPTER 4

Death Race

The bets [on the 1866 race] were the largest stakes in any sporting event well into the next century, and they were shocking.

—Queene Hooper Foster,
New York Yacht Club
Heritage Series lecturer

The idea for the first transatlantic yacht race had arisen during a dispute over dinner among four young American millionaires. On a freezing December evening in 1866 at New York's exclusive Union Club—somewhere between the wine and the brandy—they began bragging about their yachts. The discussion turned heated about which was fastest.

James Gordon Bennett Jr., heir to his father's *New York Herald* newspaper fortune, claimed it was his deep-keeled, 107-foot schooner *Henrietta*. Pierre Lorillard, heir to his family's tobacco empire, argued it was his 110-foot centerboard schooner *Vesta*. George and Franklin Osgood, heirs to their family's investment banking fortune, insisted it was their 106-foot racer *Fleetwing*. "One word led to another," reported the *New York Times*, "proposition followed proposition, claim followed claim." The argument quickly boiled into a "put up or shut up" match of epic proportion, with each millionaire outdaring the other in a monumental game of chicken.

Only a race could decide the issue: boat-on-boat. But it had to be a defining race, something more spectacular than that summer's 250-mile race off the New Jersey shore from Sandy Hook to Cape May and back. *Fleetwing,* as Franklin Osgood bluntly reminded Bennett, had already beaten *Henrietta* in that kind of match. He taunted Bennett that the *Herald* itself had called such coastal races for "smooth water gentry"—wimps in today's parlance. Seething, Bennett said he'd "wager $10,000 that the *Henrietta* could show her stern to the *Fleetwing* all the way in another race—if they went the width of the Atlantic."

Spinning the globe in the Union Club, he traced a fantastic course. Starting from Sandy Hook, New Jersey, at the entrance of New York's Lower Bay, it stretched across the entire North Atlantic—fully 3,100 nautical miles—all the way to the Needles, a rocky headland at the tip of the Isle of Wight in England.

In 1866, this distance was unprecedented for a yacht race. Racing took place in protected harbors, bays, or sounds, around carefully laid courses of 30 miles or so. The 60-mile course around England's Isle of Wight was considered a distance race. Offshore races of 200 to 300 miles were considered marathons. Ocean racing of the kind Bennett proposed was completely unknown and not without reason. A nautical mile measures 6,076 feet, or 15 percent longer than the statute mile of 5,280 feet. A course of 3,100 nautical miles therefore is the equivalent of 3,565 statute miles. By comparison, Tokyo to Singapore is only 3,350 statute miles; New York to San Francisco, a distance of just 2,568 statute miles; and Moscow to Madrid, but 2,120 statute miles. Bennett's proposed course, on the other hand, equaled the distance from Moscow to Beijing. Attempting to race lightly built, overcanvassed yachts that far—across one of the roughest oceans in the world—was tantamount to daring Niagara Falls in a barrel.

The proposal was stunning. Nobody had ever done it before. Nobody had been crazy enough to try. Nobody but "Jamie" Bennett, only son of the founder of the *New York Herald,* would've bet his life on it.

He was just twenty-five years old that December. Born with a platinum spoon in his mouth—some said a whole dinner service—he was a high-society party animal. With an assured annual income of $11 million in today's value, he had a prodigal view about spending it on whatever made him happy. He bet hugely on horses, yacht races, prize fights, billiards, and cards. He kept stables of matched Thoroughbreds and luxury carriages to carry him in style to any occasion: four-in-hand coaches, fast two-wheeled cabriolets, and four-wheeled phaetons. He dated debutantes and showgirls without showing much distinction between one and the other.

When he was drinking, which was often, his antics—then and later—were scandalous. According to a biographer, he delightedly "moved through restaurants, pulling off the tablecloths on both sides of the aisle, crunching the crockery underfoot." Invariably, "the next day a handsome bill would appear at his office, which was promptly paid." Drunk at Delmonico's, he heard a fire alarm, rushed outside in his evening clothes, and imperiously started barking orders to a company of firefighters. They turned a hose on him. When he sobered up, he sent each man an expensive new rubber raincoat.

Attending a New Year's Day open house at the home of his fiancée, a young and beautiful debutante named Caroline May, he was dead drunk. By one newspaper account, "well-served with punch from other open houses, he proceeded to insult his host most grievously." By another account, he committed "a breach of the most primitive of good manners." Whatever his drunken offense, yachting historian Ed Holm noted that it "was sufficiently gross to send New York society reeling in shock and bring his engagement to May to an abrupt end." By all accounts, it got him thrown out of the May house, resulting in a streetside fistfight (some said horsewhipping) in the snow with one of Miss May's relatives, followed by a duel with pistols at twelve paces (both men missed). The scandal drove him to exile for a time in Paris.

It didn't curb his *Animal House*–like antics. He bedeviled his neighbors by drunkenly driving through their formal gardens with a coach and four, in the middle of the night, stark naked. In his cups in Paris, he raced his coach and four under a too-low overpass, knocked himself unconscious, and was hospitalized for weeks. At exclusive Newport, he boozily bet an aristocratic English polo player that he didn't have the gumption to ride his horse up the grand staircase of the resort's ultraswank Reading Room. Bennett not only lost the bet, he also was barred from the Reading Room for life. It didn't trouble him a particle. In retaliation, he built a play-house for himself called The Casino—right on Newport's Bellevue Avenue, where the richest of the rich had their huge mansions. There he could engage in whatever shenanigans he liked.

Yet he was no drunken fool: there was a keenly honed edge to him. He'd had the finest Continental (French) education money could buy. And his entire life, his father had groomed him for business: in particular, the dog-eat-dog New York newspaper busi-ness, where his father was, arguably, the biggest, baddest dog of all. He proved startlingly adept at it—like a carnivore turned loose in its element. He had been schooled in the finer arts, too—painting, literature, and music—enough to pass easily in society, which, at the time, was extremely literate and well versed. He'd also mastered what were then called "the manly arts"—riding; shooting; angling; and, most especially, yachting.

For his sixteenth birthday, his father gave him a 72-foot center-board sloop named *Rebecca*. It came complete with a professional crew of twenty-two. He raced it that year (1857) in the New York Yacht Club's annual cruise. He had a gift for racing or, perhaps more accurately, the crew hired by his father did. Jamie Bennett was elected to membership in the New York Yacht Club when he was just sixteen years and three months old, the youngest member ever admitted. His father's money undoubtedly had more to do with his election than Junior's yachtsmanship. Still, *Rebecca*—with Jamie and his professional crew—was a fierce competitor, finishing at or near the top of the racing results until 1861, though not without controversy and protests. Nothing about Jamie was without con-troversy.

The outbreak of the Civil War that year was good news for the Bennetts. Indeed, father and son viewed it as a golden business opportunity and quickly moved to make the most of it. Bennett Sr. pledged that the *Herald* would stand solidly behind the new Lincoln administration. This was a reversal of its previous editorial policy, but old man Bennett never had any reservations about changing his spots when there were newspapers to be sold and money to be made. He also offered his son's new 225-foot schooner yacht *Henrietta* to the U.S. Revenue Service for the duration of the war.

Lincoln was duly appreciative. The *Herald* had one of the largest circulations of any newspaper in America, and the U.S. Navy had only sixteen ships in home waters at the time. Consequently the *Herald*'s war correspondents (they eventually numbered more than sixty-three) were showered with credentials and access. The paper sold wildly within the federal armies, more than doubling its circulation. By presidential appointment, Jamie Bennett, just twenty, was made a third lieutenant in the U.S. Navy and assigned to serve aboard his own *Henrietta* with the federal blockading squadron. This left the son of Lincoln's benefactor safe from any real shooting.

He looked good in his specially tailored dark blue, double-breasted, gold (not brass)-buttoned uniform coat and stiff-billed officer's cap. But Jamie didn't serve long—a year at most. And his service was anything but usual. In April 1862 he was aboard *Henrietta* off the Carolina coast. In August he was back in Manhattan to join the New York Yacht Club's annual cruise. Usual or not, at least Bennett saw active service, which is more than could be said for most millionaires' sons. He dutifully stood his watches, became practiced at navigation, and raced *Henrietta* on the open ocean in pursuit of blockade runners.

When the war ended, he was cockier than ever. Wartime duty aboard a Civil War Revenue Service cutter was quite as dashing as service aboard PT boats would be a century later. The *Herald*'s circulation was at an all-time high. He was poised to take his father's place as editor. Jamie was fabulously rich already and, as his father's sole heir, destined to be richer still. In New York's conservative social circles, however, he remained an outcast. He was "new money," after all—a flood of it, to be sure, but a dirty flood. It derived not from shipping lines, railroads, mines, or factories, but from a paper that pandered to the masses with stories of crime, depravity, divorce, domestic disturbances, prizefighting, and worse.

That made him a multimillionaire. It did not, by any means, make him a gentleman. Yet, backed by wealth and fueled by brandy, he'd issued a challenge—loudly and publicly in the Union Club.

Pierre Lorillard couldn't ignore it. He was older (thirty-three) than Bennett and an accomplished sportsman in his own right: a crack wingshot, expert angler, driver of trotting horses, breeder of Thoroughbred racehorses, and yachtsman. He was not as boisterous as Bennett. He was married, for one thing, and a fourth-generation millionaire for another. But he was as arrogant and, if anything, richer. In fact, he was heir to some of the oldest, most extensive wealth in America. The Lorillard tobacco empire was already 106 years old in 1866 (Bennett's upstart *New York Herald* was barely 20). It was certainly no stranger to self-promotion. To celebrate the centennial anniversary of the firm, $100 bills (equivalent to more than $1,600 in today's value) were wrapped at random in packages of tobacco named "Century."

What's more, Lorillard was a keystone in New York's social firmament. In fact, he was the *de facto* dauphin of established New York society and its enforcer against assaults by *nouveau riche* scalawags such as Bennett. Marshaling the venerable Barclays, Beekmans, Livingstons, and Schuylers behind him, he had barred the Astors, Roosevelts, and Vanderbilts from obtaining boxes at the *ne plus ultra* of New York's social scene, the grand opera of the New York Academy of Music. Their money simply wasn't old enough. Bennett's, by comparison, was still hot in his pocket.

Bennett's drunken notion to race across the Atlantic may have shocked Lorillard. It was new money challenging old. Furthermore, it amounted to an alleged gentleman "calling out" an established one. At a time before syndicates funded yachts and before races were ruled by clubs and committees and handicaps, it was very much a personal thing. Shocked or not, Lorillard could do nothing but accept. Neither could the Osgoods. But Lorillard promptly outbluffed Bennett. He doubled the wager, to $20,000 a side.

But the boasting and the betting didn't end there. If a man truly believed his yacht was the fastest on the high seas, there was no point waiting to find out. By agreement, all three vessels would sail on December 11—"blow high or low," as they put it, meaning regardless of weather. This elevated an already forbidding race into a dangerous one. By October, conditions in the North Atlantic are already wintry. December rings in the coffin nails of gale and storm season in the North Atlantic.

All four men could've sensibly postponed the race until the following summer and gone about their usual, comfortable routines. Bennett typically spent the morning (late morning) in the *Herald*'s offices at Ann Street and Broadway in lower Manhattan. This was usually followed by a very long lunch at Delmonico's (where he might dine on trout *à la Normande,* leg of mutton with caper sauce, or quails on toast points), a brief afternoon return to the office (to smoke a cigar), an extended supper at the Union Club, then an evening at the theater, with late-night drinking and carousing afterward. But waiting until summer to race—seven long months—was a lifetime to young millionaires, old money or new, for whom instant gratification was a birthright.

If they were going to race, December was the last and only open window in which to do it. A bad one, to be sure, but any later and none would be open. Before the blazing coal stove grates of the Union Club, it seemed a suitably "manly," "plucky," and "sportsmanlike" thing (to use the terms of the day) to do. In the foggy, tempestuous, ice-studded seascape above 45 degrees north latitude, it would seem very, very different. This fact, like others that evening, apparently passed largely unnoticed. It merely savored the wager.

By the time they stumbled out of the Union Club, the stakes had escalated. Each side put up the then fabulous sum of $30,000—equivalent to $351,000 today—to win. In current values, the owners' pot alone amounted to more than $1 million in gold, the highest purse for any sporting event to date in the nineteenth century. The money was deposited with the treasurer of the New York Yacht Club—winner take all. It was an instant sensation. When word got out to New York's bookmakers, millions of dollars more were bet.

As soon as Bennett's head cleared the next day, the stark reality of the thing descended upon him like a cold, clammy cape. It wasn't one of his typical "morning-afters," where a check for a few hundred dollars in damages would suffice. It certainly wasn't something he could walk away from. The challenge had been made to fellow members of the New York Yacht Club and duly witnessed at the Union Club. There was no backing down. Like it or not, on December 11 he was going across the North Atlantic, in winter, "blow high or low."

While he may have been brimming with brandified confidence the night before, he turned pietistical pragmatist in the morning. Like his father, he hated to lose. At once he moved to hedge his bet. A messenger was sent to "Packet Row" on New York's South Street. He was instructed to find Captain Samuel "Bully" Samuels.

Samuels, a Boston-born mariner at sea since age eleven and then forty-three, was a legendary packet ship captain, at a time when a packet was rather like the Concorde jet today. It was the fastest and consequently most expensive (if not necessarily comfortable) service across the Atlantic. More than that, it was the only regularly scheduled service across the ocean. Built to carry international mail, packet ships had finer hulls than average for extra speed, carried frightening spreads of canvas, and employed captains who knew how to make the most of both.

The average eastbound or "downhill" passage (United States to England), boosted by prevailing winds and current, was twenty-four days. The westbound or "uphill" passage (England to United States), against the wind, averaged thirty-eight days and usually was longer. Still, this was *twice* as fast as any other ships crossing the Atlantic at the time. And Samuels was renowned for making even faster passages: seventeen or eighteen days eastbound and about twenty-four days westbound.

That speed came at a price. For first-class passengers bound for America, a one-way ticket cost "30 guineas, wine included," equal to somewhat more than $2,100 U.S. today. For first-class passengers bound for Britain, the cost was $150, or more than $1,700 today (presumably because less wine was consumed on the faster eastbound passage). The cheapest fare—a one-way ticket in steerage, where passengers slept in stalls, packed in like sheep—cost $25, or the equivalent of about $300 today, a sum it might take a poor man years to save.

Yet the expense was worth it. Unlike other ships, packets sailed on schedule—"full or not full"—from New York and Liverpool twice a month (later, as packet fleets increased in number, it was weekly). For merchants shipping premium-priced cargo and for businessmen carrying time-sensitive letters of credit or bills of exchange, such regularly scheduled service was a boon. The voyage itself, however, was always punishing, dangerous, and often downright terrifying. Sailing on schedule meant packets had to sail in all seasons, in any and all weather. Furthermore, they had to sail fast.

Packet captains didn't shorten sail in a gale or heave-to in a storm. Canvas was carried until it split or snapped the spar. They didn't slow for blizzards, icebergs, or fog. The fact that their sharp-edged vessels were notoriously "wet ships," which when hard-driven in a seaway, dove deeper and broke more sailors' bones than fat merchant ships, was of no concern to them. Every single passage, Bully Samuels said, "was a race against time, night and day, winter and summer, and under the hardest conditions." For packet ship captains every voyage was literally a race to the bank. Skippers got paid bonuses for posting speed records plus a hefty percentage of everything they delivered intact: 5 percent on freight, 25 percent on cabin (first-class) passengers, 5 percent on steerage passengers, and a fat allowance for carrying the mail. Fast voyages, meant more voyages, and more voyages meant quicker fortunes. As a result, they drove their crews like slaves and their ships beyond endurance. On Liverpool packets, sailors got no rest, seldom ate hot food, and were never warm, never dry, and never safe. Roughly one out of every six packet ships that sailed either foundered, was wrecked, or vanished at sea. Quite naturally, no sailor who could find a berth elsewhere wanted any part of a packet.

To fill out crews, packet ship skippers were reduced to recruiting seamen "from the riff-raff of the waterfront dives," as one naval historian described it. "They were herded aboard by unscrupulous boarding-house runners. Raw greenhorns were marched around a cow's horn in a dive kept by one Paddy Doyle, who then vouched for them as seamen who had been around the Horn." Most of these men were about what you'd expect to find in the saloons that functioned as labor pools on the nineteenth-century waterfront: addicts, petty criminals, penniless immigrants, runaway teens, and

Legendary Captain "Bully" Samuels (right) and firearms heir Caldwell Colt (left) aboard Colt's *Dauntless,* which was sabotaged in the 1887 transatlantic yacht race.

deserters from other ships. Getting these "packet rats" to work ship was Samuels' specialty, the source of his nickname "Bully." Any man slow to turn out got a "starter," usually a kick in the face calculated to break his nose. This got his attention yet scrupulously spared his ribs, hands, and feet so he remained able to work. Any man hesitating to climb frozen ratlines, hesitating to obey any order, got "handspike hash" or "belaying pin soup." Speed was the one thing—the only thing—that mattered on a packet ship, and Samuels was the hardest-driving packet skipper on the Atlantic.

It was not always one-sided. Aboard the clipper packet ship *Dreadnought* in August 1859, the "packet rats" mutinied, tried to kill Samuels and his mates and to seize the vessel. Bully was prepared. Instead of single-shot, muzzleloading pistols, he'd equipped his officers with the latest Colt six-shot revolvers. The mutineers were cowed, locked under hatches, and the officers brought the ship in.

Bennett snapped him up like a Thoroughbred racehorse. Samuels didn't come cheap. His reputation was huge: captain of *Dreadnought,* the "Wild Boat of the Atlantic," fastest of sailing packets before the Civil War; captain of two Union warships during the war (when Bennett was a lowly third lieutenant), and present at the capture of Fort Fisher, the last Confederate port to fall. When Bennett approached him, he already had a handsomely paying job as captain of the fast American packet *Fulton* and was quite content to stay where he was. To get him to quit and skipper *Henrietta* cost Bennett $10,000, about $117,000 today. This was a fantastic sum for a race that looked to amount to less than a month's work. In fact, it was five times more than the monthly salary of the president of the United States at the time. Nonetheless, Bennett paid it gladly. Samuels demanded the money in advance and immediately bet $7,500 of it (more than $87,000 today) on himself to win.

Recruiting experienced seamen cost Bennett more. Most old hands refused the high pay he offered because, as yachting historian Ian Dear wrote, "it was generally acknowledged that the men were sailing to certain death." They knew at a glance what they saw— rich men's racing yachts—"cockleshells" and "skimming dishes," too small, too light, with open cockpits and not nearly enough freeboard to keep out North Atlantic seas in winter. Even with their tall racing masts cut down, which was usually done in such vessels prior to attempting an ocean crossing, they still carried a frightening spread of canvas. In a midwinter ocean race, despite gales or mountainous seas, especially with Bully Samuels at the helm, sail would be crowded on and carried regardless of risk.

Blue-water sailors knew full well that meant gruesome labor and unending danger. There would be no normal watch-upon-watch, where a fellow could at least catch four hours' sleep, but all hands on deck as long as a man could stand. In winter, with decks awash, subzero cold, and rigging sagging with ice, that wouldn't be long. Frostbite could take a man's fingers and toes in a few hours. ("Mittens or any kind of protection on the hands," wrote an ex-packet ship skipper, "were absolutely tabooed at sea, both for efficiency and safety.") Working ship with frozen hands and feet held exquisite tortures. Changing tons of frozen sail, tying in or shaking out reefs, and perched ten stories above a rolling deck on ice-covered lines in pitch darkness were frightening enough. Replacing split canvas or rigging carried away by winds that could carry a man away like a kite just as easily was another thing entirely. In an open cockpit, a man could vanish in the snap of a finger. For millionaires huddling belowdecks or Bully Samuels sitting on his fat stack of greenbacks at the helm, an open ocean race had appeal. The $100 bonus Bennett offered able-bodied seamen didn't. Quite sensibly, the experienced, "old" sailors held back. It was mostly younger, inexperienced "bold" sailors who signed on. Like Samuels, most bet a good part of their advance pay on the race and gave themselves up to their chance.

Wagers were still being laid on the morning of the start. Thousands of spectators, who had boated down to Sandy Hook the night before, waited until the last minute to see what final conditions were like before placing their bets. The December sun came up a pink sore to seaward, "the rawest of December days," according to Samuels. It shone intermittently, without warmth, through high, scudding clouds. The thermometer registered 29 degrees Fahrenheit. A spanking offshore wind, blowing out of the west at 25 to 30 miles per hour, made it feel bone-chillingly colder. Outside the protected waters of Sandy Hook, seas were churning 8 feet high, with white-caps and spray.

Such conditions favored no boat over another. In length and tonnage, all three were nearly identical. Osgood's *Fleetwing* was 106 feet, 6 inches long (200 tons), and Bennett's *Henrietta* just 6 inches longer (107 feet and 205 tons). At 110 feet in length overall, Lorillard's *Vesta* was the longest vessel, the traditional measure of a yacht's speed. She was also pencil-thin, with a beam of 14.5 feet compared to *Henrietta*'s 23-foot waist and *Fleetwing*'s 28-foot girth. In rig and sail plan there was no difference whatsoever. All three yachts were two-masted, fore-and-aft gaff-rigged schooners, carrying the same sails and approximately the same sail area.

Such vessels sailed fastest with the wind abeam (from either side). A fresh wind blowing from square behind, as it was that morning, caused them to roll, often violently. Waves from behind caused them to surf into waves in front, burying the bow and dramatically slowing the boat while severely straining the rig. The combination of roll, pitch, and yaw made all three boats unstable and steering a steady course next to impossible.

In such conditions, Lorillard's *Vesta* may have had somewhat of an edge. She was the only centerboard (retractable-keel) yacht in the race. With her centerboard up, she drew just 7 feet, 6 inches of water. With her centerboard down, she had a draft of 15 feet—3 feet deeper than her fixed-keel rivals. Since it was adjustable, it could be raised and lowered to make her steer better and reduce rolling to some degree. Furthermore, *Vesta*'s open cockpit had been surrounded by raised bulwarks and roofed over to avoid being swamped by high seas. Bully Samuels had taken the same precaution with *Henrietta*. Either because of overconfidence or ignorance, the cockpit of the Osgoods' *Fleetwing* was left uncovered and unprotected.

Oddsmakers divined nothing new or significant from their observations that morning. Perhaps they should have. In any case, the race remained a lottery. Those who'd waited to place their bets must have been sorely disappointed. Surely Bennett was. Both Lorillard and the Osgoods waved good-bye from Sandy Hook. Like Bennett, they'd hired professional skippers and crews to race their yachts across the Atlantic. But none of the three men was crazy enough to sail across the Atlantic himself. That was for hirelings. They would celebrate Christmas regally in their mansions on Fifth Avenue, then take fast steamers to join their vessels in England. Drinking champagne, puffing cigars, and bundled in warm comforters, they bid Jamie a fond farewell. He and *Henrietta* and his "new money" could go to hell.

All three yachts crossed the starting line almost at the same instant—"So near together that you could have tossed a biscuit from one to the other," according to Samuels. Once clear of the treacherous sandbanks lining the southern shore of Long Island, the schooners lost sight of one another. *Henrietta* veered northeast, taking a modified great circle course across the Grand Banks to make the most of prevailing westerly winds. This was the shortest passage, but the most dangerous. It took them "shaving close to the George's Shoals and Sable Island," a graveyard of ships; through the nearly constant, blinding fogs on the Grand Banks; and above 40 degrees latitude—realm of icebergs; blizzards; and sudden, unbelievably violent winter storms. *Fleetwing* shaped a similar course. *Vesta* steered a more southerly route. It was a longer passage, but less likely to be slowed by fog, ice, and storm, and gave her the benefit of riding the Gulf Stream out into midocean.

In his packet runs, Samuels had made the northern passage countless times (seventy-eight by the end of his career). But as he told Bennett, it was always "dicing with the devil." And this time he didn't have a stoutly built, oceangoing ship underneath him. There was the devil to pay as soon as *Henrietta* was fairly offshore. By Samuels' account, it blew "a half gale of wind [all the way] to the Banks, with the men constantly standing by gaff topsail and peak halyards," soaked by spray and rimed with ice. A week into the race, lashed by sleet, snow, and driven before roaring westerlies, Samuels was charging into the mid-Atlantic. Though the schooner was "fairly burying herself" in huge seas, he "carried on" with all sail. In one day's run he drove her at an average speed of 11.6 knots and logged a (then) record-breaking 280 nautical miles. "Talk about racing," he remembered, "it was a race every minute."

In winter gales, it was terrifying. Under a skyscraper of screeching canvas (*Henrietta*'s mainmast towered 12 stories abovedeck), the noise was deafening. Heeled over 45 degrees or more, the schooner's lee rail was underwater and her decks more or less constantly awash. Heavy seas repeatedly heaved her up and threw her down. Describing the impact to reporters later, Samuels "brought his open hand down upon his knee with an expressive gesture—'The slap is hard,' he said, 'yes, a bit hard.'" The pounding, in fact, was enough to jar tooth fillings loose. The rolling and yawing were nauseating.

Bennett and his guests took refuge below. Samuels remained on deck day and night, often tied to a chair. "Night is the time to try the nerve and make quick passages," he wrote in his reminiscences. "The best ship-masters are those which are most on deck after dark and rely on nobody but themselves to carry canvas. The expert sailor knows exactly how long his sails and spars will stand the strain. . . ."

Samuels may have known. Bennett didn't. He was terrified

Henrietta would be dismasted. Though he was the ship's owner, he found himself more or less an onboard captive of Samuels, like every man aboard. He was tied to the tail of his own tiger. He urged Samuels to shorten sail, but the packet skipper said with a growl, "This is yachting in earnest, Mr. Bennett."

By 4:00 P.M. on December 18, however—conditions deteriorating—even the imperturbable Bully Samuels was scared. The winds hauled around, intensified, and the seas rose monstrously. Samuels struck the topsails, lowered the big mainsail, and close-reefed—but refused to strike—his foresail and headsails, and doggedly held his racing course. He ordered two helmsmen tied to the wheel to keep it. He ordered his two officers [mates] to tie themselves into the cockpit. To keep the men on deck from being swept overboard, he ordered them to straddle the boom like a rocking horse, lashed them to it himself, and then hoisted it 6 feet above the deck "so that if a sea broke on board it would wash under them." He made no apologies. "This was a race, you know," he said later, "and we were taking chances on having our decks swept."

For the next four hours he somehow drove the wildly rolling and plunging *Henrietta* on. "We staggered through it," he remembered, "until the wind freshened into a full gale from the southwest . . . [and] the gale developed into a hurricane." That was putting it matter-of-factly. Samuels, one of the finest North Atlantic passage-makers ever, was not given to exaggeration. In pitch darkness, winds screeched at more than 64 knots (73.6 miles per hour)—strong enough to uproot trees. The waves—cresting and collapsing like 5-story buildings all around the boat—were whipped white as snow, spray flying off them like bullets. Visibility was zero.

At 8:00 P.M., still carrying sail, a monster wave swallowed half the boat. From the helm, Samuels saw it "board us abreast of the fore rig [the sails he'd refused to lower], burying everything forward—bow clean underwater and stern in the air." She hung there for an instant. Then a "terrific sea washed over her, burying her almost completely." It "ripped the foresail out of the bolt ropes," swept the jibs away, and clawed down the whole forerig.

The chaos was surreal: mangled bow boom, sails and rigging awash. Everyone knocked off their feet. The vessel nearly perpendicular, those topside hanging on for their lives. The ship's carpenter was screaming that the ship had opened up forward and the Atlantic was filling her.

Where Bennett was during all this is anyone's guess. Probably below in his cabin, thrown headlong from his berth despite its leeboard, plunged into darkness, and as disoriented and panicked as everyone else. If he was thinking clearly, he was thinking about drowning—all thoughts about races and wagers forgotten.

Only Bully Samuels kept his head. He ignored the carpenter. Getting the ship on her keel again was what mattered. He ordered the men now hanging off the main boom (none had been swept away or injured) to clear the debris fouling the bow. The crew, more afraid of him than the storm, obeyed. They went to work, *Henrietta* righted herself, and in a merciful, "momentary lull," as Samuels called it, hoisted a storm trysail and "hove to." That held her into the storm. The rest of the night, until 4:00 A.M., was spent stopping leaks, working the pumps, and making repairs.

It was later argued that he waited far too long before making sail again. That argument holds no water. Samuels knew very well when to dice with the North Atlantic devil. The other competitors did not. The same storm engulfed them both.

Vesta, in third place when it hit, was driven farthest north. Running off before the gale, under reefed sails, she overtook *Henrietta*. But running with the storm took her rather too far north. She would pay a dear price for it.

The storm ripped *Fleetwing* from her course almost to the same latitude as *Henrietta*. Though she was under storm canvas, her deck was "swept time and again, forward and aft, all hands in danger," according to the *Boston Herald*. In whiteout conditions, no one saw the rogue wave hurtling in from windward at 20 knots or more until it struck at the main rigging, sweeping the decks fore and aft. One survivor said the water smashed into her uncovered cockpit with the force of "a Niagara." Even though they were lashed in, the entire ship's watch—eight crewmen—was swept overboard. Two men, clutching desperately to the trysail that had come adrift, were eventually hauled back on board. The other six, encumbered in sou'westers and heavy sea boots, were gone in the dark. Captain

Edwards, *Fleetwing*'s skipper, hove to under bare poles and scoured the black, raging seas for five hours. Not a trace of the missing men could be found. In this gallant but futile gesture, he knowingly abandoned any hope of winning the race.

When the storm blew itself out, *Vesta* was leading the pack. In fact, she was fast pulling away, at times achieving an unheard-of speed of 14 knots. "She fairly flew," noted one of those aboard, covering 277 miles in a day's run. But the winds soon lightened, then hauled around to the southeast, directly in the direction she had to go. To reach the Bishop's Rock Light in the Scilly Isles at the entrance to the English Channel from her far northerly position, she was forced to beat into the wind.

To her south, Samuels again had the reorganized *Henrietta* well under way on a more favorable and faster point of sail. For a race of more than 3,000 nautical miles, it was a remarkably close finish. *Henrietta* had the Bishop Light in the Scilly Isles, just 50 miles from the English mainland, abeam at 10:00 P.M. on December 23—only two hours ahead of *Vesta*. Forty-one hours and forty-five minutes later—on Christmas Day 1866—she had passed up the English Channel and crossed the finish line at the Needles first. Her crew was suffering exhaustion, frostbite, and dehydration.

Samuels was thanking his lucky stars and counting his winnings. He'd faced down cannon fire, mutiny, hurricanes, and a hundred stripes of maritime mayhem. But he called "the race of 1866 the hardest human beings ever took part in. Everybody suffered terribly. I shall never forget that fearful experience."

Bennett was apparently celebrating the fact that he'd arrived in one piece. Between the time *Henrietta* entered the English Channel and reached Cowes, he and his guests indulged in some serious drinking. Gerard S. Huffam, a teenage dockyard worker at White's Shipyard at Cowes, saw *Henrietta* come to anchor. "On one of the yachts," he recollected, "was Gordon Bennett of The New York Times [sic], and there was another man named Fisk, and another one named Jerome. . . . I spoke to all three of them and heard them woozily sing Yankee Doodle."

When the battered *Fleetwing*, second to finish, arrived at Cowes with her news, any thoughts of celebration were squashed. *Vesta*, whose Channel pilot had somehow gotten lost, finished dead last.

For Bennett, his $60,000 prize purse was pocket change. Deducting what he'd paid for Samuels, crew, and fitting out *Henrietta*, it actually amounted to a little more than $30,000 (about $351,000 in today's value). The *Herald* earned him that much in ten days.

But the prize money meant nothing. What mattered was the *news*. On both sides of the Atlantic, the racing news was gobbled up by the public. An audacious race had been run, men were dead, and a transatlantic record had been set. That story was spun into gold worth far more than any prize money. The race coverage sold newspapers, increased circulation, and boosted advertising revenue. In fact, it sold so many newspapers that the following year Bennett established the *New York Evening Telegram* to augment the *New York Herald*.

Six men were dead, regrettably, but dead contesting with nature herself, which gilded an already dramatic story. The fact that they were driven more or less like human racehorses, to win a prize purse for their owners, wasn't mentioned. The "Great Ocean Race" of 1866 taught Bennett that making news was as profitable as reporting it.

The lesson was never lost on him. "I *make* news," he said later, and indeed he did. He sent Stanley to find Dr. Livingstone (1869–1871), participated in a second transatlantic yacht race in 1870, and financed Lieutenant George Washington DeLong's tragic (but newsmaking) 1879 attempt to reach the North Pole (the vessel, DeLong, and a dozen men were lost).

But winning the 1866 race remained perhaps his greatest personal triumph. Considering the winter gales *Henrietta* weathered and despite being forced to heave to in mid-Atlantic, her time from Sandy Hook was record-breaking—a phenomenal thirteen days, twenty-one hours and forty-five minutes—at an average speed of 9.36 knots. Bennett's record would stand for more than thirty years.

CHAPTER 5

Third Day at Sea

*The wonder is always new that any sane man can be
a sailor.*

—Ralph Waldo Emerson

*A*t 2:00 P.M., Ailsa's *third day at sea, an explosion shook her down
to the keel. The noise deafened Stevenson. He was sitting in the
cockpit marveling at the "cobalt sky . . . only exceeded in beauty
by the cerulean sea." Running before a "splendid flashing breeze
. . . under every kite with which a racing yacht can be smothered,"
the yawl was ripping along at 12 knots (almost 14 miles per hour).
He was mesmerized by it, especially by the ballooning spinnaker
that drove the boat forward, carving "a path through a [wave] crest
like a scimitar" and sending it "soaring over the following seas."*

Captain Miller was finally racing—full out. He had been since
shortly after midnight when, in addition to the frightening spread
of sail already aloft, he set Ailsa's massive spinnaker. The wind and
the weather were too good to waste. He was determined to put as
many miles between him, Charlie Barr and Atlantic, and any other
competitors as conditions allowed.

Stevenson found the press of canvas as unnerving as it was fas-
cinating. The spinnaker—a lightweight, three-cornered sail set far
forward of Ailsa's mainmast—was essentially a huge parachute,

intended for use in light winds. But that afternoon, in a strength-ening wind and fast-rising following sea, it took on a perverse life of its own. Yacht hands called it a spinnaker or "spinxer" because it was first used aboard the yacht Sphinx *during a race in the Solent in the 1870s. Like its namesake, the mythological lion with a human head that killed anyone who failed to answer its riddles, it was a devilish thing. In the days long before ultrastrong synthetic sails, wind tunnel tests, and vents designed to produce a steady flow of air over the sail surface and prevent wild gyrations, it was a per-fect monster.*

On the wave crests it snared the strong wind and literally wrenched the 90-ton boat forward. In the troughs of the waves, its 60-foot long boom was buried in Ailsa's frothing bow wake, only to rear up like a mustang "to the masthead at every heave," leav-ing the sail "folding and flapping like pelican wings." In the dizzy-ing roll afterward, fully 10 feet of the end of Ailsa's massive mainsail boom were plunged underwater. "No device," Stevenson noted in his spray-drenched journal, "could keep Ailsa steady in those pendulum rolls."

At the ear-splitting crack, he reflexively looked up. He glimpsed the spinnaker boom "bent like a yew bow" and then watched the wind snap it into three pieces, as if it were made of balsa wood. With a hideous ripping sound, the spinnaker sail was torn "asun-der." The fractured boom crashed into the sea, dragging shredded sail with it, beating against Ailsa's starboard side "like the flukes of a whale." The noise was tremendous; the sudden brakelike drag, worse. The heavy wreckage pitched the bow down, the following sea whipsawed her stern, and her otherwise still-filled sails almost rolled her on her beam ends.

In the pandemonium, Miller and the helmsman struggled to bring her back on course. Crewmen rushed forward to free the rat's nest fouling the bow. They hauled in what they could, chopped away what they couldn't. A 20-foot section of the spinnaker boom had vanished entirely. The splinter-ended fragments that were retrieved were quickly fished (spliced) together to fashion a replace-ment. But the jury-rigged spar was too short to accommodate the spinnaker, even if the men could stitch its shredded fragments back

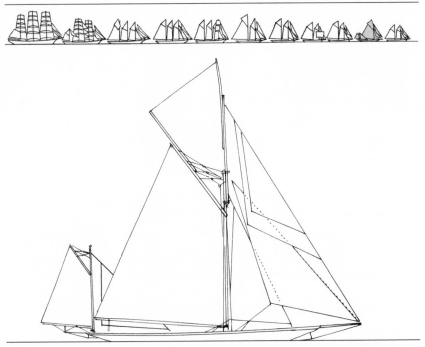

Ailsa—127 feet long overall and 89 feet at the waterline—was an inshore racer thought to be too lightly built and rigged to weather the North Atlantic. Designed as a cutter, she'd been rerigged as a yawl to boost her speed and was considered over-canvassed.

in one piece, which would take days. Instead Miller ordered them to fit the balloon jib topsail to the patched spar, but it was no real substitute.

Three days from the start of the race, Ailsa had lost her primary power sail for running before the wind. But things quickly turned uglier. The wind and the sea both increased "alarmingly," and Captain Miller was forced to shorten sail. The mainboom was hauled inboard and two reefs tied in the mainsail. A twenty-year veteran of yacht racing, Miller had no choice. Unlike the bigger two- and three-masted schooners in the race, Ailsa was now more or less entirely dependent on her single mainmast and boom. Miller couldn't afford to lose either.

CHAPTER 6

Sore Hearts and Heads

Never sail on Friday [day of Christ's crucifixion]. first Monday in April [birthday of Cain and day Abel was killed], second Monday in August [day Sodom and Gomorrah were destroyed]. Never carry flowers on board [presages funeral wreaths for a sailor or whole ship's company]. Never embark a woman [it makes the sea angry]. A naked woman in the form of a ship's figurehead, however, calms high winds and gales.

—Superstitions of sailors

No one at the New York Yacht Club was anxious for another transatlantic race after the first. The weather conditions and death toll had been appalling enough. Its members were content to race one another in New York Harbor or offshore New Jersey and take their annual summer cruise out Long Island and Rhode Island Sounds to fashionable Newport.

In 1870, however, the club was formally challenged to a cross-ocean match by English railroad millionaire James Ashbury. He was coming to the States in his 108-foot schooner *Cambria* to make the first attempt to win back the America's Cup (still known as the Queen's Cup at the time). Prior to the Cup race, however, he wanted a "go" at the club's defending yacht in a race across the Atlantic and then around Long Island. Unlike the first race, this wasn't an intraclub affair, but an international one; not a matter of wagers, but prestige. Ashbury offered a prize cup worth £250 (roughly $19,000 today). Though the memory of the 1866 race was still fresh, the New York Yacht Club could do nothing but accept.

Jamie Bennett, now the club's vice commodore, took on the challenge himself. It was, after all, his event and his record. He had a new copper-bottomed 123-foot schooner named *Dauntless,* which promised by dint of her longer waterline to be faster and more weatherly than *Cambria* on the high seas. He again reached deep in his pockets and hired Bully Samuels as skipper. This time the course was reversed and somewhat shorter: from Old Kinsale Head off Cork Harbor in southern Ireland to the Sandy Hook Lightship at the entrance to New York Harbor. Yet it was the "uphill passage," mostly against prevailing winds and currents. The start of the race took place on July 4. The mild summer season appeared favorable for a speedy westward crossing.

Winds, in fact, proved disappointingly light. At the end of a week, neither vessel had reached the 1,000-mile mark. *Dauntless,* in the lead, had logged 940 miles, *Cambria* 904 miles. Only 36 miles separated them. Nine days later, *Cambria* had taken the lead, leaving *Dauntless* 90 miles behind.

Samuels, steering a more southerly course, ran afoul of pile-driving winds and rough seas off Nova Scotia. As always, he carried more canvas and carried it far longer than his rival. The risk almost paid off. Nearing Georges Bank east of Cape Cod, *Dauntless* was ripping ahead when struck by a gale. Samuels ordered two seamen out onto her long bowsprit to reef the headsails. They were perched precariously on footropes when the vessel plunged into a deep wave trough that buried its bow. When *Dauntless*'s head staggered up, shedding tons of black water, the footropes had been plucked clean. The men were nowhere to be seen.

Unlike *Fleetwing,* there is no record that *Dauntless* came about or hove-to in order to search for them. If she did, she did not tarry long. That was neither Samuels' nor Bennett's style. There was little chance of finding them and less chance of finding them alive. *Dauntless* continued racing westward.

Sailing a more northerly course, the wind and weather favored *Cambria.* She crossed the finish line at the Sandy Hook Lightship first, after an exhausting run of 2,881 or 2,994 miles (depending on varying sources) that took an estimated twenty-three days, five hours, and seventeen minutes (nothing about this race was clear). *Dauntless,* leaving her crewmen behind, finished only one hour and forty-three minutes later—evidence, if any was needed, that she did not waste much time looking for them.

The club's defeat at the hands of an Englishman in an open ocean race was humiliating. The deaths were shocking. In two transatlantic races, run fewer than four years apart, eight men serving under the burgee of the New York Yacht Club had been lost. The dangers of ocean yacht racing had been made chillingly plain. The sole satisfaction to the New York Yacht Club was that *Cambria* was soundly beaten in the America's Cup races that followed, though it must be noted that the NYYC mustered no fewer than eighteen vessels, almost its whole racing fleet, to prevail against her (an ambush Ashbury bitterly complained about for years).

It was almost twenty years later—in 1887—before yachtsmen challenged the North Atlantic again. Oddly, the bloodied New York Yacht Club itself issued the challenge. Unsurprisingly, Jamie Bennett, elected commodore again in 1884, played a part. Ostensibly its purpose was to demonstrate that the New York Yacht Club hadn't lost its seagoing mettle.

The year before (1886), not a single member had responded to a Britisher's challenge for a short (660-mile) open ocean race between New York and Bermuda. The press had a field day lampooning "American yachtsmen [embodied by the NYYC] for being so fainthearted." To the thin-skinned, always prickly bluebloods of the club, this public chaffing was an affront. To Bennett, it was a slap in the face.

The club issued a general challenge through Brooklyn businessman and New York Yacht Club member Rufus T. Bush. He offered to race his new, wickedly fast schooner *Coronet* across the Atlantic against all comers. He backed it with a stake of $10,000 (approximately $117,000 in present value), the cash posted with

F. W. J. Hurst, NYYC treasurer. Anyone from any yacht club, on either side of the ocean, who wanted to race could do likewise.

No one did.

This was hardly surprising. Yachtsmen tend to be a conservative bunch. The sea makes certain of that. Inshore races, the port-to-port matches the New York Yacht Club so enjoyed during its annual summer cruise, were all well and good. Ocean racing, as Bennett himself had demonstrated, was another sport entirely. Win or lose, it wrecked fine yachts, incurring thousands of dollars in damages. Even for millionaires, it cost dearly to send a boat to the Continent and bring it back. Not to mention the fact that it meant being without a boat for the festivities and entertainments of the summer cruise. What's more, seamen's deaths—whether by act of God or negligence—were open to interpretation, liability, litigation, and were a positive hindrance. There were races, trophies, and sport enough to be had without running those kinds of risks. Transatlantic racing, to say the least, appeared to be anything but a paying prospect. American yachtsmen weren't "fainthearted," as the press was saying. They were simply among the most practical of men.

None of this rationale spoke to Bennett. It merely ratified the opinion of the newspapers. That left him—the penultimate newspaperman *and* New York Yacht Club commodore—between a proverbial rock and a hard place. The press had raised the issue, and the club had thrown down its gauntlet. There could be no vindication of the club's seagoing honor if no one picked it up. If no one did, well, the New York Yacht Club would just have to do it itself.

That is, in fact, very much what happened. After a suitable period of time, only one man accepted the challenge. It was another New York Yacht Club member: young Caldwell T. "Colly" Colt, dapper heir to his father's vast firearms fortune. He was, in many ways, a mirror image of Bennett in his younger days: egocentric, spoiled, and by contemporary accounts "a boaster and an exhibitionist of sorts." One gets the impression that he was not so gently persuaded by Bennett to make it a race. Colt was something of his protégé. Bennett had not so recently sold him his aging schooner *Dauntless*. As any yacht buyer, Colt had no doubt listened to its previous owner's tales of her passages—especially the transatlantic race of 1870. Tellingly, as soon as he'd accepted the challenge, Colt lured old Bully Samuels out of retirement and hired him to skipper *Dauntless*. It had Bennett's fingerprints all over it.

Samuels was sixty-four at the time. Far beyond middle age, he was as big as a beer keg and reduced to wearing pince-nez spectacles. He didn't need to go to sea again, much less make another ocean race. He'd done quite well investing his winnings, despite some speculative setbacks (he was never averse to betting). He headed several successful businesses in New York and owned a fine brownstone home in Brooklyn overlooking the harbor. But he was still Bully, just thicker in the middle and hair gone silver. The temptation to race across the Atlantic one last time—and win—was too much for the old man. He moved his gear into the captain's cabin aboard *Dauntless*. Colly Colt took up residence in the opulent owner's stateroom, filled four staterooms with guests, a wine cellar, with vintage champagne, and brought along two stewards and two cooks. Rufus T. Bush embarked four guests, one of New York's most celebrated chefs, and veteran passagemaker Captain C. T. Crosby to take *Coronet* to the finish line for him.

The race commenced on March 12, in squally spring conditions. Both vessels started off Owl's Head [Bay Ridge] in Upper New York Bay, aiming to finish at Roche's Point, off Queenstown in southern Ireland. From the outset it was clear that Samuels had lost none of his stuff. He knew *Dauntless* full well and he drove her, straining every spar, far out into the North Atlantic. In strong winds he made fantastic progress. In one day's run—averaging a rip-roaring 13.2 knots an hour—he logged a record-breaking 328 miles for a yacht. In another, he actually overtook a steamship traveling in the same direction. Colt was exuberant. The rupture of *Dauntless*'s freshwater tanks in mid-Atlantic didn't trouble him. He broke out his abundant supply of vintage champagne for all hands to take its place (the crew, it was reported, didn't like the stuff despite its pedigree).

On March 21, nine days out, *Dauntless* encountered gales. Disregarding the heavy weather, Samuels kept up every stitch of canvas that would hold. On May 23, seas monumentally high, two exhausted crewmen attempting to change sail were swept overboard. Nobody could see them—until their still-attached lifelines snapped tightly, almost ripped out the stanchions, and showed them dragging astern. This forced Samuels to heave to at once. "After great difficulty," Samuels said, "they were hauled aboard and saved," but conditions were so bad he had to heave to for another twelve hours.

The following day, still driving through pulverizing seas, a completely unforeseen emergency arose. The ship's carpenter reported a serious leak. The ship's forepeak flooded whenever its bow was buried in the sea. At first Samuels ignored it, but it soon became so bad that the ship's crew had to work the pumps every fifteen minutes just to keep her afloat. Maddeningly, Samuels was forced to heave to again. The vessel, oil bags out to smooth the crashing seas, remained hove to for twenty-four hours and progressed but 42 miles as everybody aboard furiously searched for the source of the leak. It couldn't be found. There was no help for it. Samuels kept one watch on deck, working what sail they could and the other watch below working the pumps.

Aboard *Coronet,* Captain Crosby had no leaks to fight, only the same filthy weather. He had to heave to twice in midocean: once for thirteen hours and then for twenty. But as soon as conditions moderated, he was under way again. At sunset, as one on-board reporter noted, "the vessel was, as usual, got under easy canvas for the night." As events turned out, Crosby could well afford the luxury and perhaps knew it.

The finish was an anticlimax. *Coronet* coasted over the finish line in fourteen days, twenty-three hours, and thirty minutes, after a run of 2,949 miles. Bennett's 1866 record was still intact. *Dauntless,* leaking badly, finished almost thirty hours behind. Bush walked away with Colt's $10,000.

Long after the race, the cause of the leak was revealed. According to ocean racing historian Ian Dear, "When *Dauntless* had her copper bottom stripped off [for refitting] . . . it was found that two auger holes had been neatly drilled each side of the stem [bow]." Samuels "raged and roared" about it. "There is not a doubt in my mind," he said, "that those holes were bored with the intention of disabling the *Dauntless*." It was far too long after the race to prove anything: but auger holes precisely drilled on either side of her stem could scarcely have had any other purpose. In the end, however, Rufus Bush's winning *Coronet* was dealt a rough justice. In 1905 she was sold as worthless and ended her days as a so-called gospel ship, floating missionary, of the Holy Ghost and Us Society, cruising the coast of Maine. Perhaps that penance was her salvation. She is now the chief project and one of the key attractions of the International Yacht Restoration School in Newport, Rhode Island.

Unlike previous transatlantic races, the 1887 contest had been spared death, but made odious by sabotage. The suspicion that a fellow NYYC member may have been to blame made it worse.

Any desire left for ocean racing sank out of sight.

CHAPTER 7

Fourth Day at Sea

By heavens—blue sky—and the glass don't know it.
—Captain Lem Miller,
yawl *Ailsa*

Stevenson *had gotten no sleep. Running before heavy westerly squalls, under a double-reefed mainsail and storm trysail,* Ailsa *rolled wildly all night. He noted miserably that the violent motion "nearly equalled that in a square-rigger running before the wind in the Southern Ocean." The leeboard, fitted to the side of his bunk to keep him from being pitched out of it, instead acted like a back-board. He was slammed against it so hard and repeatedly it left him bruised. At 2:00* A.M. *a snap roll sent a torrent of seawater down the open companionway. It flooded the main passageway, soaking the grand saloon forward and all four staterooms aft, including his.*

At 10:00 A.M. *the barometer, sky, and seas looked dismal. Everything was dark, wet and heaving. But by noon the wind suddenly dropped "by half, the sea moderated, [and] the sun smiled." Captain Miller, one eye on blue skies and the other fixed on the brooding barometer, was confounded but jubilant. The trysail was struck, the mainsail unreefed and headsails set.* Ailsa *came over, the helmsman brought her up smartly on course, and she bounded ahead like a greyhound glad to be out of its kennel. It was near-*

perfect weather for her. "Two hours later," Stevenson wrote, "the whole solar system changed." Squalls attacked Ailsa "from all around the compass." The headsails were hauled down, the mainsail reefed, and the trysail hauled up again.

The shifting of canvas went on all day. Miller gave the crew no rest. Whenever the squalls retreated, he crowded on canvas and raced. Stevenson marveled that the crew handled the incessant sail changes "like men on a cup defender—by no means an easy job in a lop of sea and jumble of squalls." But this wasn't anything like an America's Cup race, which, though intense and physically draining, was relatively brief, seldom lasting more than half a day. Ailsa's crew had already been more or less on the job for four days, was sore tired, and was sorely aware that, conditions being what they were, they might be facing another four days of the same. Anything that got in the way of working the ship most efficiently—a sloppily tied knot or the owner's guests—was something to be made right or gotten rid of. It was natural that sooner or later, tempers frayed.

Grenville Kane, the owner's representative, took to sitting in the companionway, sheltered from wind and wash, to watch the men scrambling to shift sail. He found the spectacle enthralling. He quickly suffered "a deft kick on the head from the second mate's [Johnathan Svensen's] nice, new rubber boots." Though followed by "frantic apologies" from the mate, it served its purpose. It sent Kane scurrying below, "killed his ardor," and rid the deck watch of an idler fouling the companionway.

Henry Reuterdahl, the marine artist aboard, was soon sent packing as well. He'd arranged his "patent, collapsible easel" on deck to capture firsthand a picture of a line squall at sea. He was, of course, a perfect nuisance to men attempting to work ship. The manifold "guys and props he arranged" to keep his easel stable were anathema. Ailsa's helmsman made short work of him, maneuvering the boat until "a sea top fell over the quarter and broke against his legs." The helmsman repeated the drenching until Reuterdahl's expensive easel "disintegrated in the elements."

Stevenson saw plainly what was going on and brought it to Miller's attention. Miller admitted no conspiracy, merely that painting on deck while racing wasn't a good idea. "By heavens, just look at the man," he said as Reuterdahl frantically tried to save his canvas, brushes, and oils from washing over the rail. The artist retreated below to the saloon.

Stevenson took the hint. He was cold, tired, and hungry. Ailsa had logged 192 miles that day at an average speed of 8 knots—an admirable performance in foul weather and confused winds, but nowhere near a racing mark. He had no idea who was leading or lagging in the race; only that a monstrous expanse of ocean lay ahead. And as their course took them progressively farther north, conditions could only get worse. Then the storms would be joined by fog and ice. As he had written in his last newspaper column before sailing, "The ice, with its almost inseparable fog, has reached remarkably far to the southward this year and will be, by far, the greatest menace." In fact, May 1905 would be one of the worst months for icebergs in the North Atlantic in a half century of recordkeeping.

Miller and his Norwegians could have the deck. Stevenson went below to join the other guests.

CHAPTER 8

Another Kind of Race

Wilhelm's one idea is to have a navy which shall be larger and
stronger than the Royal Navy.

> —Empress Frederick,
> Kaiser Wilhelm II's mother and
> eldest daughter of Queen Victoria

The motivation for the 1905 transatlantic yacht race was another
—darker—competition that commenced in earnest in 1889.

On August 2 that year Kaiser Friedrich Wilhelm Viktor Albrecht
von Hohenzollern, just thirty, newly crowned emperor of Germany and king of Prussia, dropped anchor in Osborne Harbor off
the Isle of Wight in England. It was his first state visit as German
emperor, but he wore the full-dress uniform of a British admiral of
the fleet, the highest rank in the Royal Navy.

The commission, granted by his grandmother Queen Victoria,
was honorary. The regalia, however, was official: a plumed *chapeau
de bras;* swallow-tailed, double-breasted sixteen-button royal blue
coat (lined in white silk) with gold oak leaf-embroidered collar;
heavy gold epaulettes (topped with embossed crown above crossed
batons surrounded by laurel leaves); slashed cuff flaps with gold
ranking lace to the elbows; gold embroidered sword belt; and elegant dress sword. "Fancy wearing the same uniform as St. Vincent

and Nelson," the kaiser wrote of the outfit. "It is enough to make one quite giddy."

He was aboard the imperial yacht *Hohenzollern* at the head of a German naval squadron to attend the most awesome arms display on earth—a grand fleet review of the Royal Navy.

He had brought the best ships of his own navy to the event. The battleships *Friedrich der Gross* and *Preussen* were the most powerful; each mounting four 10.25-inch Krupp breech-loading guns in revolving, armored turrets and capable of steaming at 14 knots—for brief periods, anyway. Three-masted and ship-rigged, however, they mostly cruised under canvas. The battleships *Sachsen, Oldenburg,* and *Baden* were newest (completed between 1875 and 1883), each armed with six 10.25-inch guns. But the guns were mounted in open-topped, lightly armored barbettes, completely exposed to plunging shell fire or shrapnel. *Deutschland* and *Kaiser,* despite their august names, were obsolete "central batteryships." Though each packed eight 10.25-inch guns, the majority were fixed, pointing port or starboard, and could only be brought to bear by turning the whole vessel broadside, like Lord Nelson's ships a century earlier. Other than these, the new kaiser had with him the little *Freya*—a wooden-hulled, ironclad ram with half a dozen 6-inch guns—and three unarmored "dispatch" boats.

This less-than-imperial navy was all that Wilhelm brought to his grandmother's party. In fact, it had been difficult collecting even this small squadron to accompany him. The whole German navy—still run by generals at the time—totaled only twenty-four major warships. In manpower it numbered but seventeen thousand officers and men. The vessels Wilhelm left behind were embarrassing relics: wooden-hulled, sail-powered steam auxiliaries that were a quarter century old or more.

Eight of the eleven ships he'd brought to England, in fact, were ship-rigged and more or less dependent on sail for any kind of long-range cruising. The rest were exclusively coastal defense vessels, with limited range and seakeeping ability. What's more, half were based in the North Sea and half in the Baltic, each unable to assist the other (the Kiel Canal lay years in the future).

The Royal Navy waiting to greet him was stunning in size and

Sponsor of the 1905 ocean race: His Royal Highness, the emperor of Germany and king of Prussia, Kaiser Friedrich Wilhelm Viktor Albrecht von Hohenzollern. His ambitions were as large as his ego. The race was a desperate attempt to save both.

scope. According to the *Illustrated London News,* it was "divided into seven fleets and squadrons." It filled the huge Spithead anchorage from Portsmouth and Southsea, across the Solent to the Isle of Wight. It consisted of more than 120 warships, including 20 battleships, 29 cruisers, 6 armored coastal-defense ships, 17 gunboats, and more than 30 modern torpedo boats, plus ironclad steam frigates, armored corvettes, turreted monitors, and steam rams— eighteen different types of warships altogether.

Yet this was hardly the whole of the British fleet. As the Admiralty made very public for propaganda purposes, it was merely the portion of the fleet assigned to defend the home islands. Another twenty-two battleships, twice as many cruisers, and three times as many gunboats were absent on "foreign station," protecting the empire's interests from Suez to Singapore and Hong Kong to Honduras. In fact, most of the Royal Navy's 300 warships and 97,600 officers and men weren't at the Spithead review.

Those that were, however, presented an awe-inspiring sight. Anchored in three lines, each 7 miles long, lay rank on rank of raw naval power. The vessels receded into the distance like a floating iron wall, crenellated with towering funnels and masts and bristling with mammoth-mouthed guns. Freshly painted black, white, and buff, brass and brightwork blindingly polished, each ship was "full dressed"—Royal Navy ensigns displayed from the flagstaff and mastheads and a rainbow of signal flags and pennants flown from bow to stern. Upward of 25,000 "formidable-looking tars," as the *London News* reported, lined every yard and rail. Immaculately uniformed in white sennet hats (ship's name in gold on the tally band); blue frocks with light blue tallywhackers (flaring collars edged with three white tapes); black neckerchiefs; and blue, bell-bottomed trousers, they sent up three thundering British cheers "such as only British tars can give."

The spectacle, like ancient Roman triumphs or the Soviet Union's twentieth-century May Day parades, was calculated to intimidate potential enemies. The ships included in the 1889 review were carefully selected to terrify Germany—specifically the new kaiser. In battle against the British vessels on display, his minuscule navy could not survive an hour.

The turret battleship HMS *Inflexible*'s four massive 16-inch guns alone outranged and overpowered anything in the German fleet (or any other fleet, for that matter). *Inflexible*'s armor—24 inches of compound steel and iron backed by 36 inches of teak—was thicker than that of any warship in the world. It also featured electric lights, antirolling tanks, torpedo launchers, and 39 auxiliary engines for steering, ventilation, and other operations—advances unheard of in German ships. HMS *Devastation*, the first major battleship without sails, had triple-expansion engines and a range of 5,000 nautical miles at cruising speed without recoaling—a bluewater capability no German warship could match. HMS *Collingwood*, one of the newest battleships on display, used forced draft to supercharge her engines and boasted a speed of 17 knots; fantastic for a heavily armored ship of nearly 10,000 tons when torpedo boats at the time made 20 knots.

The Admiralty's new light cruiser, HMS *Magicienne*, bristled with a hedgehog of 4.7-inch rapid-firing guns, each gun spitting out an unprecedented 10 rounds per minute. Then there was the legion of British torpedo boats, in three types, capable of closing at 20 knots and loosing barrages of 30-knot Whitehead torpedoes against German capital ships.

On Saturday, August 3, Wilhelm watched this fearsome fleet salute him from aboard the British royal yacht *Osborne*. He'd kept his host and uncle, Albert, prince of Wales, waiting almost three hours. It was an intentional slight. Wilhelm, after all, was now emperor of Germany and absolute ruler of fifty million subjects. As long as his grandmother, Queen Victoria, remained on the throne, his uncle would remain only a prince and be treated as such. The new kaiser's hubris did not go down well with his grandmother, uncle, or the British people. But Wilhelm, as rooted to protocol as Victoria (when it suited him), didn't care. He had taken his place on the world stage and would be given his due. The grand fleet review, quite obviously, was instead intended to remind him of a lower station. To the astonishment of his hosts and just about everyone else, it did nothing of the kind. On the contrary, as naval historian Bernard Ireland put flatly, "It only served to fire him with envy."

As ship after ship passed, Wilhelm saw something tantalizing: weakness. He had seen it when he first reviewed his own navy at Kiel: decrepitude in disguise. He could smell it like the mince pies with flaming brandy sauce that were his one gastronomic weakness. Despite its apparent power, as Ireland concluded more than a century later, "the Royal Navy was a metaphor for the aging monarch [Victoria] herself. Virtually unchallenged for the better part of a century, it had become arthritic and complacent. . . . A powerful sense of tradition had atrophied into powerful conservatism."

Inflexible's 16-inch guns were indeed the largest and longest-ranging in the world, but amazingly they were muzzleloaders. To load them, the muzzles of the guns first had to be depressed below an armored glacis on deck, 100 pounds or more of high explosive rammed up the barrels, and 500-pound shell rammed up the barrels after that. This process left the most powerful battleship afloat impotent during the not inconsiderable time it took to do it (approximately one round every $3\frac{1}{2}$ minutes). Virtually all European navies had adopted faster firing breechloaders; the British fleet "was almost the last Navy in the world to be equipped with muzzle-loading guns."

Certainly *Devastation* had greater range and seakeeping ability than any of the kaiser's battleships, but its 10- to 12-inch armor was no more than pie crust to the new high-velocity guns Germany's Krupp works had developed. While *Collingwood* was reputed to be the fastest battleship in the world, her overtaxed engines were notoriously unreliable and—by dint of her low freeboard—she could never achieve her vaunted 17-knot speed in anything but a dead calm. Her 12-inch batteries outclassed the kaiser's 10-inch guns, but, like his, were mounted in exposed barbettes without overhead protection. *Hercules,* like many of the battleships paraded before him, was a central battery ship—an improvement on the broadside ironclads of the 1860s, but still a ship-rigged, three-masted hemaphrodite, her masts and rigging shockingly vulnerable to gunfire, only a pittance of her heavy guns able to bear ahead or astern.

In an age of swift and sweeping advances in metallurgy, gunnery, and steam power, the world's largest naval power had been largely left behind. Indeed, the "great Victorian boast that the Royal Navy was the largest in the world," as Royal Navy chronicler Robert Wilkinson-Latham wrote, "concealed much muddle and lack of coordination."

Wilhelm saw it plainly. Certainly the British Admiralty did. In 1887 its chief constructor (naval architect) recommended that no fewer than seventy-two ships be scrapped outright. The report of the 1888 fleet maneuvers, in fact, presented to Parliament in early 1889, "revealed deficiencies in all aspects of the navy." Even the *London News* reported that the 1889 fleet review was "noticeable as an exhibition of the various forms of naval architecture which have been in use during the past half century, several of which are now quite obsolete." It was a navy that many were calling "too old to fight and too slow to run away." And—laid upon it like a banquet on a shaky table—was spread the riches of the entire British Empire.

None of this escaped Wilhelm's notice. He was new to the throne, not stupid, by no means deferential, and cat-eager to make his mark. Militarily, he was overshadowed by his grandfather Kaiser Wilhelm I, who had won the Franco-Prussian War and established the Second Reich. His father, Kaiser Friedrich, whose reign lasted only nine months (dying of throat cancer, he couldn't speak for most of it), had been a decorated war veteran. Diplomatically, Wilhelm could never hope to escape the overwhelming reputation of Chancellor Otto von Bismarck (he would shortly fire him), and routinely and dismally failed every time he did.

But none of them had ever looked to the sea. None of them had tested themselves upon it. None of them had won anything on the waves. Technology, as his naval attachés were almost certainly telling him, had dealt everyone a new hand—indeed, a whole new deck. The majority of Britain's vaunted navy was obsolete and no better than his own. If that was true of the world's supreme maritime power with some three hundred warships, it also was true of the world's second- and third-ranked naval powers (France with ninety-five ships and Russia with eighty-six).

For the new kaiser, it was something of an epiphany. The place to write his name was the high seas.

Following the fleet review, he set out with a vengeance to win everything on the waves.

CHAPTER 9

The Man Nobody Liked

There *is the dark cloud.*
> —Lord Salisbury, British prime minister
> (on Wilhelm II's accession)

To his grandmother (Queen Victoria), uncles (the prince of Wales, the duke of Edinburgh, and the duke of Connaught), and cousins (the duke of York, Czar Nicholas, and Queen Marie of Romania, to name a few), the kaiser always had been "Willy." As a child, they felt sympathy for him. His left arm and hand had been mangled at birth when—after fifteen hours in labor—he'd been wrenched from his mother's womb with forceps. For the rest of his life, his left arm remained a full 6 inches shorter than the right, atrophied and useless. His left hand, though perfectly formed, remained the size of a child's, "unable to hold anything heavier than a piece of paper," according to biographers. In public, it was forever gloved and positioned atop the hilt of a saber or hidden in specially designed pockets in his clothes.

It was cause for Victorian embarrassment, but no more so than others of Victoria's line who suffered hemophilia, dementia, alcoholism, or cancer. Otherwise he seemed nothing much out of the ordinary, as far as royal offspring went: just another precocious, perhaps somewhat more pompous, prince-in-waiting. The moment his father died, however, Willy showed fangs.

Queen Victoria was shocked at his behavior. Her son-in-law Kaiser Friedrich III had scarcely been pronounced dead when a regiment of Wilhelm's black-uniformed hussars sealed off the Neue Palais in Potsdam with orders that no one could leave. That included his own mother—the kaiserin, Victoria's eldest and favorite daughter. Victoria immediately sent him a telegram: "I am heartbroken. Help and do all you can for your poor dear mother [Victoria's daughter] and try to follow in your best noblest and kindest of father's footsteps."

Instead the palace was ransacked for the dead kaiser's private papers, personal letters, and diaries, Wilhelm himself turning his bereaved mother's bedroom upside down. He was searching for the identities of anyone opposed to his succession. He forbade any clergy, prayers, or services at his dead father's bedside. "In defiance of his father's instructions and grief-stricken mother's pleas," according to biographer John Van der Kiste, "he allowed an autopsy conducted on his father's body." He suspected that an English physician, sent at Victoria's insistence to attend his father, was culpable for his death. He ripped open his father's will, and ordered many of his last requests disregarded and his personal papers destroyed.

Three days later, Wilhelm had his father buried. The thing was done so quickly, wrote an observer, that "while the chapel was being decorated, the coffin stood in the midst of hammering workmen like a toolchest, while the short path to the church was guarded by troops." There was no evidence of grief among the new kaiser's sycophants. According to Prussian count Philip von Eulenberg, they seemed happy: "the clergy were laughing and chatting, Field-Marshall Blumenthal, with the Standard over his shoulder, reeling about, talking—it was horrible." There was a calculated paucity of state ceremony. Amazingly, the new kaiser sent no invitations to the funeral to foreign princes, even though he was inundated by telegrams from foreign heads of state paying their respects. Wilhelm's own mother and three sisters were so incensed at the rush to plant Friedrich's corpse that they refused to attend the funeral. The prince and princess of Wales managed to get there in time for the services: Albert furious at his nephew's conduct and Alexandra labeling him "a mad and conceited ass."

The new kaiser wasted no time mourning. Within three weeks he was at Kiel reviewing his fleet—in a bedazzling new *Grossadmiral's* uniform he'd designed himself. Then he was off on gaudy state visits to Russia, Austria-Hungary, Italy, Sweden, and Denmark. On each of these trips, to dispense as gifts, according to a biographer, "He took with him 80 diamond rings, 150 silver orders, gold photograph frames [with his own portrait], 30 gold watches and chains, 100 caskets and 20 diamond-set Orders of the Eagle [Germany's highest honorary order]."

While his father had been content to travel in chartered first-class railroad cars, Wilhelm indulged himself in a specially ordered imperial train. It consisted of a brace of high-speed locomotives and twelve state-of-the-art Pullman cars—lounging, dining, and sleeping cars, with plush seating, thick carpeting and stained glass—painted in the blue, cream, and gold colors of the House of Hohenzollern. He ordered a new imperial steam yacht: 383 feet long and 3,756 tons, with a ram bow, three-masted schooner rig, and two raked steam funnels. In size and speed she was equivalent to a light cruiser (nearly identical, in fact, to the German commerce raider Emden, 387 feet and 3,554 tons, which terrorized the Indian Ocean in World War I). In U.S. dollars today she cost about $25 million to build. He also commissioned exquisite blue stationery for himself, embossed "All Highest." Under his signature he routinely inked *"Suprema lex, regis voluntas"* (the will of the king is the highest law).

Despite his inheritance (140 million gold marks or about $514 million U.S. today), annual income (20 million marks or $74 million U.S. today), Berlin real estate (worth 18 million marks or $66 million U.S. today), and no fewer than fifty-three castles, palaces, and estates, he immediately demanded—and got—a pay raise. It boosted his annual salaried income alone to almost 27 million marks ($100 million U.S. today).

To Victoria, all this looked celebratory, monomaniacal, and in abominably bad taste. She had been religiously mourning her dead husband for twenty-seven years; Willy hadn't mourned at all. In fact, he'd made a mockery of every courtly ritual of mourning there was. To Wilhelm, it seemed only that he was getting his due. As emperor, at last, he no longer had to answer to anyone—about anything. He embraced the role of "All Highest" like an actor—a rather bad actor, determined to play a far larger part than he'd been given. The dual devils of his birth and his birthright spurred him to it.

When told of his newborn grandson's disabilities, Kaiser Wilhelm I reportedly remarked that he was "not sure whether congratulations on the birth of a *defective* prince are in order." The words branded him forever: defective prince. His grandfather and the Prussian royalty made no qualms about the fact that someone else—fitter in Prussian eyes—would make a better successor to the throne. Wilhelm never forgot. Throughout his life he was driven not only to demonstrate that his lifeless arm wasn't a disability—that he was any man's equal—but also that as kaiser, he was any man's superior. His Prussian upbringing cemented the two beliefs. The bond was permanent and cold.

When they yanked him from his mother's womb, the physicians thought he was dead. He was limp and turning blue. They handed him to a midwife and went to work to save the kaiserin. The midwife repeatedly slapped him until, finally, he began to breathe and scream. His mother was bedridden for a month after the ordeal. Mortified at the infant's disfigurement, she saw him little during that time. As an infant and a toddler, he was lavished with affection. After that, neither she nor the crown prince had much time to spare for the child. His upbringing was left to an English nurse, then a Prussian governess, von Doberneck, whom Wilhelm forever remembered as "a great, gaunt dame of firm character, whose method by no means excluded the use of the palm."

At age seven he was surrendered to Professor George Hinzpeter, a severe thirty-eight-year-old bachelor with doctorates in philosophy and philology. Hinzpeter's system of instruction consisted of twelve hours a day of study and physical exercise. It was part of his Spartan policy never to give the child any praise, encouragement, or approval. As Wilhelm recollected, "The impossible was expected of the pupil in order to force him to the nearest degree of perfection.

Naturally, the impossible goal could never be achieved; therefore, the praise which registers approval was also excluded." The lesson left its mark: force, not approval or encouragement, made things work; in fact, force was the *way* things worked. A person with the authority or the power to force another to do something—the backhanding governess von Doberneck, the icily commanding Professor Hinzpeter—pulled the strings.

At fifteen, he was packed off to school at Cassel. The regimen was unending: up at 5:00 A.M., lessons from 6:00 A.M. until noon, physical exercise from noon until 2:00 P.M., more school lessons from 2:00 P.M. until 4:00 P.M., a private lesson from Hinzpeter until 5:00 P.M., an hour for dinner, then more schoolwork from 6:00 P.M. until 9:00 P.M. Intellectually, he wasn't exceptional. He did well in history, poorly in mathematics. Physically, he was extraordinary.

Despite only one hand to hold the reins and inner ear damage that gave him problems with balance, he was taught to ride. The punishing expedient, as biographer Michael Balfour wrote, consisted of "placing him on a stirrupless pony and replacing him there as often as he fell off." He endured the indignity until will overcame fear. It forged him into a master horseman—one of the finest royal equestrians in Europe, in fact.

He was similarly made into an expert fencer, wielding either foil, épée, or saber. In this business, his disability became his advantage. In compensation for his atrophied left arm, his right was over-developed and powerful, tailor-made for slashing a heavy saber. He was so good with it that he was made a member of what a biographer termed "the most swagger students' [dueling] club, Borussia," whose sole, murky charter was to overcome *der innere Schweinehund* (the inner pig), or cowardice. Dueling with sabers, especially in Germany at the time, demanded sangfroid. Though a duelist's eyes and body were protected (by goggles and an umpirelike padded chest protector), the face was purposely left bare. The whole point was to cleave an opponent's cheek down to the jaw, flesh hanging, leaving a signature scar—Borussia's calling card. Any honor Wilhelm may have gained by his swordsmanship, however, was denied by his birthright. Nobody in his right mind would ever challenge the crown prince of the German Empire to a duel.

Even if he had—which was tantamount to personal and professional suicide—court law abrogated an heir's obligation to accept.

At blood sports, he excelled. On a not unusual grouse hunt in 1902, he killed more than three hundred in a day's shoot. Visiting his grandmother in Scotland, he hunted red stag, loudly complaining to his ghillie about the cold, Highland rain, as if he expected the guide to turn it off for him. In Luxemburg he shot roebuck; in Russia, wolves; in Austria-Hungary he shot chukar and Hungarian partridge. At home, in Hesse and Thuringia, he shot snipe, white partridge, woodcock, and blackcock. In East Prussia he shot wild boar. Not long after taking the throne, he raised a monument to himself in the state forest at Rominten. Inscribed in gold, it read: "Here His Majesty Wilhelm II brought down His Most High's fifty-thousandth animal: a white cock pheasant."

Obviously this accomplishment had great meaning for him, otherwise he wouldn't have kept meticulous track of fifty thousand kills. Granted, like most royal hunts, the game Wilhelm killed was largely stocked. Most hunts consisted of orchestrated *battues* or beats, wardens beating the woods and bushes to flush the game within easy range of the waiting sportsmen. Still, for a one-armed man wielding a shotgun or a rifle it was—if not particularly sportsmanlike—proof of a deadly proficiency with firearms that few men with two good arms could match. The monument at Rominten was proof of a lust not only to win but also to dominate. It was what he'd been rigorously trained and cultivated to do. Upon becoming emperor that lust turned into addiction.

It poisoned relations with those few who were closest to him. He completely dominated his wife (who was also his cousin); a lady at court described her as "completely submissive, with eyes like glass." His children avoided him. His own mother, who found him bullying and cruel as a youngster, never really forgave him for his behavior at the Neue Palais. Neither did Queen Victoria, who found her grandson's insistence upon being treated as emperor at all times insufferable. "To pretend that he is to be treated in *private* as well as public as 'His Imperial Majesty' is *perfect madness*," she wrote Lord Salisbury. "*If* he has *such* notions, he better *never* come here. The Queen will not swallow this affront." His uncle

Albert, prince of Wales, quipped that his nephew "William the
Great," he called him, "needs to learn that he is living at the end
of the nineteenth century and not in the Middle Ages." Both of them
were looking for Willy to keep his proper place.

Unfortunately for Victoria and his uncle Albert, the first place
Wilhelm chose to demonstrate his imperial dominance was at sea.
Following the 1889 fleet review, his uncle unwittingly showed
him where to begin. He and Thomas Ismay, chairman of Britain's
White Star Line, took the new kaiser on a tour of the brand-new
liner *Teutonic*. It was another blatantly obvious attempt to intimidate him. The vessel's Germanic name was rather a taunt, since it
was the first fast passenger liner built under an all new set of
British Admiralty regulations, which mandated that it could be converted into an armed merchant cruiser in times of war. An impressive 565 feet long, she was armored and fitted to carry a brace of
rapid-firing guns. Driving twin screws, her triple expansion steam
engines gave her a top speed of 20.4 knots. She could pursue, over-
take, and destroy any unarmed merchant ship afloat—which, of
course, meant every vessel in the German merchant marine, second
largest in the world after Britain's and the most likely target of such
attacks. There was little the German navy, fifth largest in the world,
could do to protect it.

The effect this guided tour had on the kaiser was hardly what
Albert or Ismay had in mind. Wilhelm spent an hour and a half
roaming the ship; marveling more at its myriad creature comforts
than its warlike appurtenances. At the end, "with the casual cov-
etousness of a man who spots a new brand of cigar or gold ball,"
noted transatlantic ocean liner authority John Brinnin, "he was
overheard to say, 'We must have some of these.'" Nobody in the
British contingent heard it the way his German entourage did.
They took it as an imperial order, to which the only acceptable
response was "As Your Majesty commands." The emperor wanted
a passenger liner. Shortly afterward he made plain that he wanted
not only a liner; he also wanted one that was larger, faster, and
grander than the *Teutonic*.

When he told his aides what he wanted it for, they couldn't
believe he was serious. He wanted to wrest the "Blue Ribband" of

the Atlantic—the record for the fastest transatlantic ocean passage—from the British. He wanted to do it in a German-designed and German-built vessel, and he wanted it done at once. All elements of common sense argued against making the attempt. The Blue Ribband was as much a British possession as Gibraltar. British steamship lines had held the record for well over half a century. Though Germany's merchant marine was nearly as large as Britain's, little of it had been designed or built by Germans. Most German steamship lines commissioned ships to be built on the Tyne or the Clyde, the epicenters of British shipbuilding, the finest yards in the world. Designing a Blue Ribband winner looked to be a daunting technological challenge, a shipbuilding nightmare, and a financial black hole.

Wilhelm bulldozed all objections. Huge construction subsidies were to be paid German shipping companies. British engineers and shipwrights were to be offered fantastic salaries to lure them to work in German shipyards. But—and on this point the kaiser was adamant—as soon as "German shipwrights had learned what they needed to know, the services of the Englishmen and Scotsmen were to be dispensed with."

The result was the tall, fast, fearsome-looking North German Lloyd Line passenger liner *Kaiser Wilhelm der Grosse,* from the Vulcan Yards at Stettin on the Baltic. At 649 feet in length, she easily eclipsed the British Cunard Line's 620-foot *Campania* and her sister *Lucania,* then the largest, fastest passenger liners in the world. The *Kaiser Wilhelm,* accommodating a phenomenal 2,300 passengers, was capable of a top speed of 23 knots. It was launched in May 1897, and the kaiser pressed to put her into service in September. Time was short. He not only wanted to snatch the Blue Ribband from the British, he also wanted to do it before the end of Queen Victoria's Diamond Jubilee year, when all things commemorated the queen's reign (and, by extension, the British Empire's maritime monopoly). On her maiden voyage, she shattered the eastbound transatlantic steamship record from New York to Southampton. In winterlike conditions, she made the 3,200-mile passage in just five days, seventeen hours, and eight minutes. Four months later, she captured the *westbound* record from Southampton to New York.

The British were stunned. The Blue Ribband belonged to the kaiser. He waved it in front of the German people like a captured battle standard. All expense and effort were quite forgotten. They cheered him, cheered Germany, cheered themselves. It was quite like the enthusiasm and pride displayed by the U.S. public during the space race of the 1960s. It also muzzled any criticism about his expensive naval ambitions. The subsidies he lavished on German shipping companies, ostensibly to carry the mail, but more importantly to build ships that, like the *Teutonic,* could be modified for military use in times of war, were extravagant. The kaiser's critics at home saw them for what they were, as did the British: appropriations by imperial decree for a "shadow navy" of big, high-speed, easily armed merchant cruisers. While all this was true, winning the Blue Ribband demonstrated to the German people that it wasn't. It was simply a triumph of German will.

For the kaiser, it was a public relations Austerlitz. It momentarily silenced those in the Reichstag opposed to opening the public purse so he could buy a navy of his own. Other than the emperor's vanity, they saw no justification for spending money on a fleet. A first-class army was expensive enough. None of Germany's few and far-flung colonies merited spending a fortune for a navy to protect. Nobody wanted them anyway.

Only one, West Virginia–sized Togoland in West Africa, was financially independent of the Fatherland, and its precarious solvency rested on exporting yams. German-controlled Cameroon, just above the equator in West Africa, was described by contemporary historian Byron Farwell as "generally regarded as one of the most unhealthy spots on the West Coast and often called the white man's grave. In a story, perhaps apocryphal, a young [German] man posted to the area who asked if his return passage would be paid, was informed that the question had never arisen." German South-West Africa, largely an arid plateau girded by the Namib Desert along the Atlantic coast and the Kalahari Desert in the interior, gobbled up millions of marks in subsidies every year. Germany's largest colony, German East Africa, which also gobbled subsidies, was infested with the tsetse fly and tenuously administered by five thousand Germans living amongst eight million natives.

In the Far East, Germany's other colonies seemed, if anything, more pathetic. Tsingtao, on the Shandong Peninsula on the Chinese mainland, had a fine harbor but little else of promise. Funded by imperial subsidies, German colonists had established a flourishing brewery there; its signal commercial success. Kaiser Wilhelm Land (modern-day Papua, New Guinea) consisted of malarial swamps and jungled mountains, much of it unexplored. Its primary use, like French-controlled New Caledonia to the south, was as a penal colony. In the vast Pacific, Germany's holdings in Samoa (1,093 square miles), the Caroline Islands (271 square miles), and the Marshall Islands (70 square miles) had nothing of value for export except guano.

Indeed, almost all of Germany's colonies were unclaimed remnants from Europe's great nineteenth-century scramble for empire. They had been plucked up by previous chancellor Bismarck, not to keep, but to trade away—bargaining chips to gain more vital territorial concessions for Germany in Europe. Kaiser Wilhelm saw them in a vastly different light. They were the foundation stones of his overseas empire. He had no intention of giving them away. He meant to build upon them. The primary tool for doing that was the blue-water navy he'd been hungering for ever since taking the throne.

With the Blue Ribband in his pocket and German nautical pride higher than ever because of it, he launched a brilliant lobbying offensive to win the massive appropriations necessary to build a fleet of his own. He ordered his new chancellor, Count Berhard von Bülow, to make "a complete overhaul of the relevant [imperial press] machinery. He ensured that press officers were placed in each ministry to provide a favorable slant on any [naval] news which was issued. Certain newspapers with wide circulations were selected to present the government case." He ordered the German Colonial Society formed to organize lectures, distribute pamphlets, and sponsor public meetings on the need for a navy. He mandated that Germany's major port cities organize yacht clubs and yacht races to excite public participation. The German Navy League—consisting of industrialists, businessmen, and aristocrats whom Wilhelm knew from his Blue Ribband venture were eager to put their snouts in the pork barrel—was organized to lobby apace with the palace for a huge increase in naval spending. The kaiser's handpicked new navy secretary, Admiral Alfred von Tirpitz, strategically painted the Royal Navy's sheer size and its implied threat of British domination as Germany's greatest enemies, and an expensive, new high seas fleet as Germany's sole salvation. The kaiser's speeches rang with suitable soundbites: "Our future lies on the water" and "The colonies must be defended in the North Sea."

It was a masterpiece of soft and strong-arm politicking. Fewer than six months later, the kaiser's First Naval Law—a plan to *double* the size of the German Navy—passed the Reichstag by a comfortable margin. The British were stunned. Wilhelm was ecstatic. He never afterward forgot the power of public relations.

He used the same well-oiled lobbying machine fewer than two years later to win the passage of the more ambitious and frighteningly expensive Second Naval Law, in 1900. Instead of building an average of one battleship a year, as budgeted in the 1898 law, Germany would henceforth build *three*. The newly coined German Imperial Navy was to number thirty-eight first-class battleships (Wilhelm had argued, unsuccessfully, for forty-eight!), fifty-eight cruisers, and countless destroyers and torpedo boats. Securing the appropriations was a triumph for the kaiser. It appalled the British, who saw no strategic German purpose for such a fast-growing fleet other than to challenge their own. They had no choice but to accelerate—or more properly reaccelerate—the building and modernization of their own navy. Driving the British to jump through such dangerously escalating hoops did not seem to concern Wilhelm. He seems to have delighted in it. In 1904, he put his lobbying juggernaut to work on a special, supplementary naval law. It was something of a Trojan horse in that it did not mandate building more ships. Instead, it materially increased the size (and cost) of the ships already being built under his 1900 law. Battleships were to more than double in size, from 13,000 to 28,000 tons. Armored cruisers were to be as big as the previous battleships.

The warships emerging in litters from the belly of the Reich would henceforth be monsters.

CHAPTER 10

Fifth Day at Sea

Last night the devil was adrift on the deep sea.
                                        —Paul Stevenson,
                                        yawl *Ailsa*

*I*t had been a wretched night, far worse than the night before. In his log, Stevenson jotted increasingly anxious entries: "huge menacing squalls," then "choking, heavy West wind," then "nasty, breaking following seas," and then "five points of yawing *at every heave.*" A compass card is divided into thirty-two equidistant points, each of eleven degrees, fifteen seconds. Five points of yawing—poleaxing Ailsa fifty-six degrees off course every time she was hit by a wave—was phenomenally dangerous.

Yaw—produced by following winds and seas—diminishes the effect of a ship's rudder, causing it to veer (yaw) off course. In a way, it's like a maritime auto skid; the wheel unresponsive, the vessel sliding downwave or downhill, so to speak, going pretty much wherever wind, water, and its own mass hurl it. A good helmsman, like a good driver, can minimize or at least control yawing to a degree. But the kind of yaw Stevenson was describing—whipsawing 116-ton Ailsa from her east-northeast heading (roughly two-thirty on a clock face) to either north-by-east (twelve-thirty) or southeast-by-east (four-thirty)—was all but uncontrollable. Under

*those conditions, the only sensible thing for Captain Miller to do
was heave to. Stevenson could not understand why the order had
not been given.*

*After midnight he stuck his head out of the companionway to
see what in the world was going on. Spray stung his face like bird-
shot. The drumming of canvas overhead was deafening. To his horror, he saw that not only was the huge mainsail still up, it was also
unreefed. Above it, the gaff topsail was full out, too. It was crazy,
reckless, stupid, like downhill skiing through a forest at night. In
knockdown conditions, Miller was driving the boat downwind.*

*Looming in the darkness astern, Stevenson could plainly see the
pursuing seas: mountainous black swells illuminated as their summits broke in eerie green phosphorescent crests. The helmsman,
braced at the wheel in his sou'wester with a lifeline fast around him,
appeared to be the only man on deck. His face was lit like a jack-
o'-lantern in the binnacle (compass) light. Despite cold and wet,
Stevenson was startled to see him—quite literally—"sweating." At
first Stevenson thought it was the brute physical effort required to
muscle the wheel in such seas. Then he realized it was fear.*

*The man looked possessed. His head seemed to swivel full cir-
cle on his shoulders. Backward, trying to anticipate the moment
when the North Atlantic would deliver its next roundhouse punch.
Forward, to apply the requisite helm to counteract it. Aloft, to keep
what Stevenson aptly described as Ailsa's "Satanic mainboom"
from jibing—swinging wildly across the deck in the inescapable yaw.
In an uncontrolled jibe, the overly canvased boom was a loose cannon, and Ailsa's boom measured 70 feet long. Anything it struck
was doomed. The best that might mean for a crewman in its path
was a quick, merciful beheading; the worst a spine-shattering cart-
wheel into the dark, drowning embrace of the sea.*

*The damage it could do to the boat was quite as catastrophic.
It might pivot with force enough to rip out the rigging screws, snap
shrouds, and stays, and to fracture, if not carry off, the mainmast.
If the standing rigging held, the momentum of the boom alone was
still more than enough to hurl the boat broadside on the sea and
capsize her. If it didn't, the percussive impact of a 50-ton wave could
fracture Ailsa's thin planking and ribs, knock a hole in the hull, or*

punch her port lights out of one side of the boat straight through the other.

All these calamities were vividly apparent to Stevenson. Dead astern, ballooning behind the helmsman's back, he saw what he called a "king roller"—a monstrous, 40-foot wave fetched up over hundreds of miles of open ocean. It hissed out of the darkness at first. But as it closed on the boat, the hiss became a rumble that amplified into a roar. It slammed into *Ailsa* square astern, with a boom that made her woodwork shriek and her rigging shudder. It pitched the stern in the air, smashed over the taffrail, and swept the deck like a waterfall. The deluge knocked the helmsman off his feet. It sent Stevenson sprawling down the companionway.

He fell on Captain Miller, who was coming up. Dripping and sputtering, Stevenson angrily told him that conditions were awful. If the mainsail and the topsail didn't come down at once, they'd either be carried away or drive the boat under. It was past time to get all that canvas down and the small storm trysail up. *Ailsa* couldn't take any more.

Miller looked at him like he was a lunatic, then smiled. "Ya, ya, ya," he shouted, "a wretched condition, but a helpless one when racing." He scrambled topside and left Stevenson speechless at the foot of the ladderway.

Belowdecks, everything seemed worse. *Ailsa,* formerly an elegantly appointed yacht, had been stripped for efficiency in the ocean race. Her grand saloon had been denuded of all movable furniture and fixtures, its fine, hardwood floors covered by rough planks. Six hanging kerosene lamps—two of which had shattered against the carlings and gone dark—provided a shadowy light. "Three tons of [spare] canvas crowded one side of the room," Stevenson wrote, and "a portentous zinc-lined icebox, bolted to the floor, with ice enough to fill a morgue" crowded the other. The only place for the afterguard to sit and eat was a red leather-upholstered banquette in the saloon's starboard side corner. But Captain Miller had commandeered its gimbaled (swinging) table as a navigation station. Except at mealtimes, it was piled with his "charts, dividers and parallel rulers."

Overhead, an eight-paned, leaded-glass skylight leaked incessantly. The steward had arranged "huge, thick glass receivers under *the dead lights to catch the drip," but with the rolling, pitching, and yawing they spilled as much as they caught. It was pointless trying to keep the place dry, anyway. Crewmen exchanging sail came and went constantly, leaving an ankle-deep slop of sea behind. The mountain of drenched canvas they piled in the saloon left the walls beaded and running with condensation. Under battened hatches, the damp cabin reeked of "kerosene fumes and the weird breaths from the big meat boxes." The latter smell no longer bothered Stevenson. It made him forget the menace outside. It made his mouth water.*

The one—the only—saving grace of the voyage, so far, anyway, had been the food. Mr. Redmond had spared no expense on provisions. The ship's white-capped Danish cook was no longer suspect. Burrowing among the cold, pallid contents of the big icebox, he produced wonders. Regardless of weather, Stevenson marveled that "hot, new-made soups confront us each noon." At supper he was flabbergasted to find "salmon steaks and egg sauce, sweetbreads, sizzling roasts and plum puddings." At the cramped banquette, he wrote that the service was better than "that of a first-rate hotel . . . all swiftly served by the gaunt-jawed Briton [steward], whose training in Albion's navy has enabled him to disregard an angle of forty-five degrees."

The whole thing must have seemed surreal to him: a white-capped chef and a British butler; serving up—as he vividly logged— "squabs, souffle, omelettes and green salads" in the middle of the Atlantic in a gale. Aboard a Fife-designed yacht upon which Mr. Redmond had lavished $1 million for no other purpose, really, than to win a garish trophy cup worth far less than his everyday service of Limoges.

All the momentary comfort the fine food provided didn't change the fact that Redmond expected a return on his investment. Stevenson now fully recognized that. Miller was obviously dead serious about producing it. The crew—whether for wages, bonus money, or sheer pride—obeyed every syllable of his orders. The wind-driven missile Redmond had launched was now far beyond its fail-safe point. In the wastes of the North Atlantic, its sole purpose now was running for its life to win a rich man's race.

CHAPTER 11

Spoiled Sports

Tournaments . . . the most exciting, expensive, ruinous and delightful activity of the noble class.

—Barbara Tuchman

There are common sports. And then there are those reserved for the wealthy. Extreme elitist sports, such as open ocean racing, are historically the realm of the very rich. Poor men (but for Sherpas) don't summit Everest. They don't race around the globe in yachts or hot-air balloons. They don't set land and water speed records. They don't hunt the "big three" trophy animals in Africa. This isn't because they lack the desire, ability, or courage. They simply can't afford it.

Elitist sports are expensive and exclusionary. That is, indeed, part of their whole purpose. The expense weeds out supposedly lower, common classes and elevates the game to one peculiarly of the rich, by the rich, and for the rich. Polo, somehow, comes to mind. But there is quite a bit more to elite sports than money. Most have their roots in blood sports, usually begun as religious rituals, a kingly form of sacrifice and worship. They later evolved, for better or for worse, as the epitome of manliness. "A knight cannot shine in war," wrote a contemporary chronicler in the Middle Ages, "if he has not prepared for it in tournaments. He must have seen his own blood flow, have had his teeth crackle under the blow of an adversary." In either case, they were calculated to prove as nearly as possible not who had the most wealth necessarily but who was ordained, spiritually or physically, to persevere and lead. In effect, elite games evolved as a kind of man-made test to reveal God-like powers or, at the very least, powers far beyond those of ordinary men.

In extreme elitist sports—mountain climbing being a relatively recent, transcendent example—money is merely the ante. The supreme test of those with the money to play is whether they're willing, quite literally, to bet their lives on the outcome. That's the thing that raises the game to a realm beyond money. That's the thing that conveys upon the winner a nobility and a prestige that no color of coin or cut of jewel can purchase.

Losers, of course, pay a gruesome price. Following the first ascent of the Matterhorn in 1865, a rich British dilettante, Lord Francis Douglas, just eighteen, a Swiss guide, and two other British climbers (Rev. Charles Hudson and neophyte climber D. R. Hadow, just nineteen) encountered "tricky rock" on the way down. Hadow panicked and, paralyzed with fear, froze in his steps. Above them, the rest of the summit party, Englishman Edward Whymper, and two Swiss guides, impatiently waited.

What happened next haunted Whymper for the rest of his days. As he watched the guide below "absolutely taking hold of his [Hadow's] legs and putting his feet, one by one, into their proper positions," Hadow slipped, knocking down the guide, and sending them both plunging down the face. Roped together, "in another instant, Hudson was dragged from his steps and Lord F. Douglas immediately after him." Whymper and the two guides—roped to the falling men—scarcely had time to brace themselves before the rope snapped taut, groaned, and broke. "For a few seconds," wrote Whymper, "we saw out companions sliding downward on their backs and spreading out their hands, endeavoring to save themselves. They passed from our sight uninjured, disappeared one by one, and fell from precipice to precipice on to the Matterhorn Glacier below, a distance of nearly four thousand feet in height."

Lord Douglas at least died quickly. American millionaire Dudley Francis Wolfe, who perished attempting to climb K2 in 1939, wasn't so fortunate. His inherited wealth had bought him a place in the expedition (his father had made a fortune in coffee, his mother was the favorite daughter of one of Colorado's great silver barons). It had already bought him estates (his nephew likened one on the Maine coast to "something out of Scott Fitzgerald's *The Great Gatsby*"), Rolls-Royces, racing powerboats, and yachts. It also purchased a way out of his boredom; unhappiness; and the long shadow of inherited, wholly undeserved fortune.

Aboard his palatial schooner *Mohawk,* he'd placed second in the 1931 transatlantic yacht race—no mean feat. The year before the K2 expedition, in his expensive cutter *Highland Light,* he won the Findlay Trophy for the 1938 Bermuda Race. In between, he'd taken up mountain climbing, and the prospect of conquering the world's second-highest—and toughest—peak was irresistible. It became, wrote Andrew Kauffman and William Putnam in *K2: The 1939 Tragedy,* his "obsession, the be-all and end-all of his dreams. . . . At last he had a chance to prove himself to the world, a chance to show he could become somebody on his own merits."

For all his ardor, Wolfe's mountaineering merits were nil. He was a novice climber, forty-three years old, overweight, unfit, with bad eyesight. In his three seasons of mountaineering experience, climbing well-established, guided routes in the Alps, "it frequently required more than one guide to haul his large bulk to the summits." Other than his money, he had no qualifications for being anywhere near the Himalayas.

Amazingly, he managed to ascend to more than 25,000 feet— far short of the 28,250-foot summit—but well within the frigid, oxygen-starved, high-altitude desert that climbers call the "death zone." Storms, his unfitness as a climber and logistical foul-ups marooned him up there—most of the time in a tent by himself, above 22,000 feet—for thirty-eight consecutive days. No human being, without oxygen support, can survive at such altitude so long and live.

Incredibly, Wolfe did. A party of four Sherpas sent up the mountain to rescue him found him alone at Camp VII, at 24,700 feet. He'd been there for seventeen days. Tsering, sole survivor of the encounter, reported he was "in horrible condition . . . lying in his sleeping bag, very apathetic . . . he had not eaten for several days, nor had he been outside his tent. He had even relieved himself in the tent. He complained that he had no matches and therefore no warm food and worse, no fluids." The Sherpas made him tea, dragged him to his feet, and told him they were taking him down.

Outside the tent, he staggered and fell drunkenly—signs he was suffering as yet unrecognized but lethal high-altitude cerebral edema or high-altitude pulmonary edema. He was delirious but still imperious. He ordered the Sherpas—as he might have his limousine driver at home—to "come back the next day when he would be ready." It didn't occur to him that this meant they'd have to descend the 1,300 feet they'd just climbed, climb it again in the morning, and repeat the treacherous descent with him as baggage. It never occurred to the Sherpas to disobey.

Lacking tents or sleeping bags of their own, they descended to Camp VI, where a furious storm left them tentbound for twenty-four hours. As soon as the weather cleared, three of them—Kikuli, Kitar, Phinsoo, expert climbers undertaking a perilous high-altitude rescue while thoroughly exhausted themselves—went back up to bring the crazy, sick, rich man down. Neither they nor Dudley Francis Wolfe were ever seen again. Only Tsering—left in reserve at Camp VI—came down from Camp VI.

Other wealthy mountain-climbing dilettantes fared better. And more decadently. In fact, it can be argued that they set the example Wolfe and others tried, but failed, to emulate. Horace-Bénédict de Saussure, the rich Swiss merchant who "invented" the elitist sport of mountain climbing—getting to the tops of places nobody in his right mind goes solely for the sake of saying so—started bagging Alpine peaks in the 1780s. He risked his life, but he did it in consummate style: the brand of a rich man's sport.

At forty-seven, he made it to the top of 15,771-foot Mont Blanc, which was quite a big, dangerous deal in 1787; Saussure's party was only the third to stand on the summit. To get him there, however, took eighteen guides and a manservant. His personal gear, carried by the guides, consisted of what he considered the barest necessities: a large tent, mattresses, bed linen, and "a green curtain" (Saussure, sharing the tent with his servant, insisted upon his privacy); two half bottles of *eau de cerises* (cherry brandy) and six half bottles of white wine; one white suit, two green jackets, three vests, four shirts "to be worn at night" and five shirts "for day wear", five pairs of shoes; and a parasol to shade him from the sun.

Rich women played this early, intoxicating mountaineering death game, too—with equal sublimity. In the late 1860s, not long after Lord Douglas had taken his death dive, a wealthy English amateur climber named Lucille Walker became the first woman to surmount the Matterhorn. She later became the first woman to reach the top of the Eiger. On both expeditions, her sole provisions consisted of sponge cake and champagne.

All that sounds like ludicrous excess today. Taken in context, it isn't. Excess—extravagance and courage—has always been the marrow of nobility's games.

Egypt's pharoahs initiated this kind of sport five thousand years ago in hunting lions. Like elitist sports ever since, it was heavily equipment-oriented: equipment being expensive to obtain; expensive to learn to use; expensive to maintain; and, consequently, a symbol of wealth. More than that—as suburbanites sporting Patagonia, Helly Hansen, Henri Lloyd, and Musto gear evidences—its possession also was an ostentatious fashion statement, a sign that one had arrived. When a pharaoh went lion hunting, it must have looked like God had arrived.

He rode in the equivalent of a Mercedes SUV: a fast, exquisitely engineered chariot, gilded with gold leaf, drawn by a team of matched well-bred horses trained by the master of the king's horse. The horses themselves were richly caparisoned in silver-mounted harness and full silver trappings—silver being rarer and more valuable in ancient Egypt than gold. Driving the team was the king's master charioteer, whose whole life was devoted to the purpose. The pharaoh—richly dressed, coiffed, and perfumed—stood with his majestic weapons, the finest, state-of-the-art stuff money could buy: composite bow (which could be fired rapidly with deadly effect at short range, the assault weapon of its day); quivers of arrows; bronze-headed spears; and an elegant dagger. Running alongside the chariot were Nubian fan-bearers, waving ostrich feather fans to keep him cool.

The end was never really in doubt. Assisted by pedigreed lion hunting hounds and legions of beaters, the quarry was quickly cornered and killed. But the act was glorified in murals, reliefs, sculptures, and hieroglyphs: god-king conquering beast. It was an extreme sport, to be sure—downing a lion with a bow and arrow at 25 yards isn't for the fainthearted—but not nearly as much as it was made to appear. It taught nobility a lesson, however: confronting death, ironically, bought a kind of immortality. When one already has everything in this world—as Egyptian pharaohs quite literally did—what better way to spend it on than the next?

Well, perhaps one other thing, one that had nothing to do with the hereafter and everything with the here and now. In 1954, during excavations at the foot of the Great Pyramid of Cheops (Khufu) at Giza, German archaeologist Hermann Junker made a bizarre find. It was a long tomb sealed with 41 limestone blocks, each weighing 16 tons. It took Junker's twentieth-century machinery more than six months to move them out of the way. Beneath, cut out of the rock, lay a plastered, airtight pit. When Junker tapped it open with a hammer and a chisel, it expelled a rush of hot air in which he said he "smelt incense, smelt time, smelt centuries, smelt history itself."

Inside, instead of finding royal sarcophagi, he saw heaps of planking whose preservation was so perfect that it looked "fresh and new, redolent of pine oil, though it was almost completely dry of natural moisture." He had found the world's first, grand, pleasure yacht—the second king of the fourth dynasty's 4,505-year-old royal yacht, in fact. Built of Lebanon cedar, it had been carefully disassembled in 1,224 pieces, laid in 13 hemp-mattressed layers, complete with its rigging, deckhouses, and oars: reconstructed, she measured a phenomenal 143 feet long, with a beam of 19½ feet and an estimated displacement of 45 tons. The double-ended, keelless vessel, world's largest for a millennium, was estimated to have a draft of 5 feet and to have floated just 15 inches clear of the water amidships.

At first Junkers thought it was Cheops's funerary "boat of the sun," a purely ceremonial vessel intended to symbolically carry the dead pharaoh into the afterlife. It proved anything but. Its hull planking, ingeniously lashed together with almost 3 miles of hemp cordage (found intact), bore deep grooves where the ropework, swelled and tightened into place by repeated floatings in the Nile, showed archaeologists "clearly that the boat had been [long] used in the water." Six pairs of well-worn oars were found: a steering pair 28 feet long at the stern, and 5 pairs of rowing oars 21½ feet long under the fore canopy.

Also found were the perfectly preserved sections of a wood-paneled closed cabin, 30 feet long, with reliefs of graceful, palm-formed columns carved on the walls. In today's parlance it would be called the owner's stateroom—600 square feet of opulent privacy. Forward of this stretched a 40-foot-long canopy supported on each side by 6 fluted hardwood columns from which were draped fine linen cloths, soaked with water, to shade the pharaoh and his entourage and, as the water evaporated, provide a very effective form of air-conditioning. A small, canopied cabin at the bow housed the king's captain and the king's pilot.

That this was a party boat, not a funerary boat, showed in the decking. Archaeologists found it was "laid as a series of hatches, each of which could easily be lifted aside to stow stores." The hatches, like the planking, showed evidence of regular use. Under them would have been stowed the pharaoh's finest beverages: choice wines (the Egyptians had reds and whites, sweet and dry, made from grapes, dates, palm sap, and pomegranates) and strong barley beer (with an alcohol content of about 8 percent). Into the hold also went a cornucopia of good things to eat: fresh, dried, or salted beef, mutton, pork, or fish; baskets of fat, live ducks, geese, and pigeons; jars of honey, milk, butter, and eggs; onions, leeks, garlic, peas, celery, radishes, and cucumbers; saffron and sesame cooking oil; and finely-ground wheat flour of up to forty different varieties for making bread, pastry, cakes, and biscuits.

Cheops had obviously enjoyed yachting, away from the palace's pressures but not its perquisites. Aboard such a capacious royal yacht he could take them all with him, basking in cool Nile breezes during Egypt's blast furnace summers, trysting with his concubines, fishing, hunting, or gambling on games of senet. He enjoyed the boat so much that he wanted to take it with him. Apparently it was a last-minute decision. The burial pit was too small to cache the big yacht intact; so he ordered it painstakingly disassembled, hermetically sealed, and covered with 656 tons of solid rock (arguably the world's most effective yacht antitheft device; four other boat pits around the base of his pyramid, not similarly protected, were found empty). It was testament in volumes to how highly the rich valued their penultimate playthings.

Even the most egalitarian of games of antiquity—the Olympics —weren't for poor men. Nowhere was this more evident than in the Olympiad's final and crowning event: the *hoplitodromos,* or race in armor, where contestants had to wear helmets and greaves (leg guards) and carry a shield. This equipment—called a panoply— wasn't cheap. Its cost was roughly comparable to that of a luxury automobile today, and possession of it was a distinguishing mark of the rich.

Like most valuables of the time, it also was heavy. The *hoplon,* the trademark shield that gave Greek spearmen their name (*hoplite*), was about 3 feet in diameter—made of solid wood, armored in bronze, backed by leather—and weighed about 18 pounds. The bronze helmet and greaves added another 10 pounds or more. While you had to be rich to buy this armor, you also had to be damned fit to race in it. Winning the *hoplitodromos* wearing it, especially in the scorching post harvest heat in which the Olympiad usually was conducted, certainly took the strength and the stamina of the gods; considering that a man actually had to win it twice in the same day, in his qualifying heat and in the final. But that was something money couldn't buy. That was its attraction.

As the last event of the games, it also was among the most prestigious. The winner received amphorae of the finest, most expensive olive oil in Greece. How much liquid wealth was awarded the champion of the *hoplitodromos* isn't known, "but the winner of the boys' *stadion* [a short, 200-yard sprint] received 50 amphorae," so the men's grand prize must have been far more lavish. The oil was contained in specially decorated amphorae emblazoned with images of the Olympiad. Twin-handled and vase-shaped, they were startlingly similar to trophy cups today. Typically the winner auctioned the oil for a handsome price. The winning cups, however, were more esteemed and seldom sold.

But—like most elite games—there was more of a prize to it than that. In the day-to-day honoring of the various gods at the Olympics, a competitor showed handsomely from a religious stand-point. The fact that winners were venerated as heroes until the next Olympiad—wine, women (or boys), and song "on the house," so to speak—didn't hurt either. Beyond that, the games were a form of diplomacy short of war and a very effective one at that. Many of the events—javelin, wrestling, boxing—had clear military impli-cations and none's purpose was clearer than the *hoplitodromos*. It was literally an "arms race," a martial demonstration of individual brute strength and stamina at a time when military superiority was all about individual brute strength and stamina. Human muscle powered war, and a city was, practically speaking, only as strong as its citizen-soldiers.

Those soldiers had to be capable of bearing an 18-pound shield on one arm (by comparison, an M-16 rifle, fully loaded, weighs only about 8 pounds), while simultaneously wielding a 10-foot-long spear or a 2-foot-long iron sword in the other, in what amounted to a murderous, nonstop shoving, stabbing, hacking, and clubbing rugby scrum. There was really no way out of the fighting once it started. Five minutes of such hand-to-hand combat, where a fresh opponent appeared in place of each one cut down, must have seemed a lifetime, ten minutes purgatory, and fifteen minutes all but unendurable. Unless, of course, a fellow had been trained for hell. And no adversary seeing the Spartans shed their customary blood-red cloaks before battle, revealing physiques muscled like knotted cords, their helmeted heads masklike and unblinking, doubted it for a moment.

The *hoplitodromos* demonstrated that such training had been highly—very highly—developed. One was hesitant to challenge a state whose champion had triumphed in the *hoplitodromos*. There might be hundreds more like him at home. Yet the race was as much a demonstration of moral as physical superiority; evidence of a supe-rior state of mind, "a conduit of virtue." Plutarch wrote of an "old man at the Olympic Games, unable to find a seat and jeered at until he came to the Spartan benches, whereupon every Spartan rose as one man to offer him a seat." This act of noblesse oblige won far higher honor than the race. It was said for centuries afterward, "All Greeks know what is right, but only the Spartans do it." Rich men's games proved far more than riches.

It took an all-new kind of nobility, richer still, to take races of this kind to sea. Only the *nouveau* peerage that rose with the tide of European commerce in the fifteenth century—signally in Venice—could have invented yacht racing. Yet a member of the New York Yacht Club in 1905 would have felt at home among his counterparts at the Great Regatta in Venice in 1450. The principal competitors, after all, were rich merchants, bankers, and insurers; the Rialto, their Wall Street. Like New York, Venice was the world's undisputed financial capital, and money was key to the city's prosperity. Many of Venice's monied class, like New York's at the turn of the twentieth century, had inherited their wealth and been rigorously schooled in its management. Instead of prep schools like Groton or Choate, they were apprenticed to a master of the abacus to learn mathematics, and a master teller to learn bookkeeping and other essentials of business. In place of Harvard or Yale, they worked in the family business until they'd mastered the intricacies— or guile—involved in accounting, banking, and commercial law.

Managing family money, of course, was much easier than making it. Spending it was even easier. The rich merchants of Venice lined the Grand Canal with hundreds of ornate palazzi, just as American capitalists lined Fifth Avenue with mansions four hundred years later. They endowed Venetian libraries, churches, and museums, like American financier J. P. Morgan would later endow the New York Public Library, the Cathedral of St. John the Divine, and the Metropolitan Museum of Art. They spent fortunes on clothes and adornment, parading around "even on everyday occasions, in elaborate, bejeweled turbans and brocaded velvet cloaks." Venetian ladies took such excess to extremes, wearing *chopines,* highheeled or more accurately platform shoes 12 to 16 inches high. To walk in them required supporting servants at each hand—another ostentatious display of wealth.

To show their sophistication, they threw money at the arts—

painting, sculpture, and particularly music. Almost everything they did with their enormous fortunes, in fact, was more or less copied (knowingly or not) by America's robber barons and their heirs, especially the ultimate demonstration of wealth and self-importance: building and racing yachts.

Commissioning a boat to compete in the Great Regatta was the once-a-year chance for Venice's freshly minted commercial princes —and especially their heirs—to stand out. A fifteenth-century Venetian racing galley was the fastest, most sophisticated luxury playtoy of its time; owning one was like having a Gulfstream jet today. The doge's state galley *Bucintoro,* which served rather as the committee boat at the regatta, exemplified that. She was 100 feet long with only a 20-foot beam and was propelled by forty-two oars, each pulled by five superbly conditioned, magnificently liveried rowers. Under muscle power alone, she was capable of making a then-phenomenal 9 knots (10.3 miles per hour). Purpose-built racing galleys could go even faster: in sprints, oarsmen could drive them as fast as 11 knots. Independent of wind, no vessel would go faster for four hundred years. They were also the most maneuverable vessels afloat. With one side of oarsmen backing water, they could turn on a ducat; with both sides backing, they could almost stop on a dime.

But Venetian yachts were as famous for beauty and ornamentation as speed and maneuverability. *Bucintoro* was stunningly opulent. She was gilded, not just in parts, but also from stem to stern, waterline to gunwales, every surface the sun might reach. Outside and in, her two decks were a wedding cake of ornate wood carvings and ostentatious decoration. Moving at speed—with gold-embroidered flags, banners, and canopies overhead, red-lacquered sweeps flashing her whole length—she must have appeared like a divinely driven machine.

Naturally, every Venetian who could afford it wanted a galley just like it, or better, for the regatta races, which all Venetians from the humblest stevedore to the doge himself watched—and wagered—on. They outbid themselves to secure the services of the city's most exalted craftsmen—master shipwrights—to build the fastest vessels to win. These men, whose trade was so crucial to maintaining Venice's maritime supremacy that they were prohibited by law from leaving it, cost dearly. So, too, did the myriad artisans—master carvers, gilders, painters, even tailors—necessary to win the regatta's other competitions, for ships' beauty, ornamentation, and the livery of their rowers. Extravagant wagers were laid on every contest, but the greatest prestige (and lion's share of the purse) went to the fastest racers.

Fast ships were evidence that Venice could move trade goods or troops—particularly troops—faster, farther, and more reliably than its rivals. For this, of course, Venetian shipowners charged an exorbitant premium, financed by Venetian bankers and secured by Venetian insurers. Conveying Crusaders to the Holy Land, in fact, fattened Venetian family fortunes for generations. The bid to transport the Fourth Crusade alone—50 galleys to carry 4,500 knights, 9,000 squires, and 20,000 men-at-arms to the Levant—was 85,000 "Cologne marks" or approximately $100 million U.S. today. The Crusaders couldn't afford it. So the Venetians—knowing full well they couldn't—instead cheaply bought their services to attack and sack Constantinople, capital of the Byzantine Empire and their principal trade rival in the eastern Mediterranean. It was called the "Crusade against the Christians." It didn't really matter to the Venetians; an enemy in trade was just as mortal as one in war. Winning over one was as good as another: Christian or infidel, the threat, and color of their money, was the same.

For the commercial crown princes of Venice, fast ships were critical—in war or in peace—to assure continued fortune. Yacht racing, much like the *hoplitodromos,* was a ceremonialized, diplomatic means of flexing muscle, both martial and monetary. At the Great Regatta, Venetian heirs could do that without lifting a finger except to open their purses. In the 1905 Kaiser's Cup transatlantic race, America's could, too.

The difference is that in 1905, seven out of eight of the American millionaires who entered the race sailed on their own boats and bet their lives on the outcome.

CHAPTER 12

Clubs and Kings

You can do business with anyone. You can only yacht with gentlemen.

—J. P. Morgan

One of the ironies of the New York Yacht Club is that you don't have to own a yacht to be a member. You don't even have to know how to sail. You must, however, have money. A lot of money. What yachting historian Ed Holm calls the "most aristocratic and exclusive aquatic fraternity in America" does not accept just anyone. It never has. It is an institution as formidable—and as quirky—as the U.S. Supreme Court. Walter Cronkite, himself a NYYC member, called it "born with a certain autocratic air." No one questions that. From its foundation in 1844, the club has been singularly "conspicuous for the prestige of its membership, which over the years included *some* of the most experienced and dedicated yachting sailors in the country as well as *many* of the most powerful and influential businessmen."

By 1900, however, the overwhelming majority of members were wealthy businessmen, not yacht sailors. Most, in fact, were not even yacht owners. Of 1,565 members in 1900, only 402 of them—about one in four—owned a yacht. At least what the New York Yacht Club deemed a yacht; its bylaws at the time stating "the New

York Yacht Club does not recognize *any* vessel of less than forty feet long as a yacht, and does *not* admit them into the club."

Consequently, the yachts flying the club's burgee were big ones—the biggest and the grandest the world had ever seen. Henry Redmond's 127-foot *Ailsa* was considered something of an economy model. In 1900 the club's squadron of large yachts—18 steam and naphtha launches (such as banker August Belmont's 72-foot, 21-knot steam tender *Scout*), 86 schooners, 109 sloops, cutters, and yawls, and 189 steam yachts—was unmatched by any yacht club afloat. Forty-seven of those yachts were more than 200 feet long. Only the richest of the rich –about one in thirty-three New York Yacht Club members—could afford one of those. But yachts more than 300 feet long really separated the men from the boys. Wall Street millionaire (billionaire in today's value) Anthony Drexel's schooner-rigged *Margarita* measured 352 feet length overall (LOA); newspaper heir Jamie Bennett's *Lysistrata,* 314 feet; and financier J. P. Morgan's *Corsair III* 304 feet (the third of four ever larger yachts of the same name he built to outdo other NYYC members).

The size and sophistication of such yachts can only be judged in comparison. At 352 feet, *Margarita* was bigger than America's Indiana-class battleships (350 feet LOA), then the largest vessels in the U.S. fleet. Designed by legendary British marine architect George Lennox Watson, who was something of the Versace of steam yachts at the time, she cost roughly $10 million in today's dollars to build and required a crew of ninety to operate. She was equipped with engines capable of generating 5,000 horsepower: roughly equal to those of the White Star passenger liner *Britannic,* sister ship of the *Titanic.* Bennett's 314-foot steam yacht *Lysistrata* was larger than the U.S. Navy's contemporary Texas-class armored cruisers (308 feet LOA) but just as fast (17.5 knots vs. 17.8 knots). J. P. Morgan's twin-screw *Corsair III*—Morgan being Morgan— could make 19 knots, and according to contemporary yachting authorities was "in every respect an ocean greyhound." Morgan had a penchant for very fast steamers. His *Corsair II,* donated to the U.S. Navy in the Spanish-American War, armed and renamed *Gloucester,* was fast enough to overtake and destroy two Spanish destroyers at the Battle of Santiago in 1898.

But the sheer number of steam-powered megayachts on the New York Yacht Club's list by 1905 had made it something of the laughingstock of other clubs, or what Holm delicately called "the focal point of derision by die-hard sailing enthusiasts." Caspar Whitney, editor of *Outing* magazine and rather the grand inquisitor of what were and were not properly manly games at the time, wrote, ". . . the New York Yacht Club, year after year, tends to become more and more a big steam-yacht affair, with ladies, chefs, and dress coats, and such like *agrements* of civilization—very charming and proper indeed, but not conducive to the best interests of yachting as a manly sport."

All that was quite true. More than half the vessels on the club's list were steam yachts—189 in all, far more than the 49 on the rolls of the Eastern Yacht Club, considered the next most steam-infatuated club in the United States. Ladies had indeed been admitted to the club's ranks since 1894 (beginning with Andrew Carnegie's sister-in-law), which was radically progressive at the time (though in 1905, fewer than one in a hundred members were women; specially designated "flag members," in that, on paper, they owned yachts, but were excluded from voting in club elections). Chefs and stewards were as omnipresent aboard luxury steam yachts as seamen. One could hardly serve the most simple luncheon without them. In "Yachting's Golden Age," Ed Holm relates the by no means apocryphal story of a journalist calling upon New York Yacht Club commodore Elbridge T. Gerry aboard his 161-foot auxiliary schooner *Electra* at lunchtime. Gerry was absent, but the journalist was seated in solitary splendor in the dining saloon, where cooks and stewards presented him salver after salver of "roasted oysters, cold game, Westphalia ham, boned turkey, filet of beef, several kinds of pastry and ices, hot-house California grapes, claret cup, coffees and liquers." The other *agrements* of civilization about which Whitney complained were also in evidence aboard *Electra*. Holm noted that many of them represented the latest technology at the time. The yacht had a newfangled "Edison generating plant, [powering] 58 incandescent lights, a 15,000-candlepower masthead searchlight, electrically powered ice plant and electrical apparatus for firing the guns when starting races."

Creature comforts aboard the club's floating mansions went far beyond that. Aboard *Lysistrata,* Bennett had three elaborate suites for himself on each of her three decks, a Turkish bath to combat hangovers, and padded stalls for two cows so he could have fresh milk. A glassed-in gallery overlooked the engine room so guests could observe the working of her massive, meticulously polished machinery. For the vessel's figurehead, he commissioned a massive carved wood owl that, a reporter marveled, was "fitted out in such a way that the eyes can be made to blaze with electric searchlights."

Railroad heir William K. Vanderbilt's 291-foot bark-rigged *Valiant* (bigger, by design, than Queen Victoria's royal yacht *Victoria and Albert*) had twenty guest staterooms, a Paris-designed Louis Quatorze grand saloon (furnished in Chippendale with a Steinway grand piano), and could palatially carry her passengers and sixty-two-man crew across the Atlantic in seven days. Other Vanderbilt

Auxiliary yachts at the time represented the acme of wealth and luxury. Railroad heir Charles Vanderbilt's *North Star* boasted "a drawing room and library [that] rivalled any found on Fifth Avenue." The yachts in the Kaiser's Cup race were just as opulent.

heirs were not to be outdone. Charles Vanderbilt's 256-foot yacht *North Star* boasted a "drawing room and library," according to a newspaper account that "rivalled any found on Fifth Avenue." Frederick Vanderbilt's 282-foot yacht *Warrior* featured what one paper described as "elaborate bathrooms fitted with hot water geysers"—discreet Victorian vernacular for bidets. John Jacob Astor IV's 221-foot *Nourmahal* (which translates as "favorite of the harem") had a dining saloon that could seat sixty, electric lighting and refrigeration, a 42-foot steam launch for ferrying guests, a faster gas-powered launch to carry their mail and fetch them whatever they desired, and four rapid-firing Hotchkiss guns to protect them from pirates on Caribbean cruises. Nothing could protect Astor from his own appetite for excess however. As an honorary staff officer in the Spanish-American War, he calmly witnessed the charge up San Juan Hill while under fire; as a first-class passenger on the maiden voyage of *Titanic,* he perished with equal sangfroid.

Even relatively modest-size steam yachts—by New York Yacht Club standards, anyway—seemed decadent to Whitney. New York businessman Eugene Tompkin's 146-foot *Idalia* steamed at speeds of up to 17 knots, seldom cruised under sail, and had a full-time crew of a dozen, most of whom were employed tending the engine (a licensed engineer, two stokers) and the owner and his guests (a chef, assistant chef, chief steward, and assistant steward). Despite being a decidedly midsize yacht for the time, her deckhouses featured a sumptuous dining saloon, pantry, buffet, ladies' lounge and gentlemen's smoking room. On the lower deck was a hardwood-paneled 21-foot-wide grand saloon, owner's suite, and half a dozen elegant guest staterooms.

"Your steam yacht is a convenience," Whitney chastised. "It is available for entertaining purposes. It is useful for cooling off and resting tired businessmen, and it is the popular craft for elderly people and yacht-owners of the 'passenger' class; but it is conducive to laziness and will be the death of yachting except in the small classes." Whitney aimed his broadside directly at the New York Yacht Club: "Just so sure as a club comes to count many 'teakettles' [steam yachts] on its list, just so sure is that club to lose its sporting tone."

The New York Yacht Club had taken about all of that kind of criticism it could stand by 1905. It was, after all, the unbeaten defender and champion of the America's Cup—sailing's Holy Grail. Its members had, under sail, three times raced across the Atlantic— the first ocean racers. It boasted a wealthier, more powerful membership than any yacht club on earth. But when the idea of another transatlantic race surfaced in 1904, it was horrified.

The problem was that it wasn't their idea. It was the brainchild of two of the club's archrivals.

Like the first transatlantic race, it was conceived during a sumptuous dinner: this one at Brooklyn's Sea Gate House in honor of the outgoing commodore of the Atlantic Yacht Club. The Atlantic Yacht Club was something of the antithesis of the NYYC. Its headquarters weren't in midtown Manhattan, but on the waterfront at Bay Ridge in Brooklyn, overlooking the Narrows and Upper and Lower New York Bay—the amphitheater of American yacht racing. By and large, its members weren't merely yacht owners, but active sailors, "Corinthians," who navigated and sailed their yachts themselves. The club "prided itself on the number of *practical* yachtsmen on its rolls," according to yachting historian Holm, "and on its hospitality toward suitably qualified small-craft sailors as well as those [only] possessing larger and more costly vessels." No 40-foot rule precluded enrollment of a boat at the Atlantic Yacht Club. Boats as small as 16 feet, if creditably sailed, entitled their owners to membership.

None of this meant that membership was open to anyone; far from it. The members of the Atlantic Yacht Club were quite as rich and status-conscious as those of the New York Yacht Club. Many, in fact, were rich and status-conscious enough to belong to both and sometimes to two or three others. The thing that was so different about the two clubs was what Caspar Whitney called the "tone." "Both [clubs] have always inclined to conservatism," observed Captain Roland Coffin at the time, "the Atlantic particularly so."

By 1905, the squadron runs of the New York Yacht Club had become largely sybaritic, social affairs. Professional crews attended to the sailing; members and their guests indulged themselves. "The party on the steamer," recalled yachting editor William P. Stevens, "included many ladies in spring costume, escorted by the beaux of the 'rocking chair fleet,' too old or too blasé to sail. A fashionable orchestra, Graffula's Band of Downing's, played the music of Julien and Strauss. The luncheon, from Delmonico's or Maresi's, was carried aboard in old, oblong champagne baskets and served by liveried waiters. There was champagne galore and general rejoicings and fireworks in the evening."

To the members of the Atlantic Yacht Club, that wasn't yachting. It was ossification. To them, the true sport of yachting was sailing their own boats, racing against wind, wave, and any man or club who thought himself better. And they were positively Cromwellian Puritans about it. An observer noted, "Nothing stronger than lemonade was served" aboard AYC racers. On annual club cruises, "grog and cards were frowned upon, and the sparkling exuberance of youth was discouraged." Chaplains and services were held in high regard. Where sea, sailing, and racing converged, there was no monkey business at the Atlantic Yacht Club.

The club's outgoing commodore at the Sea Gate House banquet —Wall Street investment banking heir Robert E. Tod Esq.—epitomized that. He eschewed steam yachts. His 150-foot schooner *Thistle* was a pure wind machine. He sailed and raced his own boat. He didn't need to hire a professional skipper; he held a master's license. He acted not only as *Thistle*'s captain but also as her

Wall Street banking heir Robert E. Tod eschewed auxiliary-powered yachts: his green-topped schooner *Thistle* was a pure wind machine.

navigator and sailing master. He liked flaunt-
ing his prowess at all three in ocean races.
Yachtingwise he was everything the New
York Yacht Club's so-called teakettle
steam auxiliary owners weren't. Caspar
Whitney, in fact, had held him up as an
example of a true American yachtsman, in
contrast to "yacht-owners of the passenger class" at the NYYC—and it rankled.

During his after-dinner remarks on
September 18, 1903, however—at least
in the eyes of the New York Yacht Club—
Tod went over the line. He said he hoped
to see the Atlantic Yacht Club schedule a
much longer ocean race than the 500-mile
contest it had completed that season—a
race more than *six times* as long, in fact,

Robert E. Tod, a
Corinthian sailor,
skippered and navigated
Thistle himself in the
race—the only yacht
owner to do so. Critics
said the trophy should
have rightfully been his.

from Sandy Hook to the Needles on Britain's Isle of Wight. This,
of course, was not only poaching on what the New York Yacht Club
viewed as its transatlantic race franchise, it also was theft of the
course the club had blazed back in 1866. But Tod went further by
proposing a shockingly different kind of ocean race altogether. It
was to be a stern Corinthian test of navigation and seamanship, not
a social event. No professional captains would be allowed. Owners would be rulebound to skipper—and navigate—their yachts
themselves. The contest would be decided by sail only. Unlike all
previous transatlantic races, which had resulted from personal
challenges between ultrarich men, it was to be an *open* race. Any
yachtsman—from any club—who met the qualifications and was
willing to undertake the risk was welcome to enter.

None of that had *any* appeal to the steam-yacht aristocracy of
the New York Yacht Club.

It was music to the ears of another banquet guest that night: the
seriously disillusioned, just-defeated challenger for the 1903 America's Cup, Sir Thomas Lipton. Not because the fifty-three-year-old
Irish tea megamillionaire was a sailor or racer himself—he preferred
remaining aboard his palatial steam yacht *Erin* and letting profes-

sional skippers do his racing for him—but because he'd just suffered his *third* defeat questing for the cup in five years, all at the hands of the New York Yacht Club, of course, and his competitive blood was boiling.

Despite his huge wealth (Lipton Tea) and royal titles (a knighthood and a baronetcy), he was starkly different from Commodore Tod or any other American and British yacht club peers. He hadn't inherited either his fortune or titles; he'd earned them the hard way. Born penniless in Scotland, at fifteen he took steerage passage to America. He labored as a field hand in Virginia tobacco fields, on a rice plantation in South Carolina (perhaps the most physically punishing kind of "stoop labor" there is), drove a dray wagon in New Orleans, and then clerked in a New York City grocery. He saved his hard-earned money and at twenty-one returned to Scotland with enough to open a small grocery himself, which he diligently built into the largest chain store the British Empire had ever seen. As he got richer, he acquired coffee, cocoa, and especially tea plantations in India and Ceylon (he practically owned the latter), meat packing houses in Chicago and Omaha, and he built the world's first refrigerated railroad line to speed his perishable goods to market.

He didn't take up yacht racing until he was fifty, when money was no object, and money, more or less, was what secured yachting success. Initially he did it more to publicize Lipton Tea than anything else ("In enterprise," he said, "you either go bust or advertise"), and he did it in a big way. In 1899, 1901, and 1903 he'd challenged for the America's Cup in three ever faster, ever more expensive yachts— all of them green-painted and named *Shamrock,* for his native Ireland.

Publicitywise, it was a fantastic success. The public loved him: the genial, white-whiskered, self-made Irish megamillionaire singlehandedly challenging America's robber barons on their own exclusive, watery playing field. He, in turn, loved playing to the American public. America's Cup historian Ranulf Rayner related that "Asked if his time in America as a youth had been the secret of his success, he winkingly replied, 'Bless yer, success with the ladies—yep.'" The press loved the whole spectacle. In short order, Sir Thomas and

America's Cup racing—and Lipton Tea—became almost synonymous. High-profile losing was almost as good as winning. Graciously conceding defeat was even better: it ingratiated Lipton with the public and sold oceans of tea imprinted with his image.

No one survived Lipton's charm offensive. He was elected honorary member of the New York Yacht Club in 1899, albeit only *after* he'd been soundly trounced in that year's America's Cup races. Even the ultrasnobbish Royal Yacht Squadron (RYS) was eventually forced to surrender to him, though he was eighty at the time and in failing health before they reluctantly elected him a member. Despite his achievements, most RYS members considered his pedigree positively puerile: born Irish, in a slum and in Scotland, for heaven's sake. No breeding, no formal education, no military service. Certainly he'd been fortunate making a great deal of money in the "grocery business," but grocers, however rich, really weren't suitable squadron material.

Yachtingwise, Lipton's cup challenges brought him only disaster after disaster. In 1899 he lost three out of three races, one because *Shamrock*'s topmast collapsed. In 1901, he lost three out of three close-fought contests. In 1903 he was whipped in three consecutive races without coming close to winning one. He took those defeats—suffered only a few weeks before that night's banquet—far harder than he let on in public. He "himself admitted that losing so conclusively [in 1903] was the greatest disappointment of his life." He has long been lionized in yachting as the archtype of "a true sportsman" and "good loser," which undeniably was true—at least outwardly.

But a man doesn't mount what eventually turned out to be *five* challenges for the America's Cup over a period of thirty-one years with *any* expectation of losing gracefully. Inwardly, Lipton was ferociously competitive. Tod's suggestion of a transatlantic race appealed to him immensely. An international ocean race would be a first: a publicity coup worth more than the America's Cup. A trophy cup—with his name prominently attached—would eclipse in interest the America's Cup he had repeatedly failed to win from the New York Yacht Club cabal. An ocean race open to all—self-made fellows like himself at the lower end of the social scale Royal Ulster Yacht Club or less-than-40-footer sailors at the Atlantic Yacht Club and count-less others—would be a stick in the eye of his antagonists at both the Royal Yacht Squadron and the New York Yacht Club.

As soon as Tod completed his remarks that night, Lipton but-tonholed him. Lipton told him he'd be pleased to give a cup for a match race across the Atlantic. There was one catch—Sir Thomas didn't get to be Sir Thomas out of magnanimity—he was looking for revenge. He'd offer a $2,500 prize cup (equivalent to about $47,000 today)—to be called the Lipton Cup, naturally—for Tod's novel Corinthian ocean race. But the management of the race was to be offered—like a sputtering grenade—to the smug gentlemen of the New York Yacht Club. They would have no choice but to run *his* race, which, as he deliciously appreciated, was the *last* thing they wanted to do.

His estimation proved quite right. Presented Lipton's proposal, the clannish New York Yacht Club was at a total loss on how to react. The event was distasteful to them for all the reasons Lipton suspected. First, it was a classic NIH (not invented here) concept, one that put its wealthiest members at a distinct disadvantage, most especially the steam-yacht-owning aristocracy of J. P. Morgan, C. Oliver Iselin, William Rockefeller, and Cornelius Vanderbilt III, who had funded syndicates to beat Lipton. Second; an open race meant admitting God only knew who to the exclusive, gentlemen's-only domain of yacht racing. Third; even though under the purview of the NYYC, the event would forever be known as the Lipton's Cup Transatlantic Race, Lipton's Great Ocean Race, or some other such thing. Having held off Lipton's three assaults on the America's Cup, the last thing the NYYC wanted was to beatify such a signal yachting trophy in his name.

It left the New York Yacht Club between a rock and a hard place. Lipton had graciously—and publicly—made the offer. They had to do something. One senses that Lipton savored watching them squirm.

What was done next—ridding the event of Lipton and his cup—is no great mystery. The all-powerful members of the club went to work to put an end to him once and for all. If a king could be persuaded to offer a cup, it would certainly trump any club's.

Sixth Day at Sea

*How the memory of foul weather fades when the stars
come out.*

—Paul Stevenson,
yawl *Ailsa*

Nothing shines quite so brightly on a sailor, even at night, as clearing skies. The moderating seas and changing of the watch brought
Stevenson on deck at 4:00 A.M. to marvel at a sky filled with stars.
There seemed to be billions of them roofing the ocean, the bright-
est seeming near enough to touch, suspended in a huge, velvet
quiet. A moderate wind was blowing finally, from the southeast, perfect for keeping their course; and the sea was smooth.

The two watches (the middle watch finishing its midnight-to-
4:00 A.M. shift, and the morning watch coming up to take over from
4:00 A.M. till 8:00 A.M.) were putting Ailsa under "all plain sail"
when a sharp-eyed crewman spotted them: stars, colored ones, on
the western horizon, the unmistakable night signals of a ship. Captain Miller glassed them. He made out a red light, beneath it a white
one, and beneath that a blinking red light. They were Coston
Lights, those specified by the race committee for each of the ocean
racers to display from their mastheads from dusk to dawn. He
checked the race identification table and couldn't believe it. It

was the American schooner Endymion, *holder of the record transatlantic yacht passage from Sandy Hook to the Needles, and—after* Atlantic—*the odds-on favorite to win the race.*

Although almost exactly the same tonnage as Ailsa *(116.20 vs. 116.0),* Endymion *was 17 feet longer at the waterline (the traditional measure of a yacht's speed), five years younger, and her raked two-masted schooner rig could spread almost twice as much canvas (including a big square sail on her foremast). In sea trials before the race, she was rumored to have achieved speeds of 17 knots. For all her power, however, she was coming from behind. If* Ailsa *was ahead of her—some 1,200 miles out of Sandy Hook, almost smack in the mid-Atlantic—then* Ailsa *was certainly among the front-runners, perhaps even the leader.*

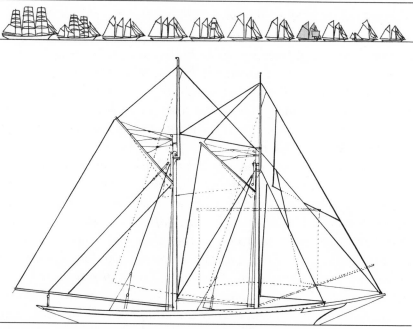

In 1905, millionaire American yachtsman George Lauder's schooner *Endymion* held the record for the fastest transatlantic yacht passage ever made. The 134-foot long, Boston-built two-master had been designed "for the express purpose of offshore work." Bookies favored her; the North Atlantic did not.

*That revelation boosted Stevenson's spirits almost as much as
the "matchless, blue morning" that came up with the sun. There was
a cloudless sky, flashing sunlight, and a lazily whitecapped, almost
black-blue sea that rose and fell in gentle swells, rocking Ailsa like
a cradle. He and the other guests basked at the helm, their first time
on deck in days. They declined going below for breakfast; the
steward brought them up coffee laced with rum. They couldn't take
their eyes off the spectacle. In full daylight, Endymion appeared startlingly closer than she had under lights before dawn. She stood up
plainly on the horizon, a shimmering tower of white canvas above
a black, clipper-bowed hull, coming on with "a bone in her teeth."
In the moderate southeasterly winds (11 to 16 knots), she closed
very quickly. By midday she was but "a few miles" astern.*

*As a yachting correspondent, Stevenson knew Ailsa was over-
matched in such a contest. She was a yawl, without much success
in coastal races. Now in the middle of the North Atlantic, she
was suddenly racing—one-on-one—with the fastest transatlantic
schooner of all. What's more, at Endymion's helm was Captain
James "Jimmy" Loesch: the man who'd set the record in Endymion
in the first place and, in the second, had been hired by her owner,
Wall Street millionaire George Lauder Jr., to break it and carry
home the Kaiser's Cup. It was only a matter of time until the bigger schooner overtook them.*

*But he had not reckoned on Captain Miller's determination. The
man had a good, fast, Fife-designed boat under him; had willed himself to beat Charlie Barr and Atlantic; and was not about to surrender his lead. Throughout the early afternoon Stevenson noted
that the two vessels "held to each other, the powerful ocean cruiser,
built to scuffle with the elements and the slender, low-sided racer,
framed up for nothing more than a few hours' thrash in the English Channel." It was a masterful piece of sailing on Miller's part.
By midafternoon, however, tactics couldn't save him. Ailsa and
Endymion were "practically abreast, with starboard tacks aboard,"
the latter coming up smartly.*

*At that moment, like in a Greek drama, there was divine inter-
vention. The moderate southeasterly winds diminished to a gentle
southwesterly breeze. It favored first one ship, then the other. But*

the ever-lightening winds favored the smaller, nimbler Ailsa. *She gradually stole away, "steering like a knockabout [small sloop], her wheel like the balance of a watch," according to Stevenson.*

Leaving Endymion *behind caused jubilation. Miller and the crew bent all sail, exhaustion forgotten. Stevenson finally had something to write about. Grenville Kane emerged on deck (no doubt minding the back of his head) to shoot the sun with his sextant. Henry Reuterdahl was painting furiously, though now his easel was lashed under the skylight in the saloon. On deck he snatched pencil sketches, careful to keep out of the crew's way. Below, he worked them into watercolors and oils. "I never knew the ocean before," he told Stevenson, "I never saw the sea until today; the color of it all."*

The beauty of two sleek wind machines racing across the sun-charged stage of the North Atlantic must have been sublime that day. Reuterdahl was no stranger to capturing action at sea. At twenty-seven, he'd been a celebrated correspondent in the Spanish-American War. His renderings of the U.S. Navy blockading squadron off Cuba had appeared in world newspapers. But in 1905 he was thirty-four, married with children, and struggling to get by as an instructor at New York's Art Students League. He supplemented his income painting nautical murals and panels for rich men's steam yachts (his commissions included Vincent Astor's Noma, *Harold Vanderbilt's* Vagrant *and G. F. Baker Jr's* Viking). *Though officially Redmond's guest, Reuterdahl was being paid to produce artwork of* Ailsa *in the race. These would take their place alongside the photographs of* Ailsa *in Redmond's Wall Street offices—part of his "rocking chair skipper's" collection. Win or lose, Redmond intended to have trophies to show for the race. That is why Reuterdahl—like Stevenson—had been invited to ship aboard* Ailsa *in the first place: a rich man's scribe to chronicle a rich man's triumph.*

Reuterdahl would become quite renowned as a maritime artist before his death at fifty-four (his works housed in permanent collections of the U.S. Naval Academy in Annapolis, the National Museum in Washington, D.C., and the Naval War College in Newport). But on that delightful day, pulling away from Endymion, *he was perhaps at the top of his form. "The colors of the belly of a sea as it curls," he told Stevenson, "it drives you mad because you've never seen how to paint deep salt water till after you've found out how little you know."*

He worked as long as there was light. In pencil he sketched Ailsa's crewmen heaving halyards and sheets, cheerfully lengthening their lead. In watercolors he captured the sunset. In oils he daubed the afterglow. He was far too busy to note the signaling of an eastbound steamer, SS St. Louis.

Stevenson wasn't. She was charging ahead at more than 20 knots.

Wind and weather had convinced Miller to shape his course across the North Atlantic by the "southern steamer route." It was a good route, longer than the more direct great circle route going north, but less exposed to ice and bad weather and universally taken by all the great passenger liners. Cyclonic gales (hurricanes) were rare in May; the U.S. Hydrographic Office reported that only six had occurred in the area since 1899, and blows of storm force had "not been especially frequent during May." Fog, however, was endemic. The Hydrographic Office emphasized that it "has always been encountered during May for a longer or shorter time nearly everywhere along the southern steamer route." On average, vessels could expect fog nine days out of thirty-one in May.

That was a long time to be blind in what, at the time, was the world's busiest shipping lane. The Hydrographic Office bluntly reminded the racers: "A word of caution must be given. The sailing directions [for the race] recommend that sailing vessels avoid these routes as much as possible. This warning is given solely because sailing craft might be endangered by onrushing steamers." Onrushing was right. Passenger liners such as Kaiser Wilhelm der Grosse, *which departed New York Harbor at the start of the race, plowed ahead at 23 knots (26.45 miles per hour)—all 14,500 tons of her, more than two football fields long. A liner charging west at that speed and a racer driving east at 17 knots (15.55 miles per hour) closed at a speed of 40 knots (46 miles per hour) or $2/3$ miles per minute, which left damned little time to avoid a collision in any kind of fog, mist, or rain. At night, of course, it was infinitely worse.*

And the Hydrographic Office reported that no fewer than thirty steamers would be on the southern course during the time of the race.

Fog blinded the racers navigationally, too. If sun, stars, and horizon were obscured, there was no way for them to take a sight, no way to determine with any accuracy where *they were. They could be smack in the middle of the southern steamer route reserved for eastbound vessels careening up from behind; or 60 miles north, smack in the middle of the northern steamer route reserved for westbound vessels closing head-on. Even with almost unlimited visibility,* St. Louis *seemed to appear out of nowhere, pass grazing close, and vanish with frightening rapidity. It chilled Stevenson. With limited visibility—at night or in dense fog or a squall—it might easily have resulted in a collision, one the big* St. Louis *would have scarcely noticed while vanishing over the horizon with equal rapidity, leaving the wreckage of* Ailsa *behind.*

No one else seemed to notice.

CHAPTER 14

Contests of Will

As a sporting event, nothing could be more absurd and more fated to be inconclusive than the ocean race instigated by the German Emperor.

—*New York Times* editorial,
December 10, 1904

On January 14, 1904—eight months before issuing the transatlantic race challenge ridiculed in the *New York Times*—Kaiser Wilhelm's dinner was interrupted by a completely unexpected visit from his sixty-seven-year-old chief of foreign affairs, Baron Friedrich von Holstein. He bore telegrams just received from German South-West Africa, one of the empire's most remote colonies, an arid wasteland on the African coast with somewhat fewer than five thousand German inhabitants that cost the imperial treasury 9 million marks a year in subsidies to maintain. Two days earlier, without warning, the native nomadic Herero tribesmen in the interior had rebelled en masse. Outlying German farms, trading posts, and settlements had been overrun and burned; 123 German soldiers and settlers had been massacred. The railroad and telegraph line between the main port at Swapokmund on the Atlantic coast and the inland colonial capital at Windhoek, just completed at great expense in 1902, had been cut. The last telegraphic messages reported all remaining German towns, including the capital, under siege by thousands of well-armed Herero tribesmen. By every appearance, the revolt seemed well organized and meticulously planned.

What, inquired Holstein, did His Royal Highness wish done?

The kaiser, stunned, demanded that the colonial governor counterattack and crush the uprising at once. Holstein explained that was all but impossible. There were but three companies of German troops, roughly 450 men, in the entire colony, which—at 318,000 square miles—was twice the size of Germany itself (roughly the size of Texas and Louisiana combined). One of those companies was besieged in Windhoek by 3,000 Herero, if it had not been overrun already; there was absolutely no way of telling. The other two were laagered on the colony's southern border 400 miles from the fighting: too few and too far away to do anything.

The kaiser dismissed the objection. He directed the Imperial Navy to land marines immediately and march to the relief of the capital. How many could be sent? He was told that one of the navy's newest gunboats, the 209-foot *Habicht,* carrying three 102mm (4-inch) guns and capable of steaming 14 knots, was patrolling off the coast. She could land her entire marine complement at Swapokmund the following morning. The only problem, Holstein explained, was that the complement consisted of only eighty-five marines. At best they might be able to hold on to the port—if the Herero didn't come down from the highlands and attack it in force, which, of course, they could easily do at any time. Still, they were the only troops immediately available, it was vital the port and its railroad terminus be held at all costs, and they would be landed at once. All, Holstein emphasized, eighty-five of them.

There were other gunboats like the *Habicht,* the kaiser reminded him: expressly designed for colonial service, on station off Germany's other African colonies, carrying marines precisely to put down insurrections of this kind. They should all steam for Swapokmund at flank speed, without delay.

Holstein pointed out that Germany had never anticipated an insurrection of such magnitude; the colonial office estimated as many as sixteen thousand Herero fighting men in the field. The gunboats the kaiser mentioned amounted to just three: one in Cameroon, more than 1,200 nautical miles from Swapokmund, one in Togo, 1,800 miles from the port; and one in German East Africa, fully 3,000 miles away. None was designed to make fast ocean voyages; indeed, to make long voyages at all, they were forced to steam at their most economical speed—a sluggish 7 knots, half their maximum. As coastal and riverine patrol vessels, none was designed to carry more than a company of lightly armed marines. Discounting the gunboat in faraway East Africa, the other two could deliver only 170 marines—a drop in the bucket. And it would take two weeks for that drop to arrive. During that time the port could fall and, with it, any hope of saving the colony. Clearly, the gunboats weren't an option. It was imperative to get as sizable a contingent of troops to Swapokmund as soon as possible.

To the kaiser that seemed simple enough. He had the second-largest army in the world; more than three-quarters of a million regulars, which in firepower and efficiency was second to none—and the envy of Europe. Since taking the throne, he'd built sixteen battleships, three armored cruisers, and six light cruisers. His new navy could carry as many troops as necessary from Germany to Africa. One of the avowed reasons for building it in the first place, after all, was defense of Germany's colonies. Here was the test. How soon and how many troops could the navy land in South-West Africa?

Holstein undoubtedly had been expecting, and dreading, the question. His answer—an explanation on the limits of logistics and power projection—almost knocked the kaiser over. The only troops equipped for overseas service and ready to sail at a moment's notice were five hundred imperial marines. The only naval vessels with the capacity and the endurance to carry them to Swapokmund, cruisers of the Kaiserin Augusta and Gefion class, had a maximum range of 4,000 nautical miles. The voyage to South-West Africa was somewhat more than twice that distance. At their most economical cruising speed of 10 knots, their coal bunkers would be empty long before they reached the nearest German coaling station, at Togo on the West African coast.

Accompanying colliers wouldn't help. Recoaling turn-of-the-century steamships was an agonizingly slow, manual process that could not be accomplished in any kind of seaway. It mandated deep, well-protected anchorages along the African coast, which the German navy singularly lacked. The cruisers would have to stop to recoal in Spain or the Canary Islands or other non-German harbors en route. With the proper cash outlays, Holstein assured the emperor arrangements could be made. In that case, the marines could be delivered at Swapokmund in thirty-five or thirty-six days.

That was anathema for the kaiser. What about sending the new battleships: the just-completed *Kaiser, Wittelsbach,* or *Braunschweig* classes? They were bigger than any cruisers and practically as fast. They were indeed, but they were designed for short, fast ship-to-ship actions in the North Sea and not for much of anything else; certainly not for carrying troops halfway around the world. With crews of 350, the battleships had no room to carry more than 100 soldiers apiece. Loaded with heavy guns and armor, their maximum speed was 18 knots, but that could be maintained only for a brief duration; otherwise the hellish operating temperatures melted machinery and stokers. For sustained steaming, their most economical speed was half that. Consequently they would take longer to get to Africa and require more recoaling stops on the way than the cruisers and longer to return. In the interim, the Imperial Navy, outnumbered as it was by the British, would be stripped of their services.

Holstein, a protégé of the great Bismarck (and who'd been instrumental in getting rid of him), suggested an alternative that was really an endorsement of his original, if marginal, plan to deliver a token force. Once he'd arranged recoaling in the Canaries, it wasn't necessary for the cruisers to hold to 10 knots. They could press ahead at 15 knots or more. That meant they'd have to recoal again at German-held Togo and Cameroon—but at that speed they could deliver the marine contingent in twenty-one days. The battalion of marines would not be enough to relieve the capital or even commence a counteroffensive, but they would be enough to hold the port and show the flag. That was the best that could be done at the moment.

The kaiser couldn't believe his ears. Three weeks? It would take the empire three weeks to put a paltry five hundred men ashore? It was, Holstein explained, largely a matter of recoaling stations. The British had them the length of the West African coast: in Gambia, Sierra Leone, the Gold Coast, Nigeria, as well as in German South-West Africa itself (Walvis Bay, the only good harbor in the colony, had been a British naval station long before the Germans arrived; Swapokmund, in contrast, was an open, windswept anchorage). British cruisers could steam at flank speed, fill their bunkers at one, and proceed at flank speed to another. If the mainland coaling stations did not suffice, they had Ascension Island and St. Helena in the South Atlantic, each fewer than three days' steaming time from South-West Africa. That was the fact of it.

Incredulous, the kaiser asked how soon Germany could put a real army in the field, one capable of crushing the Herero. Holstein's aides had undoubtedly prepared him to address this question, too. Six years before, many of them had served as military attachés in the Spanish-American War. In that conflict it had taken the United States almost two months to assemble and land an expeditionary force of ten thousand men in Cuba—an island 90 miles off its shores. To transport the troops and a modicum of small-arms ammunition and provisions required chartering thirty-two transport steamers and five barges. Most artillery, cavalry (unless dismounted), transport, and medical units had to be left behind. Steaming in a three-column convoy at 7 knots proved overly optimistic; 5 knots was the fact. The roughly 1,000-mile voyage from Tampa to Santiago de Cuba (via Key West, across the Florida Straits, down the Old Bahama Channel, through the Windward Passage, then due west) took nine days. The landing was farcical: merchant skippers of the chartered transports refused to take their ships close to shore, overloaded boats of troops overturned in the surf, and horses were thrown overboard to swim ashore themselves. Things were so bad that Colonel Leonard Wood, commanding the First Cavalry Brigade (dismounted), wrote that he "felt embarrassed that the landing was being witnessed by a score of foreign observers."

Adequately supporting even this small army by sea, near as it was to the U.S. mainland, proved devilishly difficult. Within a month of its arrival, more than 30 percent of the troops were debilitated by malaria, yellow fever, or dysentery, and the rest were short on ammunition and starving on half rations in the sweltering trenches besieging Santiago. It was fortunate for the Americans that the war in Cuba was short. But Germany had learned invaluable lessons from their experience. Drawing a deep breath, Holstein told the emperor that to send ten thousand troops to German South-West Africa—with the necessary supplies, transport, and supporting units to sustain them—would take *five* months.

This, quite naturally, came as another incredible shock to the kaiser. He was facing what Thomas Pakenham, a leading historian of European imperialism in Africa, described as the imminent "prospect of a great colonial disaster, destructive to German prestige, as well as costly in blood and treasure"—and was being told there was nothing he could immediately do to prevent it. The army, the navy—and, by extension, himself, the "All Highest"—looked impotent, unable to strike a blow against, much less suppress, a rabble of Bantu cattle herders who'd slaughtered 123 Germans. Unable to protect the most miserable, bankrupt colony in the empire. The public display of Teutonic weakness was humiliating, particularly to Wilhelm.

He was acutely aware that the eyes of the world—Germany, its allies, and its enemies—were on him. While the Herero uprising "might only be a small war in an almost unknown corner of Africa," wrote Pakenham, "it was the first war of his reign and the first opportunity for nationalistic Germany to show the power of its huge army." For Wilhelm it was the supreme test, the time to show he was a warrior king. It was a test for which he was singularly unprepared.

Though he delighted in uniforms (in his first twelve years as emperor, he redesigned the uniform of the German army no fewer than thirty-seven times) and enthusiastically attended army maneuvers and naval reviews, he had no military training or experience. At home, biographer Michael Balfour noted he was "much ridiculed in military circles" and criticized for "a disturbing element of dilettantism in his handling of the army and navy." As a commander in chief who'd never commanded more than courtiers, he knew he was compared unfavorably with his namesake Kaiser

Wilhelm I, who had won smashing victory in the Franco-Prussian War of 1870. "He is less a soldier than his grandfather," a high-ranking Prussian officer observed, "because he lacks the steadiness of view which only down-to-earth work can give." Indeed, Queen Victoria judged that his only martial qualification was a grand talent for "uniform fishing."

He had more than a thousand, representing every service, branch, and unit in Germany (three hundred for every Prussian regiment in his army alone) and every army and navy in Europe. Biographer John Van der Kiste noted that he delighted in the paraphernalia of each with "their own individual badges, sashes, epaulettes, shoulder points, belts, caps, helmets, busbys, capes, greatcoats, swords, lances and firearms." His cousin Marie, queen of Romania, wrote that he "changed his uniform several times a day, as a smart woman changes her gown." To visit the Berlin Motor Club he donned a general of engineers uniform; to visit the city's aquarium, an admiral's uniform; for morning rides, a cavalry general's uniform. In Britain he wore the scarlet regalia of a British field marshal or the sea blue of an admiral of the fleet or the spruce green of a colonel in the Royal Rifle Regiment. In Italy he wore the uniform of elite *carabinieri* regiments; in Spain, light infantry; in Austria-Hungary, uhlans and lancers; in Russia, imperial guards. All these commissions and uniforms were honorary, of course, and in the crisis irrelevant and they made Wilhelm look even more so. He looked more like a mannequin than a field marshal. He plainly knew nothing about waging war, everybody knew it, and everybody was watching what he would do.

He immediately issued a flurry of orders. The imperial marines would sail at once. The colonial governor, regardless of the number and positions of his troops, would counterattack as soon as possible. The overseas army would prepare. For its commander, he chose General Lothar von Trotha, an officer whose reputation for brutality had been made leading the German contingent in the international 1900–1901 punitive expedition against the Boxer Rebellion in China. He ordered Trotha to "crush the Herero by fair means or foul." Trotha did not need to be told twice.

All these orders produced only deepening disaster. The colonial governor, with marines and his own troops, about eleven hundred men, counterattacked in April. At a dusty outpost called Oviumbo, he was encircled by three thousand Herero tribesmen, soundly defeated and escaped only by beating a hasty, humiliating retreat. The army wasn't delivered to South-West Africa until late June—a month behind schedule. It didn't commence offensive operations until late July, almost seven months after the uprising began. And the operations Trotha conducted amounted to an undisguised extermination program against the Herero population. He drove twenty-four thousand of them—men, women, and children—into the Omaheke Desert, dynamited the waterholes behind them, and sealed the border for 155 miles with barbed wire and fortified outposts. He then issued a chilling proclamation: "Within the German boundaries, every Herero, whether found armed or unarmed, with or without cattle, will be shot. I shall not accept any more women or children. I shall drive them back to their people—otherwise I shall order shots to be fired at them." He signed it "the Great General of the Mighty Kaiser, von Trotha."

The proclamation ignited worldwide outrage: all of it aimed at the kaiser. At home, the Reichstag was appalled. Criticism of Wilhelm's colonial policy—which, in essence, was the whole justification for his ruinously expensive naval buildup—glowed white hot. Both were in danger of collapse. Worse, the day after Trotha's proclamation, the native Nama of South-West Africa joined the Herero in the revolt. The cost in blood, treasure, and prestige to regain control of one miserable colony, which had cost German taxpayers millions of marks in annual subsidies before the rebellion, was escalating out of sight. There seemed to be no light at the end of the tunnel the kaiser had dug. The pride Germany had heretofore taken in its army and navy, in the kaiser himself, plummeted.

Accelerating Wilhelm's plunge in the polls was an unparalleled series of accompanying international incidents that made a mockery of his grandiose naval and colonial aspirations. One day after his five hundred marines landed at Swapokmund, war erupted between Russia and Japan when the Japanese navy launched a surprise attack on Russia's Asian fleet anchored at Port Arthur in China. Under cover of darkness, ten Japanese destroyers raced into the heavily fortified harbor and crippled two battleships and a heavy cruiser with torpedoes. It was a striking success for the British-built, British-trained Japanese navy and a sobering reminder to Wilhelm's critics of what it would cost to ever tangle with the British navy itself. Five days before the Herero humiliated the German colonial army at Oviumbo, France and Britain signed an *entente cordiale,* carving up North Africa between themselves and tilting the whole balance of world power out of Germany's reach, leaving Wilhelm (cruising in his yacht in the Mediterranean at the time) to theatrically storm ashore at Tangier on a white horse in impotent protest. Challenging the combined navies of Britain and France was unthinkable, even for the kaiser; which led almost everybody, except the kaiser, to thinking about why Germany was spending such prodigious amounts of money on a naval arms race it clearly could never win. The same week as von Trotha turned his extermination campaign against the Nama in earnest, the Japanese navy destroyed the remainder of the Russian Asian fleet, still in its anchorage at Port Arthur.

Wilhelm's expensive, fast-building navy, confined to anchorages in the North Sea and Baltic, suddenly looked shockingly vulnerable. It didn't look like it could protect the home seas, much less Germany's colonies and interests on the high seas, the South-West African and North African debacles demonstrating the point. His opponents in the Reichstag and at court fixed on it. Despite all the money the kaiser had lavished on the navy, it could not do what he'd advertised it could do.

For the kaiser, who was putting the finishing touches on yet another of his monumentally expensive naval laws, the firestorm of criticism at home and abroad was withering. To distract public attention from these problems—disasters, more aptly—and push through his agenda, he desperately needed a success somewhere. Anywhere. A big one. And quickly.

It presented itself—like a gift horse—when his popularity was at its lowest ebb. It came in the form of a cablegram from one of his very few close friends: forty-eight-year-old Hugh Cecil Lowther, the fifth earl of Lonsdale, an English landowner, yachtsman, and something of the kaiser's personal yachting adviser. It came from

New York. Lonsdale informed him that Sir Thomas Lipton had offered a challenge cup for an open, international transatlantic yacht race—the first of its kind. The New York Yacht Club, to whom Lipton had submitted the offer, hadn't acted on it. If the kaiser offered a cup, Lipton would be protocolbound to withdraw his in favor of the emperor's. If he did, a worldwide stage would be his. Lonsdale left it at that.

Wilhelm pounced upon the idea. In fact, he outright stole it. An ocean race with his name on it appealed as much to him as to Sir Thomas, and Wilhelm had no compunction about elbowing the man aside. Lipton was, after all, a *grocer*. At Cowes, Wilhelm had loudly and often criticized his uncle Albert, the prince of Wales and now King Edward, for "yachting with his *grocer*." The world's first international ocean race ought to be dignified by sponsorship more regal than a *grocer's*.

Yet holding the torch of yachting high was hardly uppermost in Wilhelm's mind. The event was the perfect chance to win a resounding victory at sea—and at home—without firing a shot. His vast propaganda machine couldn't have invented anything better. It took the spotlight off the utter failure of his colonial policy in South-West Africa and shined it on his chief goal: staking Germany's claim to the high seas and what he called its "place in the sun." It united his subjects behind Germany's nautical ambitions and unfanged his critics in the Reichstag. It clanged like a touched shield to his adversaries: never discount German will. Like the Greek *hoplitodromos*—and Wilhelm was a student of antiquity—it was tantamount to war short of war. Even better, sponsoring the race almost magically transformed him from the bad boy of Europe to the chief benefactor of international sportsmanship and peaceful relations on the high seas. It was—domestically and internationally—a public relations mother lode.

Wilhelm didn't hesitate. He telegraphed Lonsdale that it was "splendid undertaking" and immediately offered a prize cup. The event would be called the German Emperor's Cup Race.

The rules were few and brief and were calculated to attract the largest field of contestants and the greatest publicity. Any yacht over 100 tons—of any type or rig, belonging to any recognized yacht club—could enter. There would be no handicaps or time allowances whatever. The kaiser detested them, considering them unmanly; once sending a public telegram to the Royal Yacht Squadron after the Queen's Cup race complaining "Your handicaps are perfectly appalling," even though his yacht had won the race by benefit of handicaps. The international rules of the road—which the kaiser was notorious for routinely ignoring when racing himself—would govern. Owners of competing yachts, or their representatives, had to be aboard their vessels for the duration of the race. The meaning of such Spartan rules was crystal clear: come out and contest for supremacy of the sea, man to man, no holds barred. It was a challenge straight out of the kaiser's dueling club days.

The one rule the kaiser most insisted on was the starting date of the race. His Royal Highness wanted to present the winning trophy on the opening day of his favorite personal, highest-profile maritime event: June 22, 1905, at the Kiel Week regatta. For the contestants to reach Kiel by that date, they would have to battle not

The prize—a solid gold trophy, designed by Wilhelm II himself and called the Kaiser's Cup. The world's richest, most privileged men risked fortunes and lives to win it.

only each other but also dangerous spring conditions in the North Atlantic. Any European competitors would have to face that challenge twice. Wilhelm stipulated that all competing yachts had to *sail* to the starting line in New York. That was certain to chill the ardor of the Royal Yacht Squadron and increase his chances of beating the British. For the same reason, it was certain to attract the biggest sharks in the New York Yacht Club, which guaranteed the race the headlines he wanted.

As a personal fillip, the emperor offered to design the trophy cup himself. He considered himself a Renaissance man. He painted, composed music, and choreographed ballets, rather dreadfully by all accounts, and was a keen student of the art of antiquity. He modeled his trophy upon the dual-handled, vase-shaped amphorae awarded to the first Olympians. It was fashioned of solid gold.

CHAPTER 15

The Germans

It's odd you have no yacht here. I shall never come to dinner
here again until you have one.

　　　　　　　—Kaiser Wilhelm II
　　　　　　　(at a banquet held in his honor
　　　　　　　by the businessmen of Hamburg)

That is pretty much how sixty-one-year-old Adolph Tietjens—
director of the Hamburg-America Line, Germany's oldest transatlantic steamship line and the biggest shipping firm on earth in
1905—got drafted into yacht racing. His sovereign, the man who
had been instrumental in making Hamburg-America the biggest
shipping firm on earth with lavish subsidies for everything from
shipbuilding to carrying the mail, called in his dues. Tietjens was in
no position to refuse. "The German company," wrote North
Atlantic shipping historian John Brinnin, "basked in Imperial favor,
was staffed by brilliant, ambitious executives and, as time would tell,
competitive to the point of madness." The company's house flag,
after all, was emblazoned with the motto *"Mein Feld ist die Welt"*
(My field is the world), which might have been the kaiser's himself.

Led by Tietjens, a syndicate of Hamburg industrialists duly
ponied up the money for a yacht. Since the kaiser wasn't coming
back to dinner until they had one, they elected to buy it, not build

it. They bought the very finest: a large, wickedly fast, two-masted schooner named *Rainbow.* The fact that the 158-foot vessel was British-designed and -built caused them little concern. She'd been designed by the legendary George Lennox Watson, and she won races. "If the emperor wants caviar," explained one syndicate member, "he cannot object to the waters where it originates." The syndicate renamed her *Hamburg* and placed her at the emperor's disposal. He raced her, used her as an Imperial Navy training ship when he wasn't, and came to dinner regularly after that. Tietjens' stock with the kaiser rose commensurately. It seemed a small but profitable investment.

When the 1905 German Emperor's Cup challenge was announced, however, the kaiser drafted him again: straight to the front line of his self-declared ocean war—as his *personal* representative aboard *Hamburg* during the race. He seemed the perfect man to keep an eye on the kaiser's interests. He was, Brinnin wrote, "a cold, Roman-eyed shipping executive." His Hamburg-America Line was the most fiercely competitive on the North Atlantic. In 1900 its German-designed and -built liner *Deutschland* had shocked the world and delighted the kaiser by again winning the Blue Ribband from the British—and rival North German–Lloyd Line—with a record-breaking transatlantic crossing. He'd packed its vessels with steerage passengers—for whom there were no lifeboats, by the way—and shuttled them to America at high speed and a handsome profit, with little regard for risk. He'd carried the torch of yacht racing for the kaiser, for Germany. He would do whatever His Royal Highness asked.

Yet Wilhelm was asking quite a bit. His rules for the race required owners or their representatives to personally sail in their yachts: not just in the race, but to the race as well. For European entries that meant making a westbound Atlantic crossing to New York in stormy, early spring conditions—always an unfavorable passage. This condition went a long way (as perhaps Wilhelm intended) to discourage European, especially British, entries. If the British owners of numerous low, light-built inshore racers—who'd routinely beaten him at Cowes with their Byzantine handicaps— wanted to try him in an open ocean contest, without any handicaps, they'd have to cross the ocean *twice* in their frail vessels, back-to-back with virtually no rest. Unfortunately, so would the sixty-one-year-old, sedentary Tietjens.

Accustomed to luxury accommodations aboard Hamburg-America liners, the outward-bound voyage to New York aboard *Hamburg* was a shock to him. He wrote that three of the schooner's guest cabins—"and all the bath tubs"—had been "commandeered" to stow sails and stores. He was forced to share the owner's stateroom with his son, Captain-Lieutenant John Tietjens, whom the emperor had given leave to accompany him. The comfortable saloon was crammed with spare canvas. The decks were chock-ablock with spare spars and booms. The thing that most disturbed Tietjens, however, was that there was no room left for the ship's boats. *Hamburg*'s stout launch, cutter, and gig—the only lifeboats in event of emergency—had been sent ashore. There remained only an 8-foot-long dinghy hung in the davits and four flimsy, experimental "folding boats" lashed on deck. Examining the latter, Tietjens muttered to his son that it would have been better to ship "folding chairs," at least they were useful.

He knew better than to complain to *Hamburg*'s captain. Captain-Lieutenant Edward Peters was—to the core—an officer in the Imperial German Navy. What's more, he was a select officer on a fast career track. It was no secret that he was a favorite of the emperor. On detached duty, he'd skippered a number of Wilhelm's racing yachts to victory, often with a delighted Wilhelm in tow. Of all the officers in the Imperial Navy, the emperor had chosen him to win his namesake cup for the fatherland in the coming transatlantic race. There was no mistaking the way the wind was blowing from the Berlin *Schloss*. And keeping his nose to whatever the All Highest was sniffing was all Tietjens needed to know.

Peters had been preparing *Hamburg* for an Atlantic crossing for a month. Besides sending her boats ashore, he'd struck the topmasts, stepped a new mainmast, raised her bow bulwarks, rigged a square sail to her foremast, doubled or tripled the reefing on sails, and installed additional water tanks below. Tietjens, a veteran shipping executive, didn't have to be told what all that meant. "The looks of the yacht," he wrote in his log, "were absolutely indicative of high

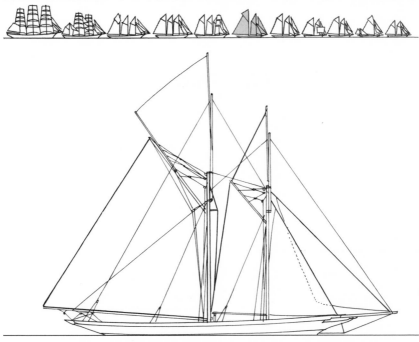

Germany's entry—the black, raked-masted schooner *Hamburg*—was selected by "many judges of well-known abilities in such matters as the probable winner." Ironically, she was British down to her keel: designed by legendary George Lennox Watson, built in Glasgow, and considered one of the fastest racers Watson ever produced.

seas" and a punishing, perhaps extended voyage. He noted that Peters had packed the boat with seventy days' provisions. But even with the new water tanks, *Hamburg* could carry only a thirty-four-day supply for her thirty-three-man complement: 6 liters per day per man. For drinking purposes, that was cutting things thin. All washing and shaving, even for Herr Direktor Tietjens, would be done with salt water.

It was some comfort to know that—given explicit orders and *carte blanche* from the emperor to recruit an all-German crew—Peters had assembled the finest blue-water sailors in the Imperial Navy; veteran seamen who had weathered the worst latitudes on earth.

CHAPTER 16

The British

I decided to enter my yacht for the honor of British yachting.
—Thomas Brassey,
first earl of Brassey

If there was one man who understood better than any the kaiser's real reason for sponsoring the race, it was the oldest man sailing the oldest yacht entered. Lord Thomas Brassey, sixty-nine, brought his thirty-one-year-old topsail schooner *Sunbeam* across the Atlantic to compete on behalf of the Royal Yacht Squadron or, more precisely, the British Empire.

To all appearances he was a perfect, white-haired specimen of a proper English yachtsman, right down to his natty "Cowes jacket" (a comfortable compromise among a mess jacket, a smoking jacket, and a dress coat invented for Albert, prince of Wales, and first worn by him aboard his yacht at Cowes). His title wasn't inherited, but hard-earned and a long time coming (he was fifty before he was raised to the peerage as Baron Brassey). He had not earned a gold sovereign of his great fortune. Like so many American millionaires, it was inherited from Daddy (Thomas Brassey Sr.), who had made millions building railroads in Britain and France. That money paid for a regal education at Rugby and Oxford (he took honors in the school of law and in modern history), and while still in school, two fast racing cutters, *Zillah* and *Cymba*. Upon graduation at age twenty-two, it paid for an iron-hulled schooner of 110 tons named *Albatross* and election to Britain's ultraexclusive Royal Yacht Squadron.

Family fortune freed him to pursue a comfortable parliamentary career (eighteen years representing Hastings), philanthropy (the East End Immigrants Association), and various prestigious government posts (civil lord of the Admiralty, secretary to the Admiralty, and later governor of Victoria, Australia). It also allowed him to indulge himself in bigger and bigger yachts, designed to his order. Before he was forty, he'd replaced the *Albatross* (a pure sailing yacht) with *Meteor* (a steam auxiliary schooner), followed by *Eothen* (a steam yacht of 350 tons) and finally *Sunbeam* (a three-masted steam auxiliary schooner of 576 tons). He spent every parliamentary recess on his yachts: cruising the Mediterranean and

The British topsail schooner *Sunbeam*—the first private yacht to circumnavigate the world—was the most famous vessel in the race. She was also the oldest.

the Baltic, crisscrossing the Atlantic, and becoming the first amateur British yachtsman to obtain by examination a Board of Trade master's certificate—tantamount to a mariner's green beret.

At sea he was cordial with everyone, regardless of birth or station. He made it a point to get to know his crew; something British peers and American millionaires avoided. Every morning, when the men were washing the decks, he took his turn at the pump brake like a common sailor. He said it gave him "exercise and a chance to talk to the man pumping with me about himself, his home affairs, how many children he has and all that." He didn't hesitate going aloft either. Once, after he'd ordered a newfangled rigging device installed in the uppermost yards of *Sunbeam,* a topman struggling with it exclaimed: "I wish the old _____ was up here to see it hisself." He was startled to hear a familiar voice say: "The old _____ is."

Brassey also was one of the foremost experts on naval affairs of the day. Twenty years before entering the race, he'd written a landmark five-volume work, *The British Navy: Its Strength, Resources, and Administration,* which, in fact, excoriated the navy's weaknesses. At the time he was civil lord of the Admiralty, and his revelations about obsolete warships, antiquated dockyards and the dry rot of Nelsonian administration were shocking to an empire wholly dependent on seapower and that, to that point, believed its navy was still the finest in the world.

Soon afterward he issued his first *Naval Annual* (precursor to *Jane's Fighting Ships*), which included the particulars of not only the British, but also of all the principal foreign navies. This served as a continuing, very public reminder of the Royal Navy's shortcomings. One result of his initiative was Britain's sweeping 1889 Naval Defence Act, a massive program to modernize the Royal Dockyards and build an all-new British fleet. "Massive" is an understatement. Its goal was to build a "two-power" navy, "one capable of defeating an alliance of the next two strongest maritime powers." In fewer than ten years Britain laid down and built no fewer than twenty-nine first-class battleships; an unprecedented number. There was, in fact, enough excess capacity in Brassey's new shipyards to build battleships for export (six to Japan alone).

The act also lit the fuse of a twenty-five-year international naval arms race that would culminate in—some said cause—World War I. The other two great naval powers at the time, France and Russia, quickly followed suit. The United States and Germany passed landmark naval acts of their own. The Americans appropriated money to build warships of "every class." The Germans initially funded the construction of seven large battleships and nine cruisers, a number which would soon expand exponentially.

When Brassey left the Admiralty, his interest in maintaining Britain's naval superiority didn't lessen a molecule. As a leader of the Royal Institution of Naval Architects, he authored a profusion of papers all of which, no doubt, made the kaiser's blood boil. There was *Defense of Coaling Stations,* of which Britain had many and Germany almost none. There was *The Future Policy of Warship Building,* which could be practiced in Britain's large, modernized shipyards but not in Germany's smaller, inefficient ones. There was *The Conversion and Re-armament of Ships on the Effective List,* which would revitalize vast numbers of obsolete British warships that Germany could never hope to match. The year before the race there was Brassey's paper *Merchant Cruisers and Steamship Subsidies,* whereby the government funded the building of the huge liners *Mauretania* and *Lusitania,* aimed not only to win back the "Blue Ribband of the Atlantic" from the Kaiser's Hamburg-America Line but also to provide the British fleet with a reserve of very fast ships for scouting/merchant raiding service.

It may be said without much exaggeration that Lord Brassey was "Britain's Mahan," the empire's equivalent of American admiral and naval historian Alfred Thayer Mahan, whose landmark 1890 work *The Influence of Sea Power upon History, 1660–1783* convinced the maritime nations of the world to expand and modernize their navies. As such he'd been widely read, undoubtedly by both the kaiser and Admiral Tirpitz. That the challenge for the German Emperor's Cup had netted one of their greatest protagonists must have been a source of great satisfaction to them. The chance to beat Brassey himself and publicly humble Britain in an open ocean race was more than they could have hoped for.

For his part, Brassey could hardly have refused the challenge.

He knew full well the propaganda value of the race. In the end—kings and emperors be damned—winning the appropriations to build what were, in effect, fantastically expensive *Star Wars* fleets of their time took public approval. Brassey had been successful in doing this with Parliament, and the kaiser had been equally successful in doing it with the Reichstag. But both knew that incalculably greater sums of public money were necessary. The winner of the Emperor's Cup stood to reap a very rich harvest.

How deeply Brassey's involvement with the Royal Navy went is anyone's guess, but he was definitely an invaluable intelligence asset. What he publicly released in his *Naval Annual* was probably a good deal less than what he privately shared with the Admiralty. His intelligence-gathering may have gone farther.

Consider this: during the 1914 Kiel Regatta (during which the news of the assassinations at Sarejevo was received), the then seventy-eight-year-old lord was caught rowing his dinghy alone amid the anchored warships of the German fleet, in waters specifically *verboten* by the Imperial Command. He was immediately detained by the kaiser's harbor police and held until his identity was established and he was released. His explanation—that he'd gone for a "short row" and had "unwittingly ventured beyond the limits prescribed for visitors"—was incredulous. Brassey was, after all, Britain's first amateur yachtsman to obtain by examination a Board of Trade master's certificate. He had circumnavigated the globe three times and had regularly attended the Imperial Regatta at Kiel since its inception in 1897. With any kind of a bottom beneath him, the man never ventured "unwittingly" anywhere. That he got lost rowing about the Kiel anchorage was a virtual impossibility.

Lord Thomas Brassey, sixty-nine, *Sunbeam*'s owner, was among the foremost naval experts of the day and determined to deny Kaiser Wilhelm a propaganda victory in the race.

Yet it made a very plausible cover story: a seventy-eight-year-old man bobbing about in a dinghy, seemingly confused, seemingly harmless, and practically invisible from the decks of Germany's big new battleships. At the same time, within the old man's head was an encyclopedic knowledge of naval architecture and arms and a journalist's eye for recognizing things of consequence. In the hours before he was spotted, Brassey had ample opportunity to quite literally run his hands over the armor belts of Germany's latest Konig-class battleships and Von der Tann-class battlecruisers, note their antitorpedo defenses, gauge the size and weight of their main batteries, and much, much more.

When he sailed *Sunbeam* to New York in 1905 to compete for the Kaiser's Cup, Brassey was intimately aware of Germany's furiously growing naval construction program. He clearly intended to deny the kaiser a propaganda victory to fuel it further. Brassey knew full well that the 170-foot *Sunbeam* was no racer. She was old (launched in 1874) and heavily built—a composite vessel of steel frames, planked with teak and copper-bottomed. Her topsail schooner rig—square-rigged on the foremast, fore-and-aft-rigged on her other two masts—was designed for comfortable cruising, not speed. She was not fast. Under canvas on the outward voyage to the United States, she averaged only 9 knots before favorable northeast trade winds.

But she was undeniably the best-known yacht in the world, the first privately owned yacht, in fact, to circumnavigate the globe (1876–1877). Lady Brassey's book about the cruise, *A Voyage in the Sunbeam*, sold millions of copies and was translated into seven languages. By 1905 Brassey had logged more than 300,000 miles in her: including seventeen voyages to the Mediterranean (each of more than 5,000 miles), six to Scandinavia and the Baltic, four to North America and the West Indies and countless shorter cruises along European shores. In visiting virtually every port of call and potentate in the world, Brassey became the acknowledged dean of the international yachting fraternity. Autographed photos of European royalty blanketed the walls of *Sunbeam*'s library. Her grand saloon resembled a seagoing British Museum, filled with rare and precious gifts from leaders of every corner of the empire. There was a teak sideboard from the raja of Sarawak, ivory elephants from the

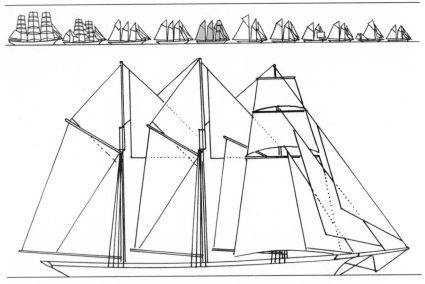

Despite her age, *Sunbeam* was a strong-built, oceangoing schooner, renowned for making long passages and well-suited to weather the North Atlantic. Her three-masted, topsail schooner rig, however, was designed for cruising, not racing.

sultan of Johore, and a majestic pair of carved sandalwood doors from the sultan of Perak. The poet Tennyson and Prime Minister Gladstone were such frequent guests that their cabins were named for them. The famous long-distance cruiser was nothing less than Britain's unofficial ship of state and Brassey its ambassador at large. Despite their relatively advanced ages, it was unthinkable that either of them sit out the race.

With Brassey at the helm—assisted by Captain Echard, his navigator, and sailing master Fayle, both of whom had been with him for thirty-six years, and an all-British crew of Cornishmen and Jerseymen, he steeled himself for the contest. He did not expect to win the race. He did, however, intend to beat the Germans. "I have now no higher aim," he told the press, "than to utilize every opportunity to contribute in all possible ways to a victory of the English-speaking people."

The other British challenger, Lord Lindsay, had no such notions. In his mind, the British Empire needn't trouble itself about anything.

He certainly didn't. As twenty-sixth earl of Crawford and eighth earl of Balcarres, James Ludovic Lindsay had titles, estates, bottomless wealth, endless connections, and could well afford to be that most cherished of Victorian institutions: an eccentric dilettante.

At fifty-eight he looked every bit as quirky as he was. Bearded and mustachioed to the eyes, he wore pince-nez spectacles and confronted the world with a perpetual squint. Though his valet dressed him every day in formal morning attire—black cutaway coat, gray and black-striped trousers, and black silk tie—he insisted on wearing carpet slippers instead of shoes. Whenever there was the slightest suspicion of rain, he donned a bright yellow oilskin coat; whether inside or outside. He suffered considerably from asthma and, as a result, lived aboard his yacht *Valhalla* for ten months a year, seeking out more salubrious

The owner of British entry *Valhalla*, Lord James Lindsay—twenty-sixth earl of Crawford and eighth earl of Balcarres—had titles and fortunes enough to be what he wanted to be: an eccentric dilettante. His passions included astronomy, orinthology, philately—and yachting.

climates. He spent most of his time poring over his vast, eclectic stamp collection (which included forty volumes alone containing every stamp issued by the United States), rare books, broadsides of the French Revolution, and archaic Oriental manuscripts illustrating the history of handwriting.

His other passions included astronomy, orinthology, and photography, all of which provided thumpingly good excuses for taking long yachting cruises in pursuit of them. Down to Cádiz to see a solar eclipse, off to Mauritius in the Indian Ocean to observe the transit of Venus, to the Comoros and Seychelles Islands and Trinidad seeking new species of birds. His observations and discoveries were alternately meticulous and credulous. His astronomical work helped establish the solar parallax, and his orinthological endeavors documented eight new species, three of which—a white tern, *Gygis crawfordi*; a paradise flycatcher, *Terpsiphone lindsayi*; and a heron, *Butorides crawfordi*—were named for him. On the other hand, he steadfastly insisted he'd sighted a sea serpent off Brazil.

When yachting, he habitually wore a formal white captain's cap, complete with badge insignia, gold cord, and "scrambled eggs" bill. Beneath it—to his valet's chagrin—his uncombed hair stuck out like a scarecrow's.

He was in the race—quite simply—because his 245-foot ship *Valhalla* was the biggest yacht in the Royal Yacht Squadron. A steel-hulled, three-masted, ship-rigged, steam auxiliary of 648 tons, she would in fact prove to be the largest vessel in the contest, by far. Everyone who laid eyes on her was impressed by her sheer size. But she was, first and foremost, the earl's oceangoing palace. Comfort was her primary purpose.

It showed in what Lindsay called his "workroom"—a 1,600-square-foot deckhouse. A *New York Times* reporter likened it to "the most comfortable lounging room, in the most comfortable club you can imagine." With white and gold walls and plush red uphol-stery and carpet, its centerpiece was an enormous globe of the world. Its mahogany lockers were filled with the earl's stamp col-lection, valued at more than $3 million at the time. The latest, most advanced nautical instruments and telescopes were everywhere.

But the deckhouse was merely the tip of *Valhalla*'s palatial ice-berg. A broad companionway staircase delivered guests below-decks—to a skylit main passage more than 90 feet long. Off this Fifth Avenue-like promenade, double doors opened onto a formal dining room that could seat 30 and a sumptuously furnished draw-ing room with fireplaces and a grand piano. There were six vast guest cabins (four for gentlemen and two, with attached dressing rooms, for ladies); three bathing rooms with chest-deep, 9-foot long bathtubs; and three water closets or heads. There was also the earl's luxurious private suite: a sleeping stateroom, book-lined study, and private bath. A large pantry, manned twenty-four hours a day with stewards summoned by buzzer, provided whatever *Valhalla*'s owner or guests might require. In all, this rigidly segregated area— but one door, through a midships bulkhead, admitted stewards— occupied more than 60 percent of the lower deck and comprised more than 3,800 square feet of space, yet accommodated, at most, the earl and six indulgently pampered guests.

Immediately forward lay the ship's engine room: an open area of polished machinery, boilers, and piping, three decks high. Since use of engines was prohibited in the contest and propellers had to be removed, this area was to be blissfully silent during the race. The forward third of *Valhalla*'s lower deck was not. It was crammed with nine cabins, which housed the ship's twelve officers, mates, doctor, cooks, and stewards; two messrooms (one for officers, one for subordinate officers); two large, constantly working galleys (one for guests, one for crew); and a forepeak sided with triple-decker bunks, and deck-bolted benches and mess tables for sixty seamen.

Valhalla's dimensions bespoke power. Her 208-foot waterline length dwarfed that of her closest competitor by almost 25 percent. With all sail set—fifty-five sails altogether—and wind on her quarter, she could make 16 knots (more than 18 miles per hour). By dint of her sheer size and massive spread of canvas, if the prevailing westerly winds in the North Atlantic blew hard and the seas were rough as expected, she stood perhaps the best chance of winning the transatlantic race. That alone was quite enough reason for the twenty-sixth earl of Crawford to enter her. He did so as soon as the race was announced, the first yacht to pick up the kaiser's gauntlet.

He could scarcely have done anything else. He was plugged into just about every "old boy" network in Victorian England and knew what was expected of him. He'd attended Eton, followed grudgingly by a "short residence" at Trinity College, Cambridge. As wealthy and intuitively brilliant as he was, rote education seems to have bored him silly. He suffered it only because duty required him to append the *curriculum vitae* to his résumé. That's why he'd served briefly in the Grenadier Guards, the oldest infantry regiment in the British army, and not incoincidentally, one of the most socially prestigious and expensive. He wore his uniform and commission uncomfortably—he was the antithesis of martial—and resigned it (or more properly sold it back to the government) as soon as he honorably could. Pro forma, he'd been elected to Parliament, and upon the death of his father, dutifully assumed his seat in the House of Lords.

Most of his life, however, was very comfortably lived in between these events, pursuing whatever he fancied at the moment.

At 245 feet, *Valhalla* was the largest and only ship-rigged yacht in the race and one of the most formidable. Under full canvas, she spread over fifty sails, far more than any other entry.

And whatever he fancied, he mastered. He was made a fellow of the Royal Society and elected president of the Royal Astronomical Society at thirty-one, named chief British commissioner to the electrical exhibition in Paris at thirty-four, made an associate of the Royal Prussian Academy of Sciences at thirty-six, and elected trustee of the British Museum at thirty-eight. In between, he was an active member of the Royal Photographic Society, the Philatelic Society, and the Camden Society. After age forty, he all but retired from public life: first donating his telescopes, instruments, and astronomical library to the nation, for the purpose of establishing a national observatory at Edinburgh.

Despite the fact that he was filthy rich, never had to work a day in his life, and was a true eccentric, nearly everybody liked him. On the voyage to America via the Caribbean for the race, he ordered a 500-mile detour to pick up fresh ice for his guests—nine tons worth. Since he was coming to the States, he brought his entire collection of U.S. stamps with him. He stopped in Key West, Florida, for no other reason than to say he'd visited the southernmost point in the United States. He anchored in Charlotte Harbor on Florida's western coast for two weeks to fetch and bend new sails for *Valhalla,* but spent almost all his time tarpon fishing or scouring nearby Sanibel Island to collect seashells. With Lord Crawford aboard, life was relaxed. "You can't have naval discipline aboard a yacht," he told a friend, "we have sea discipline and everything shipshape, but there's no standing at attention or saluting or any nonsense of that sort."

Yet he plunged into the business of winning the race very seriously. He attended to all the ship's navigation himself. As a prominent astronomer, he was an excellent one. In an ocean race, especially a transatlantic one of more than 3,000 miles, winning or losing rested as much on the navigator as the captain. It was the navigator's job to interpret the weather, find the wind, and divine—there is no other word for it—the fastest, not necessarily shortest, route across the ocean to the finish. In 1905 it was as much art as science. Once a racing yacht vanished over the horizon, lost sight of land and other yachts, and was swallowed in the immensity of the sea, fate pretty much rested in the navigator's hands.

Toward that end, Lindsay had equipped his yacht with what a stupefied reporter called "every contrivance known to navigators." On the outward voyage Lindsay had also developed some secret weapons of his own to give *Valhalla* a technological edge over its rivals. The same reporter noted that he had devised "an ingenious invention that shows, by means of electrical connections, the ship's course by dead reckoning. When the course is set by use of a pelorus [a navigational instrument resembling a mariner's compass but without magnetic needles, and having two sight vanes by which bearings are taken], which is connected with a clock and with the patent log, the course of the ship is traced automatically and accurately on a slate." The thing was the first "heads up" navigational display of its time. He also designed and built an "automatic sentry that warns those on the bridge when shoal water is found"—the first depth finder.

For all his forward-looking gifts, however, the twenty-sixth earl of Crawford was unable to divine the future. Though he scarcely suspected it, he was an endangered species.

CHAPTER 17

Crown Princes of Capitalism

Wealth is represented in the race. Vessels have been fitted out regardless of expense. That does not matter to those concerned: it has been determined by the American contingent that one of its members shall be the winner.
—*New York Herald,*
May 14, 1905

The mercantile American princes who took up the German emperor's challenge had but two things in common: they were fabulously, almost unbelievably rich; and they were fiercely competitive, perhaps nowhere more than in the clannish, ruinously expensive realm of yachting.

The fortunes of American capitalists at the time can only be judged in comparison with today's. According to *Forbes,* oil magnate John D. Rockefeller's wealth at the turn of the twentieth century amounted to $189.6 billion in today's dollars, steel tycoon Andrew Carnegie's $100.5 billion, and railroad heir William Vanderbilt's $95.9 billion. By comparison, Wal-Mart heir S. Robson Walton, eldest son of the retail chain's founder Sam Walton, and identified as the richest person in the world in 2001 by the *Sunday Times* of London, is worth only an estimated $65 billion. Microsoft cofounder

Bill Gates, whom the paper listed the second richest, is worth about $54 billion. Third is Oracle chief and yachtsman Larry Ellison, valued at $42.5 billion, followed by King Fahd of Saudi Arabia at $28.9 billion and investor Warren Buffet at a rather paltry $24.9 billion. By any measure, America's billionaires at the turn of the twentieth century were far richer than those at the turn of the twenty-first. They were, in fact, the richest men in history. Furthermore, their wealth was, more or less, permanent, undiluted by any federal income taxes—individual or corporate—and untouched by inheritance taxes.

They quite literally had money to burn. Jamie Bennett reportedly once tossed wads of bills amounting to $5,000 into a fireplace so he could comfortably put his hands in his pockets. James Buchanan Brady (a.k.a. "Diamond Jim"), who'd made megabucks in railroad supplies and stocks, thought nothing of ordering a dozen gold-plated bicycles for himself and giving his girlfriend, actress Lillian Russell, one with mother-of-pearl handlebars and diamond, sapphire, ruby, and emerald-studded spokes that cost $10,000, or about $182,000 in today's value. But those displays of conspicuous consumption were penny ante. America's gilded aristocracy spent vastly more on the more serious business of outdoing one another.

As a birthday present in 1891, railroad heir William Vanderbilt's wife, Alva, surprised him with a mansion in Newport called Marble House. Built of African marble, with a gold-paneled ballroom, it cost $11 million, or roughly $200 million in today's dollars. It didn't save their marriage: Alva was one of America's first high society wives to seek a divorce, and kept Marble House for herself. Relative Cornelius Vanderbilt II topped it in 1895, with a 70-room northern Italian Renaissance-style mansion called The Breakers. Over its library mantelpiece he inscribed the motto: "Little do I care for riches." Others piled in. The Wetmores, whose family fortune had been made in the Far East shipping trade, built Château-sur-Mer. Its centerpiece was an eye-popping China Room that featured an exquisite collection of thirty-five hundred pieces. At Crossways, the Newport mansion of billionaire Stuyvesant Fish, guests were blinded by a gold table service for three hundred.

The one-upsmanship extended beyond Newport. It encom-
passed more mansions at New York's tony Saratoga racetrack,
great camps in the Adirondacks, quail hunting plantations in Geor-
gia,and seaside palaces in Florida. In New York City, America's *nouveau riche* practically annexed upper Fifth Avenue, outspending each
other on castles, manors, palazzi, villas and *châteaux* in Gothic,
English, Italian, French, baroque, and Far Eastern styles.

To demonstrate their sophistication, they ransacked the art
world to decorate them. Their orders—for furniture, paintings,
sculpture, tapestries, carvings, mantels, staircases and ceilings—went
out, and the art of the Old World was packaged up and shipped
back. Darius Mills, who'd made a fortune in California gold mines,
spent $8 million in today's dollars on ancient Oriental art to deco-
rate his Fifth Avenue mansion. He neither knew nor cared much
about Oriental art, except that it was in fashion at the time.
Financier and yachtsman J. P. Morgan, whose imperial acquisitions
would later make the New York Metropolitan Museum of Art, was
notorious for the same attitude. "One day a noted art dealer showed
J. P. Morgan a small, but exquisite Vermeer," recounted historian
Matthew Josephson in *The Robber Barons:* "'Who is Vermeer?'
asked Morgan. Vermeer's importance was explained to him, also the
commercially important information that Vermeers were almost
unobtainable by private collectors. Whereupon Morgan asked the
price, which was $100,000 [almost $2 million in today's value]. 'I'll
take it,' he said, and transferred a fortune to possess a painter of
whose existence he had never heard, though he was one of the most
illustrious names in European art."

In outdoing themselves at frivolous excess, however, the costume
ball given at the Waldorf-Astoria Hotel by New York billionaire
Bradley Martin in 1897 took the cake. The ballroom duplicated the
Hall of Mirrors at the palace of Versailles, right down to original
Louis XIV tapestries on the walls. Crystal chandeliers and mirrors
illuminated rose trees in full bloom, filled with clipped-wing,
singing nightingales. Only wines and liqueurs dating from before the
French Revolution were served. Relays of orchestras provided
music. But the extravagance of the guests' costumes was what
floored everyone. "One lady, impersonating Mary Stuart," accord-

ing to the newspapers, "wore a gold-embroidered gown, trimmed with pearls and precious stones." New York banking heir August Belmont Jr. showed her up. He clanked into the Waldorf in a full suit of gold-inlaid armor that reporters calculated cost $10,000, or almost $200,000 today. The sheer indulgence of the event, according to a contemporary historian, "dazed the entire Western World." In its wake, Bradley Martin's minimal property tax assessment was doubled. In a huff, he immediately moved his family abroad.

This kind of competition to excess—keeping up with the Vanderbilts, so to speak—naturally carried out to sea, to yachting and particularly yacht racing. In a yacht race it was not only possible to *keep up* with the Vanderbilts but also to *leave them behind*. In front of all the right people, in all the best places—regattas at swank Newport, sumptuous New York, elegant Cowes, and imperial Kiel. On those watery playing fields, America's robber barons, *nouveau riche* princes, and prodigal sons raced for wagers, which though astronomical by today's measure, were pocket change to them. Mostly, however, they raced for trophy cups that, though worth far less than their everyday service of Baccarat, bestowed upon them a sort of title, peerage, and distinction they craved. For turn-of-the-twentieth-century American billionaires—mushrooms of a crassly commercial, egalitarian society—competing for the prestigious Queen's Cup at Britain's venerable Cowes Week and rubbing shoulders with royalty at Germany's Kiel Week were about as near achieving nobility as they could hope to get. And they spent fortunes to get it.

They fell all over themselves to get in on the Kaiser's Cup race. Understandably, the New York Yacht Club led the charge. Financier J. P. Morgan immediately moved to bring two-time America's Cup winner *Columbia* into the contest. Frederick Bourne, head of the Singer Sewing Machine Company and the club's commodore, proposed entering his 253-foot auxiliary schooner *Delaware*. Railroad heir Cornelius Vanderbilt offered up his luxurious auxiliary yacht *Tarantula*. Self-made oil magnate Henry Huddleston Rogers—he'd worked as a paperboy, railroad baggage man, saved $600, and turned it into $25 billion in today's value in developing Pennsylvania oil fields—offered up his equally big auxiliary *Kanawha*.

W. Gould Brokaw, one of Jay Gould's railroad heirs, wanted to throw his small but furiously fast 90-foot yawl *Sybarita* into the ring. Leading club officers wanted to enter the unsuccessful America's Cup candidate *Constitution*. There was even talk of bringing the club's venerable cutter *America*, which had won the cup half a century earlier, back into commission.

Competing American yacht clubs up and down the East Coast, from Boston to Philadelphia, proposed champions of their own for the race.

The whole thing, as the New York Yacht Club feared from the start, dissolved into a messy business. Their paragon designer, Nathaniel Herreshoff, vehemently objected entering his *Columbia,* writing emphatically that she was not designed or built for ocean racing. Nor, he added, was his *Constitution.* In fact, Herreshoff peremptorily forbade *any* yacht he'd designed to participate in the race. His light, heavily canvased yachts—built to win short America's Cup and coastal races—weren't built for transatlantic competition. Both yachts were immediately withdrawn, the *New York Herald* noting that "Commodore Morgan was so disappointed that he was out of humor with his yachting friends for days." The leadership of the New York Yacht Club itself, after careful consideration, convinced other members who'd precipitately responded to the challenge, to withdraw. Vanderbilt's and Rogers' yachts were pure pleasure cruisers, not racers, without much chance of winning. Gould Brokaw, who apparently got a case of cold feet about taking his small yawl across the Atlantic, withdrew *Sybarita*. The club focused on fielding a range of proven racers and demonstrated transatlantic passagemakers, of varying size and rig, that would afford it the best chance to carry off the Kaiser's Cup, blow high or low. They would eventually number five: far more than any other club in the race.

Irony marbles the Kaiser's Cup. Wilhelm II, perhaps the most conservative and backward-looking monarch in Europe, made it the most egalitarian yachting contest ever held to that time. But he did so only to attract the most contestants, generate the greatest publicity, and level the playing field so that Germans had an even chance to prove they were the best seamen in the world—quickly, while the publicity lasted. Lords Brassey and Lindsay, two of the most egalitarian-thinking men in Britain, in practice if not policy, entered the race for the most backward-looking reason of all: to demonstrate the superiority of "English-speaking people." The Americans who finally entered the race, however, did so for the wildest, most ironic reasons of all.

Allison Vincent Armour—owner of the 190-foot, three-masted auxiliary schooner *Utowana*—was pushed into it by the leadership of the New York Yacht Club. A genteel forty-three-year-old widower with a love for botany, he was among the heirs of Philip Danforth Armour, the legendary Chicago "pig-killer" and meatpacking mogul. The family fortune, equal to about $20 billion today, caped him with a mantle he found difficult, if not impossible, to escape.

American meatpacking heir Allison Vincent Armour could never escape the mantle of his wealth. He bought the luxurious three-masted auxiliary schooner *Utowana* to sail away from his troubles, but the yacht's ocean-racing record plunged him into the race for the Kaiser's Cup.

Family patriarch Philip Armour had lived a true rags-to-riches American success story, the kind members of the New York Yacht Club loved to tell. As a schoolboy at a priggish academy in Watertown, New York, he was expelled—according to the newspapers for "riding out with a young girl, a pupil in the same academy," though one suspects the consummation of a teenage romance was the real cause. He immediately lit out for the newfound California gold fields, almost dying of cholera on the long, overland wagon journey west. He spent five years panning the sierras for gold, alternately going flush and bust, but returned in 1857 with enough gold dust to start him in business as a pork packer in Milwaukee.

Like Bennett, the Civil War made him rich. Other than hardtack and coffee, the vast Federal armies subsisted almost entirely on salt pork, bacon, and side meat. Demand and prices soared, and Armour profited hugely. But it was in foreseeing the end of the war that he made millions. Before the collapse of the Confederacy, he sold pork futures at $40 a barrel. After Lee's surrender, he bought them back for $18 a barrel, pocketing $2 million (equivalent to more than $22 million today). With the windfall, he built Armour & Company, which, at his death in 1901, was the largest meat-packing and provision business in the world.

Allison turned his back on it. There were more than enough Armours in the Midwest to tend to that sort of thing. After graduating from Chicago's elite Harvard School at seventeen, he left by luxury train to join various and sundry East Coast Armours who were representing the firm in New York. He had money and no worries: gliding to a B.A. at Yale in 1884 and marrying Anne Louise Kelley in a gala society wedding a year later. Like so many ultraprivileged heirs of the time, he dabbled in this and that, without having to do much of anything but be an Armour. In 1890, however, his young wife suddenly died; no fortune could replace her, and he looked for something, anything, to relieve his anguish. He found it in two things about as far from the landlocked Midwest and meat-packing as imaginable: yachting and botany.

He bought the elegant Beavor Webb–designed steam auxiliary schooner *Utowana* from a fellow down-on-his-luck millionaire heir: William West Durant, scion of Union Pacific Railroad magnate

Thomas C. Durant. Young Will had bankrupted his fortune trying to develop the family's vast upstate New York real-estate holdings in the Adirondacks into a millionaires' playground. To attract rich investors, he built four successively larger and more ruinously expensive "grand camps" in the heart of the mountains. Camp Pine Knot, the most modest, was a village of twenty-nine fantastically crafted log buildings on a peninsula overlooking Raquette Lake; complete with six luxurious guest chalets; a glass dining pavilion; boat houses and bath houses; a dairy; a laundry; an icehouse; a photographic darkroom; guides' and servants' quarters; a wood shop; waterworks; stables; a carriage shed; dog kennels; and, to escape the black flies, a 60-foot-long houseboat moored on the lake. Spending beyond his means an embroiled in lawsuits, he was forced to sell all four camps.

Fellow New York Yacht Club members had no pity taking advantage of him in his distress. Financier J. P. Morgan bought 1,100-acre Camp Uncas, along with Lake Mohegan, at fire-sale prices. Railroad heir Alfred G. Vanderbilt picked up Sagamore Lodge, considered the most luxurious of Durant's camps, for a mere $162,500. At the end of his rope—he would end his days as an Adirondack innkeeper, "often serving the men he had once employed"—Durant offered his yacht *Utowana* for sale at a fraction of her cost. Armour snapped her up for a song. Leaving Durant to drown in misfortune, he quite literally sailed away from his own.

Before the race, he happily logged more than 100,000 miles in her. He made eight ocean voyages indulging himself in botany, conducting philanthropic plant research for the U.S. Department of Agriculture. When he wasn't collecting plant specimens, he was supervising amateur archaeological digs. And when he wasn't botanizing or digging—being an Armour—he regularly took *Utowana* on cruises to Europe, completing nearly twenty Atlantic crossings. Under the New York Yacht Club's burgee, he also raced her (rather her thirty-man crew did) for what the papers counted a slim "two or three seasons in German and English waters." But it was those seasons that earmarked him—or more properly his yacht—for a place in the great race.

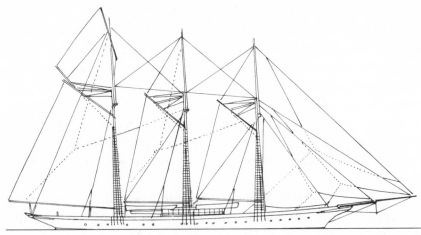

The three-masted, auxiliary schooner *Utowana*, designed by legendary marine architect John Beavor Webb, was as fast as she was opulent. Her large size (190 feet long overall) and vast rig proved themselves in offshore races. In 1901 she'd won the Coronation Cup, handily beating *Valhalla*, and then beat all challengers in the 1902 Channel Race.

In 1901, *Utowana* had won the Coronation Cup, offered in honor of Edward VII's accession to the throne that year. The 300-mile race—from the Solent to Eddystone Light and back—was considered a long one at the time. And the boat she beat was none other than the earl of Crawford's big *Valhalla*. In 1902, *Utowana* won the so-called Channel Race—from Cowes on the Isle of Wight, across the English Channel to Cherbourg, back across the Channel to Eddystone Light, and back to Cowes. The run—almost 400 miles, crisscrossing the notoriously rough Channel—was considered one of the few, true ocean races of the day. The victory, coupled with that over the *Valhalla* and *Utowana*'s successful Atlantic passagemaking history, were enough to convince the leadership of the New York Yacht Club that she was a prime contender to carry away the Kaiser's Cup.

The club's smallest entry in the race, on the other hand—the little American 108-foot (86 feet at the waterline) schooner *Fleur de Lys*—didn't look to stand any chance at all. In fact, at 86 tons (net, registered) she was 14 tons under the minimum size allowed by the rules. But her owner, Dr. Lewis A. Stimson, one of the wealthiest, most eminent physicians in the United States, wouldn't take no for an answer. He seldom did. Just three months short of his sixty-first birthday, he was determined to enter his yacht, and he appealed to the race committee to make an exception. It was almost immediately granted; perhaps because among the eight Americans vying for the Kaiser's Cup, Dr. Stimson was undoubtedly the most exceptional of all.

Like Armour and the rest of the Americans, Stimson had been born to wealth and privilege. But the Stimson family's roots went far deeper than those of almost any family in America, from Pilgrim stock dating back to 1635, and its wealth was much older, generation after generation holding its seat on the New York Stock Exchange. In America's newly-minted aristocracy of the dollar, the Stimsons were bone

American doctor Lewis A. Stimson, one of the wealthiest, most eminent physicians in the United States, lobbied hard to get his little schooner *Fleur de Lys* into the race.

fide royalty, and Dr. Stimson was something of a grand duke. He was not just a Stimson. He had done what very few rich heirs ever did: make a name and a reputation for himself that transcended his birthright.

It did not start out that way. Son of a successful Wall Street banker, he entered Yale at fifteen. When he graduated in 1863, the Civil War at its height, he was packed off on the "grand tour" of Europe, which was practically compulsory postgraduate education for rich men's sons at the time—more so with the war raging. Unfortunately, the war was worse when he got back, so his father arranged a captaincy—and comfortable staff job—for him in the

Federal army. It was a measure of his family's wealth and influence: James Gordon Bennett Sr., a "new money," immigrant newspaper millionaire, could only swing a third lieutenancy in the Federal navy for his son Jamie Bennett. Young Stimson served a year as an aide-de-camp for bigwig generals, was incapacitated by typhoid fever that almost killed him, and was invalided home. He was twenty-one.

On recovery, he took his expected place in the family banking office. Shortly afterward, as was expected, he took his father's seat on the New York Stock Exchange. Shortly after that, he was married off to the eligible daughter of another rich New York businessman. What was totally unexpected was that they both fell madly in love with one another. The wedding—which took place in Paris on November 9, 1866, at almost the same time as the first transatlantic yacht race—changed Stimson's life forever.

Newly wed and an ocean away from his father, he began to study what truly interested him: medicine. By another unexpected coincidence, his studies brought him together with Louis Pasteur. With the backing of his bride, he soon quit banking altogether. As Pasteur's protégé, he studied medicine in Paris, returned to New York's Bellevue Hospital Medical School, and took the degree of M.D. He was not yet thirty. In 1875 he won the James Woods Prize with a landmark paper dedicated to his mentor: *Bacteria and Their Influence upon the Origin and Development of Septic Complications of Wounds.*

The following year marked the apogee—and the nadir—of his life. He was appointed surgeon at New York's renowned Presbyterian Hospital, inaugurated use of antiseptics in American medicine and performed infection-free operations by the Lister spray method. At age thirty-two he was a celebrated physician, enjoyed a thriving private practice, a blissful marriage, and was—at last—his own man. In June of that year, however, his wife, Candace, died. Nothing he could do could save her. She left him with a nine-year-old son—Henry L. Stimson, who would become U.S. secretary of war during World War II—and a six-year-old daughter named Candace. The thing almost killed him. At one stroke, everything he'd achieved was suddenly meaningless. His detachment as a surgeon dissolved. For three years he was lost in grief and depression.

Two things helped him live through it. The first, as he put it, was
"years of constant grinding work." He buried himself in medicine
for fifteen years: visiting surgeon to Bellevue; then successively professor of physiology, anatomy, and surgery at the Medical College
of the University of New York (later NYU); surgeon to New York
Hospital; and author of two classic treatises on surgery and countless papers. In 1898 he was made professor of surgery at Cornell
University Medical College, which he helped found by securing
endowments from his friend and Yale classmate Oliver Hazard
Payne, who, by chance, also was a member of the New York Yacht
Club. It was largely through Payne that Dr. Stimson found his sea
legs—and a prescription for what ailed him.

His joy became a little schooner named *Fleur de Lys*, which he
purchased from Wall Street banking heir George Lauder Jr. Compared to most yachts on the New York Yacht Club's list at the time,
she was positively tiny. But she was also a rare gem: one of the last
boats designed by the great Edward Burgess, a self-taught, Boston-
born marine architect of "meteoric brilliance," whose bright light

Fleur de Lys was the smallest, most Spartan boat entered in the Kaiser's
Cup, but the pride and joy of Dr. Lewis Stimson and his daughter Candace.
She was the first woman to participate in a transatlantic race, enduring
withering criticism, yet winning universal acclaim.

was snuffed out by typhoid fever at age forty-three. His career lasted only seven years. In that time, however, he designed *three* consecutive America's Cup winners (*Puritan,* 1885; *Mayflower,* 1886; and *Volunteer,* 1887), gaining "nationwide acclaim," as historians put it, "as three times saviour of the Cup." He also produced designs for no fewer than 137 other vessels: not only racing yachts but also pilot boats, fishing schooners, steam auxiliaries, even battleships. In the annals of yacht design it was called the "Burgess era." A year before it ended, he designed *Fleur de Lys.*

Her diminutive size caused many to question her oceangoing capabilities. But like the redoubtable Gloucester fishing schooners Burgess used as her model, she was made for deep water, "con-

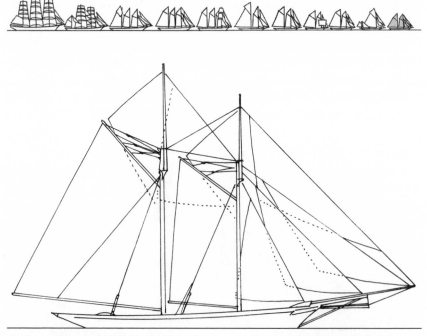

Tiny compared to other yachts in the race—108 feet long overall and just 86 feet at the waterline—*Fleur de Lys* was a rare gem, designed by the great Edward Burgess, a self-taught, Boston-born marine architect of "meteoric brilliance." Built chiefly for ocean work, she was "one of the best heavy weather boats in the fleet of starters."

structed chiefly for ocean work," reported a yachting journalist at the time, and "one of the best heavy weather boats in the fleet of starters." Of composite construction—steel frames covered with white pine planking—she was strongly-built to withstand the pile-driving seas of the North Atlantic. And her deep keel (draft, 13½ feet) made her an exceptionally stiff sailer in heavy winds. Yet according to yachting correspondent Julian Hawthorne, who saw her in trials before the race, Burgess's "easy, flowing lines let her take the seas lovingly. No seagull rides the waves more smoothly, or with less sass and froth. Her sail plan is just the thing for her, sending her forward without pressing her down. She is the sweetest little craft imaginable."

She certainly was to Dr. Stimson. He made long, blue-water cruises in her: from New York up to Labrador and across the Atlantic to Iceland, Norway, and England. Accompanying him on every voyage, enjoying them just as much, was his now thirty-five-year-old daughter, Candace—the very image of her mother. *Fleur de Lys* was really their boat: both the vehicle and the excuse for father-daughter outings, away from the rigid, often suffocating roles each had to play in New York society.

Aboard *Fleur*, the good doctor could shed his French silk shirt (with separately attached collar and cuffs), bow tie, suspenders, alpaca vest (with solid gold watch and heavy chain in opposing pockets), black Luzerne Cheviots suit, velvet-collared topcoat, mirror-shined "Bals," kid gloves, lacquered silk top hat, and cane in favor of a weathered flannel shirt, loose-fitting duck trousers, and bare feet. His daughter could exchange steamer trunks' more clothing—society ladies of the day were expected to make four or five complete wardrobe changes between breakfast and supper—for a bloomerslike "sailor's suit," mackintosh, and "soft, white felt storm hat." Out on the sea, there was time: for long talks, informal meals in *Fleur*'s cozy, oil-lamped saloon, whale watching, star gazing, and reading. There also was shared excitement: sudden squalls, ethereal fogs, wet decks, strange landfalls, new anchorages. The two delighted in it, so much so that one gets the distinct impression that Dr. Stimson lobbied hard to enter *Fleur de Lys* in the race for the soundest and simplest reason of all: Candace wanted to go.

Whether it was her idea or his doesn't really matter. Both jumped at the opportunity to share a once-in-a-lifetime adventure together.

Almost nobody else saw it that way. Yachting generally, yacht racing particularly and ocean racing especially was a testosterone-charged fraternity of the most exclusive order. The Kaiser's Cup race was perhaps its penultimate manifestation: a field of 314 officers and crew and 51 owners and guests—all of them male. When word got out that Dr. Stimson's daughter was to sail aboard *Fleur de Lys*—the sole female in the great ocean race—there was outrage. Critics pointed out that *Fleur de Lys,* the smallest, most Spartan yacht entered, was certain to be the wettest, most uncomfortable, and potentially dangerous to sail in: no place for a woman.

The press expressed admiration at her pluck, while noting what it considered unfeminine competitiveness: "This will not be Miss Stimson's first race, for she has accompanied her father on many off-shore trips; indeed in some races, she practically took charge of the yacht," the *New York American* reported indignantly. The papers neglected to mention that she had steered *Fleur* to two very competitive finishes in Cape May ocean races. It dismissed her "presence on board [as] an interesting feature of this great transatlantic contest;" concluding that "Miss Stimson may prove a mascot in this race." All the papers took pains to refer to her as Miss Stimson. This was perfectly proper and polite usage at the time, but it also—not unintentionally—served to remind readers that she was the unmarried, middle-aged daughter of a rich man.

To be fair, the press pointed out that *all* eight of the American yachts entered in the race were owned by the sons of rich men. The three-masted schooner *Atlantic,* a very fast, practically brand-new auxiliary flying the New York Yacht Club's burgee, belonged to Wilson Marshall, son of Jesse Marshall, who'd made a fortune running New York's Broadway Stage Line. The schooner *Hildegarde,* under the burgee of the Philadelphia Corinthian Yacht Club, belonged to Edward Coleman III, son of William Coleman, Andrew Carnegie's partner.

The other four American contestants were sons of Wall Street bankers and brokers—the crown princes of capitalism. By itself, this wasn't particularly surprising. Since 1868, the New York Stock

The two-masted American schooner *Hildegarde* was the proud possession of steel heir Edward Coleman, whose father was Andrew Carnegie's business partner. He lavished a fortune outfitting her for the race.

Exchange (NYSE) had vested each seat with property rights. That meant a membership could either be sold at the market price or given to heirs. But in 1903, the seat price was at its highest ever to that point: $82,000, or equivalent to $1.56 million in today's dollars, so most seats comfortably passed from father to son.

In many ways, that made the New York Stock Exchange America's only real hereditary aristocracy: an aristocracy of the dollar, to be sure, but at least an aristocracy, and a jealously guarded one. It was an all-male, all-white, insiders-only club. No women were permitted to work on the trading floor. None would until 1943, when World War II manpower shortages made it an unwelcome necessity. There were no women members until 1967, no black members until 1970. By comparison, the New York Yacht Club—which admitted women in its ranks beginning in 1894—appeared positively progressive.

In 1905, with the Dow Jones (which consisted of twelve bell-wether stocks, including American Cotton Oil and Standard Rope and Twine) nearing 100 for the first time, the New York Stock Exchange's new building at 18 Broad Street was undisputably the high temple of America's old-boy network. Under its gilded ceiling, illuminated by huge window walls, sons and grandsons of rich men went about the business of getting richer—from 10:00 A.M. until 3:00 P.M. on weekdays and from 10:00 A.M. to noon on Saturday. Even working these genteel hours, staying rich or getting richer wasn't too difficult to do. There really were no rules or regulations about how you went about making money. There was no Securities and Exchange Commission to regulate the stock market and prevent insider trading. No Federal Reserve System to control banking or credit. No Commodity Futures Trading Commission to ride herd on speculation in everything from gold, silver, oil, and coal to corn, wheat, soybeans, and pork bellies. No Federal Trade Commission to prevent monopolies, unfair business practices, and false or deceptive advertising. In short, you could legally get away with just about anything.

With the latest technology installed on the trading floor—five hundred telephones (more than at any other address in the United States), "annunciator" boards to instantly page members, and a pneumatic tube system to speed the exchange of paperwork—you could get away with it with the deftness of a three-card monte dealer. In 1901, in fact, annual turnover of shares on the New York Stock Exchange reached an all-time high of 319 percent.

That kind of high-octane laissez-faire fed a blast furnace of American speculation at the turn of the twentieth century. Investors may have gone boom or bust, but insiders with seats on the NYSE—scions of the ultrarich—really couldn't lose. The profits made them prodigal sons who, having never experienced failure, much less trial, felt supremely confident of success in any and every endeavor. Since yachting was unquestionably the most expensive, as well as most ostentatious endeavor of all, they flocked to it. William Travers, a prominent attorney at the time, was invited by one to watch a yacht race at Newport. Marveling at the magnificence of the boats, he asked who owned them. When told they all belonged to stockbrokers, he asked: "And where are the customers' yachts?" His question was answered by an embarrassed silence.

So it was with the four American Wall Street heirs who entered their yachts in the Kaiser's Cup race. Other than Robert Tod Jr., owner of *Thistle,* none was known for his business acumen, yachting skill, or any kind of charisma. In fact, they elicited far less interest and admiration than Candace Stimson. Indeed, the *New York Herald* noted, "Interest in the personality of these owners does not appear to be great. They are millionaires, not especially known in yachting."

The papers observed that Edmond Randolph, son of well-known New York investment banker E. D. Randolph, had "embarked on the sea of large yacht ownership only about a year" before the race. He knew little about sailing and nothing about racing. But his fortune had afforded him the second-largest vessel in the contest: the steel-hulled, 307-ton, 198-foot (LOA), bark-rigged auxiliary *Apache.* Though he was a complete neophyte, she was the nearest thing in size and rig on the New York Yacht Club's list to

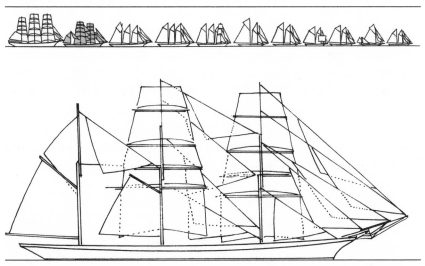

Wall Street banking heir Edmond Randolph's auxiliary bark *Apache* was the second largest vessel in the contest—the nearest thing in size and rig to the feared British *Valhalla*—and the New York Yacht Club's counter. Almost 200 feet long, 168 feet at the waterline, with a 28-foot beam, she registered 307 tons, net.

the much-feared British challenger *Valhalla*. If strong westerly winds and heavy weather prevailed—under command of professional Captain J. H. MacDonald, with a crew of forty—*Apache* looked to be the perfect counter.

Henry Redmond, another Wall Street banker, was rather an embarrassment to the New York Yacht Club. While he was adamant on entering his *Ailsa*—lavishing money to rebuild her and spouting off to the press about her chances—he positively refused to sail in her. He was the only New York Yacht Club owner in the race to do so. This was made doubly embarrassing by the fact that Candace Stimson, sole woman in the race, had volunteered to sail in the club's smallest entry. Redmond's money papered over his own lack of intestinal fortitude. *Ailsa* was a Fife-designed racer, after all, entirely refurbished at his own expense, and—if the prevailing winds were light and easterly and the seas not large—stood an excellent chance of winning. What's more, Redmond had obtained the services of Captain Lem Miller as her skipper. And next to Captain Charlie Barr himself, the club leadership knew and trusted Miller most of all.

Wall Street heir George Lauder Jr. had as comfortable an upbringing as Randolph and Redmond, but considerably more seagoing mettle and experience. This and the fact that he was former commodore of the rival Indian Harbor Yacht Club and owned the schooner *Endymion*, holder of the transatlantic yacht crossing record, gave the New York Yacht Club pause. The fact that he'd hired professional racing skipper James Loesch, the captain who'd set that record, scared the daylights out of them.

CHAPTER 18

Hired Guns

Of the skippers of the cruisers entered in the contest this much can be said: the professional men have been engaged just for the race.

—*New York Herald,*
May 7, 1905

America's yachting millionaires played a very rough game. While they publicly talked about sportsmanship and the good of the game, privately they were determined to capture the Kaiser's Cup at any cost. Wealth was their weapon. They fitted out their vessels regardless of expense: state-of-the-art winches and fittings; the latest Ratsey-made silk sails; lightweight, hollow steel masts and spars—anything to give them an advantage. Robert Tod Jr. rerigged the already overcanvased schooner *Thistle* to carry a second spinnaker on the mainmast; a watersail set under the bowsprit like on Spanish caravels; and a huge, double raffee sail of his own design. He installed two "wave-quelling pipes" in the bow to dispense oil and smother heavy seas, and acetylene gas lighting below.

Edmond Randolph one-upped him by equipping his bark *Apache* with cutting-edge communications technology—a Marconi wireless apparatus, something only a handful of navies and steamship lines could afford. The gear filled a stateroom, required a

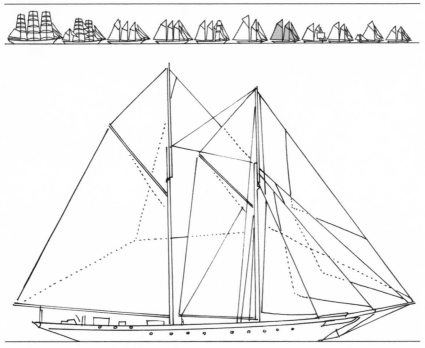

Robert Tod rerigged his 150-foot long, two-masted schooner *Thistle* to carry more canvas in the race. A huge squaresail and triangular raffee were added to the foremast and a spritsail rigged under the bowprit "like a Spanish caravel."

skilled operator to use and maintain, and even then was notoriously unreliable, but every yachtsman wanted one. Guglielmo Marconi, as brilliant a marketer as inventor, had targeted the yachting class. In 1898 he wirelessly reported the Kingstown Regatta races for the *Dublin Express*. Queen Victoria, who closely followed the races, was so impressed that she had Marconi sets installed at her residence in Osborne House, on the Isle of Wight, and aboard the royal yacht *Osborne* to keep tabs on her wayward son—the all-too-often absent, ostensibly yachting prince of Wales. In 1899 Marconi reported the America's Cup races as they unfolded off Sandy Hook—real time, from a tugboat following the racers. The publicity—the first sporting event in the United States carried by wireless—won him fat contracts with the U.S. War and Navy Departments.

Randolph told the press he wanted the Marconi device to "communicate with westward-bound steamers to obtain valuable [weather] information," but having the newest gadget of any vessel in the race figured into it, too.

When it was over, the press estimated that from $20,000 to $40,000—equivalent to $380,000 to more than $760,000 today—had been spent fitting out each boat. Those were remarkable amounts at the time, considering that big, new one-design racing sloops then built by Nathaniel Herreshoff—the so-called New York Seventies, measuring 106 feet LOA and 70 feet LWL—sold for $26,000 ($494,000 today), sails included. "That does not matter to those concerned," noted the *New York Herald*: "It has been determined by the American contingent that one of its members *shall* be the winner."

To make doubly certain of that, the Americans outbid one another to hire the most professional, competitive yacht racing captains money could buy. It was the skipper, after all, who conducted their dearly bought orchestras of sail, sheet, and helm in high opera with wind and wave. And it was on the afterdeck that the American millionaires saw their rivals' jugulars. The two British entries were more or less skippered—Corinthian-style—by their owners. Lord Brassey had sailed yachts for fifty years and had skippered Sunbeam himself for more than thirty. But he was, after all, sixty-nine years old and decidedly not a racing skipper. The earl of Crawford was an excellent navigator, which would count for much in an ocean race; but he also was asthmatic, something of an invalid, and dependent on Captain Caws—who had no real racing credentials—to manage sail and drive the big *Valhalla*. The German entry *Hamburg*, at the kaiser's insistence, was skippered by a captain in the German Imperial Navy with but a few seasons' yacht racing under his belt, seasons in which he had been soundly defeated by American boats with professional skippers.

None of that was difficult to divine. To win called for winners, and America's millionaires went shopping for them with very deep pockets. Pedestrian yacht skippers at the time were paid $500 to $1,000 for the typical five-month racing season, equivalent to $9,500 to $19,000 in today's value. Successful yacht racing skippers, who also had to be good hosts to shipboard guests and amiable with owners, might make $2,000 to $3,000 a season with winning bonuses, or about $38,000 to $57,000 today. At a time when the average American worker earned $2 per day or $600 annually (about $11,400 today), that was fantastic money.

But so-called "professional men"—the winningest yacht jockeys, retained to run the most prestigious cup races—commanded far more. The $10,000 Bully Samuels was paid for the first transatlantic race in 1866, equivalent to $190,000 today, represented something of a cellar offer to top-gun yacht racing captains in the 1905 Kaiser's Cup. For a race expected to take no more than three weeks, that was an incredible sum—the highest, in fact, paid any sports figures for generations to come. In a bidding war for the world's best racing skippers, the price rapidly went higher: $30,000 per captain, more than $570,000 in today's value, is a conservative estimate. Seven of the eight American yacht owners in the race paid that or more for great skippers to take them first to the finish. In the history of yacht racing, there have probably been none finer.

At the helm of Wall Street banking heir George Lauder Jr.'s *Endymion* was Captain James Loesch ("Captain Jim"), who held the record for the fastest transatlantic passage ever made by a sailing yacht to that time. In 1900 he'd charged 3,100 miles across the ocean from the Sandy Hook Lightship to the Needles, a rocky headland at the eastern tip of the Isle of Wight in the English Channel, in thirteen days, twenty hours, and thirty-six minutes at an *average* speed of 9.66 knots. A barrel-chested, broom-mustached Swede, he'd set that record in *Endymion* and was now back, itching to break it.

Under his command, *Rudder* magazine noted, "Few living yachts hold a better all-round record than the two-master *Endymion*." The *New York Herald* cited the reason, calling Loesch "a driver." The *Boston Sunday Herald* darkened that, saying; "He hangs on to sail until the last gasp."

In fact, he was a driver known to risk everything on a roll of the dice. At the outbreak of the Spanish-American War in 1898, he was skippering *Fleur de Lys* for Lauder in European waters and promptly found himself blockaded in a neutral port by a Spanish cruiser. The Edward Burgess–designed schooner yacht was a rich prize the Spanish captain very much wanted; one that Loesch was equally determined he wouldn't get. At night "in a gale of no mean strength and seas that suggested annihilation," according to the *New York Herald,* Loesch cut his anchor cables, got up every stitch of canvas that didn't blow away, and took her screaming out the harbor mouth into the blackness. Getting underway at night in the teeth of a gale took superb seamanship; risking demolition by grounding, storm, or Spanish cruiser took perfect sangfroid; succeeding took that most estimable trait of all great captains—luck. Loesch had all three qualities. Dawn found him well off-

Captain James Loesch ("Captain Jim") set a transatlantic yacht passage record in *Endymion* in 1900 and was itching to break it in 1905. He was known as a "driver" who "hangs on to sail until the last gasp."

shore, the clearing horizon empty, and *Fleur de Lys* racing away at 12 knots or more.

"He has a good ship," reported the *New York Herald,* "and a dangerous one to the [racing] fleet if the winds have fair strength." He was supremely confident in himself and his vessel. Asked by reporters if he thought he thought his old *Fleur de Lys* had any chance of beating *Endymion,* "he simply smiled. Comment he knew was unnecessary." Asked if he would win the Kaiser's Cup, he said simply, "I'm not worried about the race."

Dr. Lewis A. Stimson, the wealthy New York physician and new owner of *Fleur de Lys,* hired his own special maverick; a man who wasn't a professional racing skipper at all. Captain Thomas Bohlin ("Captain Tommie") didn't look intimidating. The *New York Herald* dismissed him as "a plump little man with rosy cheeks, sandy hair and big goggle-like glasses." He was, in fact, one of the most profane and successful Gloucester fishing captains alive. He'd spent more than thirty years on the Grand Banks and everyplace else in the North Atlantic where his nose told him there were fish. He had

Captain Thomas Bohlin
("Captain Tommie"),
hired by Dr. Stimson to
race *Fleur de Lys*, looked
meek—but he was perhaps
the most fearless, profane,
and fastest-sailing Gloucester fishing skipper ever.

weathered atrocious conditions and brought
in legendary hauls without losing a man or
suffering serious damage to a ship.

To get his catch to market and fetch
the best price, he also sailed fast. His
passages from the Grand Banks to
Gloucester were some of the fastest ever
registered in the "Crow's Nest," the fish
syndicate's observation tower. Against
prevailing winds he once made the
"uphill" transatlantic passage from
Stavenger, Norway (just south of
Bergen), back to Gloucester in the phenomenal time of seventeen days. Before
getting under way on that voyage, he
called all hands aft. "From this out, no
more sleep for anybody—not until we
get into Gloucester," he told them. "It's
wet decks and everybody standin' by.
No sail comes down until it *blows* down. There's your orders."

The *Boston Sunday Herald* called him "one of the most daring
men of the Gloucester fleet of fishermen," which spoke volumes
about his seamanship and judgement, not to mention raw
endurance and animal courage. He also was one of the hardest-
working, which was what made him such a successful skipper in the
first place. He dared the North Atlantic because he had to. His living was out there and, in essence, he had to outrace the Atlantic
every voyage to fetch it. The simple, but terrifying, way he did that
was to carry every inch of sail, regardless of conditions. The harder
it blew, the better he liked it. He was riding the Atlantic outward
bound or home, and one was as good as the other.

Overcanvased in gales, his standing order, if he had to leave the
deck, was "Let me know if it moderates." According to the *New
York Herald*, "His fellow skippers at home [Gloucester] know
three things about him: 'The sailor does not exist who will outcarry
Captain Bohlin; they would like to see the gale he couldn't stand off
with an able vessel; and that he has always been of the opinion that

any vessel can sail in the daytime, but it takes a fisherman to do her best sailing at night.' "

Dr. Stimson went personally to Gloucester ("home of the best fore-and-aft sailors in the world")—checkbook in hand—to hire him. The unlikely meeting, between the most eminent physician in New York and the most respected fisherman in Gloucester, went swimmingly well. The idea of racing the smallest yacht for the Kaiser's Cup seemed to appeal to both more than money. They came to terms with a handshake.

Bohlin, the cagiest businessman in Gloucester, doubtless got his price. He had only one, nonnegotiable condition. He'd race *Fleur* for the doctor and get the best Gloucestermen he knew to do it. But there'd be no New York Yacht Club "flubdubbery" about it. He and his men would not wear fancy uniforms. They'd sail like they always did: in their old woolens, oilskins, and rubber boots. Stimson, a surgeon accustomed to working in blood-spattered gown, agreed at once.

Bohlin was brimming with confidence. "We shall force her [*Fleur de Lys*] more perhaps than she has ever been forced in past experience," he told reporters. "I do not mean by that that we will take heedless risks, but we will not be afraid to take a chance, night or day, if it will drive her across fast enough to carry off the Kaiser's cup."

Philadelphian Edward R. Coleman Esq., owner of the schooner yacht *Hildegarde,* could afford to buy any racing skipper he wanted. He was the son and heir of William Coleman, steel magnate Andrew Carnegie's business partner, after all. The skipper he wanted was no-nonsense, stern-faced Captain S. M. Marsters. Marsters wasn't at all colorful, like Loesch or Bohlin, just as quietly and relentlessly competent as a jeweled watch. The *New York Herald,* whose yachting staff was among the press's most knowledgeable at the time, called him "a deep water veteran of the most pronounced type." The *Herald* didn't give any other skipper in the race that portentous an accolade.

He'd spent three years as a mate aboard *Hildegarde,* and now—back as her captain—was consumed with showing what she could do. Unlike the rest of the skippers, he kept her out of the media circus in New York, fitting her out in New London, Connecticut, far away from reporters. But Coleman had been spending enormous sums to prepare her for the race, and these leaked to the press. "All of her spars, rigging and sails are absolutely new," reported the *New York American*. In fact, Marsters had secretly replaced her old-fashioned solid wood spars with lighter, hollow steel ones. He'd treated her deck with a mixture of shellac and sand to keep sailors from slipping in wet weather. And he'd replaced her old flaxen sails with a new suit of the finest silk, identical to those used by Reliance in the 1903 America's Cup contests—the most expensive, high-tech sails of the day.

Marsters' crewmen let slip that he had fine-tuned the boat to perfection. To pick up a new square-sail yard, he drove her from

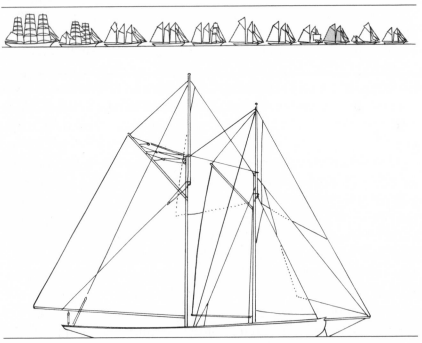

Though the two-master *Hildegarde* was among the smaller yachts in the race (134-foot length overall, 106 feet at the waterline), the A. S. Chesebrough-designed schooner was fast. She was among the New York Yacht Club's most successful racers.

New London to Boston—which before the building of Cape Cod Canal meant sailing clear around the Nantucket Shoals and the cape itself—in just twenty-two hours. The next day he drove her back—in twenty hours. "Fifteen [knots] she logged at times," said one of her crew, "and that isn't any yarn."

In the weeks before the race, Marsters sent telegrams almost daily to cable stations on both sides of the Atlantic "with a view of getting tips on the weather conditions," according to the press. He prepared for every eventuality and revealed nothing of his plans. "He will not follow others," the *Boston Sunday Herald* concluded, "but will strike out for himself." Of all the skippers vying for the Kaiser's Cup, the usually reticent Marsters was the most outspoken. Asked if he thought he would win, he boldly predicted; "When *Hildegarde* reaches the Lizard, the timekeepers will be wanting to know the news of the race and where the *other* fellows are."

Wall Street investment banker Henry S. Redmond, on the other hand, was desperately trying to find any skipper at all willing to take command of his little, sorely neglected yawl *Ailsa*. None of the professional captains he approached wanted to stake their reputations—or their lives—on the boat. When Wilson Marshall cut Lem Miller loose from *Atlantic,* Redmond fell on him like a ripe apple. He was not only out of a job skippering a favorite in the Kaiser's Cup, he was also out of a job, period. He was angry, with a sorely bruised ego, and if not seeking vengeance, seething for vindication. Redmond had been a Wall Street shark long enough to sense blood in the water. All the other owners with yachts entered in the race had already engaged captains. *Ailsa* was all that was left. If Miller wanted a crack at the cup, perhaps they could do business together.

But it would have to be on Redmond's terms. He'd already committed a prodigious sum to get *Ailsa* ready to race. He'd hired two experts from Lloyd's of London and one from the Federal Insurance Commission to survey the vessel and recommend repairs. Shockingly, they unanimously recommended what amounted to a complete rebuild. The expense, almost $50,000 or more than $9 million in today's value, was as staggering as it was unexpected. The only place left for him to cut corners was on the outlay for a skipper to race her. He set his sights on frustrated, unemployed Miller.

Miller—in his midforties, pomaded hair formally parted down the middle of his head, sporting a fierce handlebar mustache—was painfully uncomfortable wearing a suit and completely at sea negotiating with Redmond. Off the quarterdeck of a racing yacht, there was no guile in him. The *New York Herald* called him "a salt sea lad, pure and simple." Summoned to Redmond's Wall Street offices, he walked into a carefully set trap. The walls, according to one reporter, were hung with photographs of *Ailsa* in her glory days, "shown walking away from the famous *Vigilant,* romping across the mark a winner of the [1902] Astor Cup," and "sweeping across the finish line off Sandy Hook in 1903 with a record of 33 miles around the outside course in three hours—a record that has since stood." There were no photographs showing her in her current state: hauled out of the water at Jacob's Yard at City Island, masts, rigging, and fastenings gone, decking pried away, rudderpost and rudder stripped off, defleshed of planking. That was Redmond's business until a skipper was signed.

Redmond sold *Ailsa*'s promise to Miller like he sold stock. He told him the Fife-designed boat was being made "faster than ever." Not a penny was being spared. Commanding her was the chance of a lifetime to show the ability of 90-footers in ocean contests. He gave Miller the same hype he'd given a reporter from the *New York World* to whom he'd shown the same photos: "Come what may, sweeping zephyrs, flukes or twisters, the *Ailsa* likes them all."

Miller was suitably impressed. When it came time to talk terms, he was awkwardly direct. He demanded what he thought he deserved: a salary commensurate with Barr's. Redmond refused, pointing out that Barr had skippered three America's Cup winners, while Miller had only been mate. Their salaries never could be equal. Miller almost certainly countered by pointing out that, without his services, *Ailsa* didn't stand any chance of winning. Redmond didn't budge. *Ailsa* was Miller's—if he wanted to command her at Redmond's price. Apparently that was considerably less than what Miller was asking. The negotiations turned protracted, then pyrotechnic. Miller walked out of them at one point and sulked for several days. But after due reflection—and no other offers—he returned to the bargaining table with a much weaker hand.

Redmond obviously wasn't going to pay him a dime more than he'd originally offered and time was running out. It was scarcely more than two months to the start of the race, precious little time to recruit a crew, outfit the boat, and conduct any kind of sea trials. If Miller was going to jump, he had to do it. In the end, as Redmond calculated, the money didn't matter half as much to Miller as the chance. More than anything, the "salt sea lad, pure and simple" wanted command of a yacht—any yacht—in the greatest race of the century.

They signed a deal—on Redmond's terms. Miller hurried to Jacob's Yard to see exactly what he'd bargained for. Nobody could believe he was betting his future on tiny, still-in-pieces *Ailsa*. But Miller, who, in his own words, loved nothing more than to "bet a wager," believed he could win.

Following announcement of his engagement as *Ailsa*'s skipper, he told the *New York Times,* "They think we won't figure, except by a fluke, but you can bet we will be racing all the time. The boat that beats us will have to be better than I think most of them are. We'll be in it all the way."

Oddly, the most feared hired gun on either side of the Atlantic —Charlie Barr—didn't want to race at all.

CHAPTER 19

Greatest of All Yacht Captains

*We think that there can be no question that Charlie Barr stood
first among the racing skippers of the world.*
> —*Field* magazine, 1911,
> on Barr's death

In the spring of 1905, "Wee" Charlie Barr (he was barely 5 feet, 3
inches tall) had fewer than six years to live. To look at him, no one
would ever have thought it. He'd just turned forty, was sun-bronzed,
as compact and muscular as a coiled spring, and dime-novel-hero
handsome. He was in the prime of his life, happily married and happily employed as the most widely acclaimed, highest-paid professional yacht racing skipper in the world.

But the first time he laid eyes on the long, graceful, three-
masted schooner *Atlantic*—in dry dock at Morse's Ironworks in
Brooklyn—it was not love at first sight. He wanted nothing whatever to do with her. Or the Kaiser's Cup race, for that matter.

The 1904 racing season had been very good to him. Skippering
Florida railroad tycoon Morton Plant's 127-foot schooner *Ingomar*
in European waters, he'd won an unprecedented string of victories
at the Cowes and Kiel regattas. The bumper crop of winning trophies he brought back to America led to a nice, fat contract for the
upcoming 1905 season, skippering New York Yacht Club member

William Ross Proctor's pretty 70-footer *Mineola* in home waters. And Barr desperately wanted to stay home.

He'd been away almost six months: sailing *Ingomar* across the Atlantic, taking Mr. Plant and his often insufferable guests on a cruise through the Mediterranean, then taking the boat up to the regattas in Britain and Germany, and returning to the States via an extended tour of the Caribbean.

Long cruises of this sort sorely tried even the best professional yacht skippers. For the transatlantic passage, vessels had to be refitted with an oceangoing rig: shorter bowsprit, shorter topmasts and gaffs, shorter mainboom, and smaller sails. On the other side of the Atlantic, all that had to be struck and replaced with racing rig, the longer racing spars and larger racing sails having been shipped ahead by steamer. During the outward voyage, Barr was expected to whip *Ingomar*'s crew—two mates, two stewards, two cooks, and sixteen abled bodied seamen—into racing shape. At the same time, he was entrusted with the care of Mr. Plant's favorite dog: a spoiled, snappish fox terrier.

When the "sports," as crewmen called the owner and his guests, joined the schooner in the Mediterranean, Barr had to play a role not far removed from that of the captain in the long-running TV series *The Love Boat*. Fat gentlemen with fulminating cigars, inflated opinions of themselves, and no seagoing ability had to be indulged at the wheel. Good sailing weather and fast courses were sacrificed to avoid wet decks, rolling, and seasickness for the ladies. When progress was slow (*Ingomar* had no auxiliary steam engine), guests complained about going nowhere. When becalmed, they complained about the heat, forcing Barr to rig awnings to shelter them from the sun. Anyplace Plant or his guests wanted to go—to visit antiquities, shop, fish, or view sunsets—Barr was obliged to find an anchorage or, if none presented itself, make one as best he could. He constantly had to make sure there were fresh ice, milk, butter, and produce. At the regattas, he had to make certain the ship was freshly painted, polished, and in "Bristol fashion," fully dressed in appropriate flags, ensigns, and burgees. In the races that followed, he was expected to win. Throughout, he had to be cheerful and deferential with all the gentlemen guests, attentive and flattering to their wives, and a charming conversationalist at every meal—work only a diplomat can truly appreciate. At the same time—all the time— he had to tend to the unerring navigation and working of the ship.

A half year of such work was quite enough to stretch any man's patience to the breaking point. When Charlie finally got home to New London, Connecticut, his patience abruptly and uncharacteristically snapped. He returned to find his wife so sick with tuberculosis that she wasn't expected to live. The doctors could do nothing but advise him to stick close to home and await the inevitable. It came as a complete shock. Her letters to him abroad had been chatty and cheerful, filled with praise for his racing success, never once mentioning her illness. Now his success seemed thumpingly hollow, and he blamed himself for not being at home to take care of her. He forswore making any more long ocean cruises for rich men and determined to remain as near by her side as he could. Racing *Mineola* in the summer squadron runs of the New York Yacht Club was the only job that would enable him to do that.

He couldn't have cared less about the Kaiser's Cup race. It was plainly a publicity stunt. It couldn't reasonably be considered anything else. Entries of virtually any class, size, and rig, in a run clear across the Atlantic, without handicaps? That was like putting prizefighters of any division—flyweights, welterweights, middleweights, and heavyweights—into a boxing ring, turning off the lights, and giving a trophy to whoever was left standing. The *New York World* agreed: "How can anything conclusive be expected from an ocean race in which the contestants range from a schooner of 86 tons and a yawl of 116 tons to a full-rigged ship of 647 tons? The affair as a yacht race is the height of absurdity."

The early starting date struck Barr and almost everybody else as downright foolhardy. In Britain, leading sporting journals voiced concern about spring storms and ice in the North Atlantic. *Yachting World* called the timing of the race "amateurish . . . with genuine possibility of danger." *Field* warned British yachtsmen away from the event: "If a catastrophe occurs, those participating will be held up to censure." Opinion in the United States was similar. "It is the judgement of experienced yachtsmen," wrote the *Boston*

Herald, "that the date of starting, May 16, is too early. Early in July the racing would be better and the chances of accidents few. When the attention of the German naval attaché was called to the matter of date he said no change could be made because of the regatta at Kiel." Racing across the North Atlantic in boisterous, possibly dangerous, spring conditions to flatter the vanity of Wilhelm II at Kiel had zero appeal for Barr.

He'd met the kaiser the summer before at the Kiel Regatta, had raced against him, and had found him a bumptious, not altogether on-the-level yachtsman. At the helm of his yacht *Meteor,* the Kaiser repeatedly ignored the rules of the road, refusing to yield the right-of-way whenever it gave him advantage. The first time it happened, Barr was forced to put *Ingomar* about to avoid a collision, costing her the race. The second time, fast closing with the imperial yacht while holding the right-of-way close hauled on the starboard tack, Barr refused to yield. The German courtesy officer aboard *Ingomar* begged him to alter course. Barr shook his head. "But it's the kaiser!" exclaimed the officer. "When he steps behind the helm of a racing yacht," replied Barr, "he ceases to be the kaiser." At the last moment, *Meteor* gave way, and *Ingomar* won the race. Barr was not troubled by the kaiser again. In fact, the kaiser seemed to relish his bullying reputation and getting his picture in the newspapers more than the finer points of yacht racing. The transatlantic challenge had certainly done that.

All the newspapers could write about was "the German Emperor's Cup contest," "the Kaiser's Ocean Race," or simply "the Kaiser's Cup." But at best, as far as Barr could determine, the event was nothing more than a weather lottery, with the North Atlantic as judge. He was not alone in thinking so. His old friend Nat Herreshoff loudly refused to let any yacht he'd designed participate, informing their owners that his boats "were not designed for that purpose [ocean racing]." Such was Herreshoff's clout with millionaire American yacht owners that none of them dared enter, lest they never get another boat from "The Wizard of Bristol" again. All those were reasons enough for Charlie Barr to legitimately sit out the race.

The leadership of the New York Yacht Club didn't see it that way at all. An American boat—preferably one on the club's list, but nonetheless *American,* by God—was going to carry away the Kaiser's Cup. And Charlie Barr was America's finest racing skipper, in no small part because the club's members had commissioned extravagantly expensive boats for him to sail and paid him enormous sums to sail them. To club members it was a matter of quid pro quo. Charlie's services were required. Period. The inordinately powerful inner circle of the New York Yacht Club—to whom Barr owed everything—made no bones about it.

He was made an offer he couldn't refuse. Club member Proctor would grant him leave from his season contract with *Mineola* to sail club member Wilson Marshall's *Atlantic* in the transatlantic race in May. Proctor would guarantee his job while he was gone and continue him at full salary. Marshall would pay him handsomely for the race itself, with an extravagant bonus should he win. Upon conclusion of the race, the club would ship him back to the States on the fastest steamer: first class, all expenses paid. In his absence, his sick wife would be tended by the finest physicians in America; physicians he never could afford.

It was the last condition that swung Barr over. He didn't know Wilson Marshall, didn't know *Atlantic,* and had never raced a steam auxiliary schooner in his life. In taking the job, he realized full well it would cost Lem Miller his. But he also realized that his wife was deathly sick and growing sicker. Hovering over her sickbed wasn't likely to make her well. Going to sea again—racing—might. She'd be far better cared for that way than if he stayed at home. He'd be earning double salary while he was gone and unimaginably more if he won. If he raced as life itself depended on it—which, considering his wife's condition, he would have to if he hoped to see her again—he would be gone no more than a month and a half, maybe two. Leaving her was the last thing he wanted to do. Yet, in the end, it was the only thing left for him to do.

He didn't need to risk his reputation on a free-for-all ocean race. He'd already won just about everything in yachting there was to win. Three consecutive America's Cups—not only beating three challengers, but also *sweeping* all three. On both sides of the Atlantic, he'd won Queen's Cups, Cowes Cups, Morgan Cups,

Astor Cups, Bennett Cups, Lipton Cups, Goelet Cups, Commodore's and Vice Commodore's Cups, Brenton's Reef Cups, Cape May Cups, you-name-it cups. He dominated international yacht racing at the 1904 Cowes and Kiel Regattas, winning nineteen of twenty-two races in British and German waters. He was the favorite champion of the New York Yacht Club, skippering yachts for J. P. Morgan, E. D. Morgan, Cornelius Vanderbilt III, C. Oliver Iselin, August Belmont, and a dozen other American millionaires. He'd hobnobbed with titled aristocracy such as Kaiser Wilhelm, the prince of Wales, and Sir Thomas Lipton as well as William Fife Jr., George Lennox Watson, and Nat Herreshoff, three of the greatest yacht designers of all time

Nobody ever expected "Wee" Charlie Barr would reach such heights. Born poor in Gourock, Scotland, a fishing village at the confluence of the Clyde River, Loch Long, and the Firth of Clyde, he had only two options for a livelihood: go to sea or stay ashore. Growing up in a fishing town, Charlie had no desire to go to sea. He apprenticed instead as a grocer, but failed dismally. Desperate for work, he spent one cold, hard winter aboard a flounder trawler. This wasn't trawling in the modern sense of the word. Before steam or gas engines, sail-powered trawlers generally didn't drag nets. They heaved to on the fishing grounds and lowered dories, which rowed out, baited, and set long lines (trawls) of bottom-lying hooks. It was brutally hard, wet work in the best of weather. In a mid-Atlantic winter it was perdition.

Work started midnight or midday, with or without sleep or food, whenever the skipper "smelled fish." Rough seas, subzero temperatures, sleet, snow, fog, didn't matter. Short of a full gale, everybody worked as long as fish were to be caught. As a green hand, young Charlie was paired with an experienced fisherman, never a happy pairing since the men were paid by the catch of their two-man boat, which cost the latter money. On the fishing grounds, their first order of business was to manhandle a 15-foot-long wooden dory weighing about 250 pounds, across a slippery, pitching deck and lower it over the side. With one man holding it alongside, the other loaded it with cast-iron anchors, buoy lines, buoys, tubs of tarred, coiled fishing line, and nests of steel hooks. Pulling at two sets of oars worked between thole pins, they rowed 1 to 1½ miles away from the ship, laying anchors, buoys, and trawl lines all along the way. The trawl lines, extending down up to 50 fathoms (300 feet) to reach bottom-feeding flounder, consisted of gangs of baited, razor-sharp hooks. Accomplishing this work in winter, in mid-Atlantic swells—from a wildly bobbing dory fewer than 3 feet wide at the bottom, with but 22 inches of freeboard and a draft (light) of fewer than 4 inches—was punishing. Dory and rowers were encased in ice and exhausted before dropping the anchor buoy that marked the outer end of the trawl. The long row back to ship, invariably against the wind, was numbing. That, however, was only the beginning of the work.

Retrieving the trawl—one, six, or twelve hours later, depending upon the skipper's intuition—was worse. The dory had to be heaved over the side again. There was a hard row out from ship to find the outer buoy, a very hairy midocean endeavor in a small boat in winter conditions. Once found, there was the wet freezing, business of hauling fast-fixed anchors up from the depths, then the backbreaking business of hauling in miles of line, spiked with more than forty lengths of hooked trawls. Some hooks came up stripped of bait or attached only to skeletons, predatory fish or carnivorous sand fleas eating the catch. Some hooks were hauled up heavy and thrashing—sometimes with flounder, sometimes with sharks. The flopping catch (filled, a dory could carry almost 2,000 pounds worth) and all the slimy, reeking paraphernalia were then rowed back to the ship, if the overloaded dory didn't capsize first. With two-tined pitchforks, the catch was pitched aboard and the dory heaved up again. All hands then went to work gutting fish, slathering them with salt, and stowing them below. If the catch wasn't large, the captain shifted a few miles away, heaved to, and sent out the dories to bait up and try again. It went on like that until a trawler filled with fish or ran out of water and provisions.

A winter of it was more than enough for Charlie Barr. In 1884, swallowing pride, he took a job working for his older brother, John, delivering a 55-foot Fife-designed cutter named *Clara* to America. Charlie wasn't signed as mate, quartermaster (helmsman), or even deckhand. He shipped as the cook. It was his first transatlantic passage, and the whole world suddenly widened far beyond Gourock.

In America, *Clara* won most of her races, to the delight of her owner. John Barr's stock as a racing skipper quickly went high— high enough so he was tapped to command the British challenger *Thistle* in the 1887 America's Cup. He was soundly beaten by *Volunteer*. Scotland—and the Royal Clyde Yacht Club, which had paid for and bet on *Thistle*—never forgave him. According to L. Francis Herreshoff; "They blamed him so much for the failure of *Thistle*, that he came to the U.S. and settled in Marblehead, Massachusetts." He brought Charlie with him.

A singular American alchemy sparked by money, greased by connections, and galvanized by ability transformed him after he arrived. It was one part American millionaires: with money to burn on yachts, yacht racing, and skippers to do it for them. His brother's notoriety opened doors, and Charlie found there were a great many more doors with yachting millionaires behind them in America than back in Scotland. *Thistle*'s loss was the Barrs' gain. It was two parts association with the legendary American yacht designer Nathaniel Herreshoff; the men were made for each other. And it was three parts pure magic. By whatever divinity, Charlie Barr was somehow born to fit the helm of a racing yacht. He had an uncanny natural instinct for that one and only thing.

After arriving in the States, he successfully raced "extreme" cutters such as *Shona* (waterline length of 36 feet, with but 6-foot beam), made a reputation winning races in 40-footers such as *Minerva,* and was soon winning races for the millionaire owners of 46-footers such as *Oweene, Wasp,* and *Gloriana*. It was *Wasp,* which he sailed for American industrialist Archibald Rogers, that brought him together with its designer, Nathaniel Herreshoff. For the rest of his life, with two exceptions, Barr would race Herreshoff's boats. The combination was sublime.

But Barr wasn't perfect—just yet, anyway. Quick success may have gone to his head. In 1893, just twenty-nine, he was hired by American millionaire R. P. Carroll to skipper his brand-new, Herreshoff-designed yacht *Navahoe* across the Atlantic to England for the racing season. *Navahoe* was the largest vessel Barr had commanded to that time, a cutter 84 feet at the waterline, almost twice the size of the 46-footers he was accustomed to. It was also the first all-steel boat he'd sailed; in fact, it was the first all-metal sailboat Herreshoff had designed and built. And it was Barr's first transatlantic passage with the owner aboard. Typically they traveled to the Continent in comfort by steamship and joined the yacht later. But Royal Phelps Carroll (American millionaires of the period seemed to use three names or initials to distinguish patriarch from heir and heir from heir—witness the Vanderbilts) was determined to sail on *Navahoe* to Europe and determined to show his wife how fast it could go. He seems, in fact, to have strongly suggested that Captain Barr drive *Navahoe* to make a record transatlantic passage.

Barr heard his employer loud and clear. According to Herreshoff's son, who knew him well, he sailed "practically under a racing rig," which he never would have done on a transatlantic crossing unless he was specifically racing to make a record passage. As soon as he was clear of Newport and "squared away for the eastward, he clapped spinnaker and all on her," a ratification that he was racing. Mr. and Mrs. Carroll were suitably impressed. Rounding Nantucket Shoals, however, Barr ran headlong into a fogbank—and straight into Nantucket Light Ship.

That kind of thing happens, but not to professional yacht racing skippers—not more than once, anyway. It was either a result of supreme navigational indifference or pinpoint accuracy. L. Francis Herreshoff, son of the designer who knew Barr very well, excused the collision and called Barr's navigation "remarkably good . . . for you might say he was less than a ship's width off the course." Regardless, the collision sprung *Navahoe*'s mast; soured her rigging; and severely dented, but didn't hole, her steel hull.

It was a terrible humiliation for Barr. The Carrolls were surely shocked—their new purchase wrecked after driving it out of the showroom. Charlie and *Navahoe* limped into Boston to make repairs. Afterward, all thoughts of forcing a record transatlantic passage appear to have been gratefully forgotten by all parties. Barr comfortably delivered the Carrolls to England. Easing their bruised egos and any sense of buyer's remorse, he promptly skippered *Navahoe* to a win over the prince of Wales's yacht *Britannia* in a match across the English Channel. It was enough to keep his job and restore his reputation.

But it was winning *three consecutive* America's Cups that rocketed Charlie to the center of the world yachting stage. Until that time, no one had ever won the Cup twice, much less three times. Three wins—back to back to back—made him into something of the Tiger Woods of yachting. Ironically, he won his first Cup exactly five years after ramming Nantucket Light Ship. Sailing *Columbia* for the New York Yacht Club in 1899, he beat Sir Thomas Lipton's *Shamrock I* in three races. Yet it was hairier than the outcome made it seem.

Shamrock I was a William Fife Jr.–designed racer, a pureblood pedigree of speed under sail if there ever was one. Furthermore, she'd been built by Thorneycroft & Company, the most famous torpedo boat builders of the day, so her bottom was plated with manganese bronze to minimize water resistance, and her topsides were of lightweight aluminum alloy to minimize weight. She was driven by 13,492 square feet of sail, more than any America's Cup contender to that time. What's more, in racing against her, Charlie Barr faced not one skipper but two: "Archie" Hogarth and Robert Wringe. Nat Herreshoff, no light judge of proficiency or daring in racing skippers, considered "both of these men as particularly able and perhaps better than any we had in this country"—including Charlie.

In the first race, Barr won by more than ten minutes. That comfortable margin, however, resulted largely from an error by *Shamrock*'s skippers: though the wind was light, they failed to hoist the yacht's big jackyard topsail. The second race showed why. In a 12-knot breeze, *Shamrock* was over the starting line a few seconds ahead of *Columbia,* and for the next twenty-five minutes both yachts remained locked in a dead heat. Suddenly, according to observers, *Shamrock*'s topmast snapped "clean off and her huge club topsail collapsed like a falling church steeple." Barr won by default, which to his mind and everybody else's wasn't truly a victory at all.

In the third race, along the New Jersey shore, reports noted "half a gale blowing from the north which at times got up to over

30 miles per hour"—horrific conditions for big, overcanvased boats
(each vessel could carry over 13,000 square feet of sail) without bulwarks, smashing through rough seas at up to 13 knots. *Shamrock*
again crossed the starting line first—not by seconds this time, but
by almost a full minute ahead of *Columbia*. On the downwind leg,
Barr couldn't catch her. It was blowing so hard, he was running
under only three lower sails. So was *Shamrock*. Setting more canvas looked suicidal—sure to cost sail, very probably the mast, and
definitely the race. Yet if he didn't catch her on the downwind leg,
there wasn't a prayer of catching her on the homeward leg beating
into the wind. Charlie—betting on his ability and his supreme confidence in the design and strength of Herreshoff's boat—rolled the
dice. He ordered *Columbia*'s huge spinnaker and its topsail hauled
up. The instant the canvas caught the wind, the boat was sledge-
hammered and the rig winced. Miraculously, everything held
together.

At the turn, *Columbia* had passed *Shamrock* and led, but by
only seventeen seconds. The run to the finish line, both yachts' rails
under water, was by one reporter's account "the finest 15-mile run
in international yachting history." Barr drove *Columbia* over the finish line first, beating her rival by six minutes and thirty-four seconds,
corrected time. Despite this feat, many observers believed that
Shamrock, through tactical errors and accidents, had largely beaten
herself. Charlie had won his first Cup. But he would soon have to
prove himself all over again.

In 1901 Lipton was back, challenging with an all-new, wickedly
fast, George Lennox Watson–designed cutter, the 137-foot *Shamrock II*. She was state-of-the-art: the first yacht in history to be
designed not "by guess and by God" but based on scientific tank tests.
Testing no fewer than eleven different scale models in sixty permu-
tations, Watson created the most extreme and threateningly fast
racing hull yet seen. Plated with a new metal alloy called immadium,
Shamrock was very lightweight yet strong, and literally flew over the
waters. In trials she reached speeds of more than 14 knots.

Defending the Cup against her was Charlie, back at the helm of
Columbia—a vessel not only older, but also smaller and carrying
almost 900 square feet less canvas. Worse, *Columbia*'s canvas was

old and badly overstretched. Not even the fortunes of her owners, J. P. and E. D. Morgan, could buy her a new mainsail in time for the race. The only sail loft in the United States that could make sails the size *Columbia* needed—the Herreshoff Company—could make only one of the huge crosscut sails at a time and was busy sewing them for their newest racer, *Constitution*. J. P. Morgan was so furious at their refusal to give *Columbia*'s order precedence that he afterward bankrolled, the famed English sailmaking firm Ratsey, to open a loft in the United States to compete with Herreshoff. That was no consolation to Barr, who was left to improvise a solution (seizing the peak of the mainsail as far out on the gaff as possible, while at the throat making a fold in the headrope).

Yet in three races, Barr came from *behind* to win. It was a phenomenal sailing feat. In the first race, he crossed the starting line two seconds behind *Shamrock II*. Rounding the weather mark, he was forty-one seconds behind. On the run to the finish, however, Barr

Three-time America's Cup winner Captain Charlie Barr (left, at the helm of *Columbia* in 1899) had won just about everything there was to win in yachting in 1905. The last thing he wanted to do was risk his reputation on the Kaiser's Cup race, but—in the end—it was the *only* thing he could do.

not only overtook her: he beat her by thirty-five seconds. The second race was an apparent disaster. *Columbia* made a very bad start, crossing the line one minute and thirty-four seconds behind *Shamrock II*. During the first two legs of the race, Barr battled back, but at the second mark he was still forty-two seconds behind. On the last leg, sailing to windward, he somehow managed to catch *Shamrock,* pass her. and cross the finish line one minute and eighteen seconds ahead. In the third race, *Shamrock* rounded the first mark forty-nine seconds ahead of Barr. Beating back to the finish line in a dying breeze, he coaxed *Columbia* nearer and nearer, until both vessels were literally nose-to-nose. In the light air, Captain E. A. Sycamore edged *Shamrock* over the finish just two seconds ahead of *Columbia*. The victory, however, went to Barr. Because of her larger size, *Shamrock* had to allow *Columbia* a forty-three-second handicap. With this time allowance, *Columbia* was judged the winner by forty-one seconds.

It had been a near-run thing, a finish the yachting magazine *Rudder* called "remarkably close by any standards." In fact, it was the closest contested match ever held for the America's Cup until that time, one that gave the New York Yacht Club a severe scare. Of the 90 miles the yachts had covered in three races, Barr and *Columbia* had prevailed by only three minutes and thirty-six seconds less than *Shamrock II*. When George Lennox Watson was asked why his high-tech-designed racer didn't beat Herreshoff's intuitively designed boat, he quipped, "Herreshoff did not have a test tank."

Close or not, *Columbia*'s victory shot Charlie Barr's reputation sky-high. The New York Yacht Club had a winner. It would never let him go. When Lipton challenged for the America's Cup again in 1903, Barr was their champion. He sincerely wished he wasn't.

Lipton had expended yet another fortune building the 134-foot *Shamrock III*. She was another William Fife Jr.–designed greyhound, a predatory cutter with almost the maximum America's Cup permitted waterline length of 90 feet (she was 89 feet 10 inches LWL). "In model," according to Herreshoff's son, "she resembled an enlarged [and improved] *Columbia,*" Lipton's nemesis: an indication, if any was needed, that he did not intend to be beaten by a Yankee-designed boat of her type again. Her hull was built of lightweight nickel steel with a coating of white enamel to slide her over the sea. She spread 14,154 square feet of sail, more than any America's Cup yacht to that time.

In response, the New York Yacht Club commissioned Nathaniel Herreshoff to build "a radical new boat" to beat her. The members tendering the commission—including C. Oliver Iselin, William Rockefeller, and Cornelius Vanderbilt III—gave him complete design freedom and an unlimited budget. The result was *Reliance,* a penultimate racing machine: the largest single-masted, most frighteningly overcanvased racing sloop ever built.

Everything about her was Brobdingnagian. Officially—stem to stern—she was almost 144 feet long overall. Actually, from the tip of her bowsprit to the end of her 116-foot mainboom, her rig measured a colossal 202 feet. Her spinnaker boom alone was 84 feet long. Her hollow steel mainmast, with its telescopic topmast, soared 196 feet—almost 20 stories—abovedecks. Hung from this single stick was a cathedral of 16,159 square feet of canvas. That was more than 2,000 square feet more than *Shamrock III.* It was more sail than any sloop had ever carried before.

Between this massive sail plan and her 70-ton lead keel, there wasn't much. She was built ultralight for speed—steel frames covered with a veneer of aluminum topside and a veneer of tobin bronze below the waterline (which, unlike steel, could be polished to a mirrorlike finish for minimal resistance). She was the limit in light construction and scientific design, a limit that wouldn't be equaled until aeronautical designs of the 1940s.

Herreshoff also packed her with innumerable other technological advances. To work her heavy sails (her mainsail alone weighed 1½ tons) he'd engineered no fewer than nine ingeniously designed belowdecks winches: two-speed and self-releasing, these enabled the crew to work the sheets and halyards without venturing on deck. Her rudderpost and rudder were hollow and, by means of a pneumatic pump, could be flooded or emptied with seawater to harden or soften her steering. She had dual steering stations and brakes on the steering gear to mechanically aid her helmsmen. In trials, in light air, the gigantic wind machine ripped through the sea at a phenomenal 18 knots (almost 21 miles per hour).

All these radical advances would have gladdened the heart of any racing skipper. But Charlie Barr, who watched every stage of *Reliance*'s building and fitting out and who went to extraordinary lengths to understand what they all meant and how best to use them, felt otherwise. Her rig was just too bloody big. Nobody could control that much canvas. In trials he found her a brute of a boat to sail. In light winds she required a crew of sixty-four precision-trained seamen to manage her. In moderate winds she proved wildly tender ("As tender around the flanks as a virgin," as one of her crewman said). With her long overhangs and low freeboard she took a brutal beating and drenching in any kind of seaway. In heavy weather her flat displacement hull proved almost totally unseaworthy. During trials off Newport with quite a sea running, her unseaworthiness was so obvious that L. Francis Herreshoff, son of her designer, reported that "the [New York Yacht Club] race committee decided to take no chances and to amend the rules by banning racing in severe weather." He applauded the decision for safety's sake. He noted that "at the speed of the larger yachts [meaning *Reliance*, the largest and fastest of all], these yachts without bulwarks or other protection are very dangerous." In fact, the old *Columbia* (under command of Lem Miller), racing against *Reliance* in the trials with a far less intimidating spread of canvas, lost four men overboard in the blow. Three were picked up. The fourth was never seen again.

Changing the rules to favor *Reliance*, however, little more than a month before the race, could not have made Barr—competitor that he was—particularly happy. He spent the time before the start drilling his crew to perfection and learning to tame the wind-driven monster under his command. He defended the Cup resoundingly, whipping Lipton in every race. Yet despite appearances, it wasn't easy.

Herreshoff's *Reliance* falls in the same category as Howard Hughes's *Spruce Goose,* the largest amphibious aircraft ever to take wing. *Spruce Goose* flew only once and was forever mothballed. *Reliance* was scrapped nine months after she was built. The reason was the same: both magnificently overengineered giants were far too dangerous to operate.

To Charlie Barr, *Atlantic* looked like the same kind of animal.

CHAPTER 20

Too Many Cooks

Captain Barr was not at all pleased with the state of affairs
before the start.

—New York Sun,
May 18, 1905

Charlie Barr didn't really know anything more about the *Atlantic* or Wilson Marshall than what Lem Miller had told him—before the race, back when they'd been on speaking terms. Lem had worked for the man two years and had only good things to say about the boat. She was a flier. Marshall, however was a cipher: a nattily dressed, clipped-mustached thirty-six-year-old widower with enormous wealth who seemed to get little joy out of it. Perhaps because of that, he insisted on getting his money's worth—whether he was yachting, golfing, tarpon fishing, or shooting quail. It made him a hard man to work for.

His obituary headline would eventually read: "Wilson Marshall, Yachtsman, Dead." In an age when yachting was for the rich and when yachtsman meant someone rich enough to do nothing else, it pretty much summed him up. Marshall, a New Yorker who'd inherited his father's Broadway Stage Line fortune, had the particular distinction of doing almost nothing else his whole life.

New Yorker Wilson Marshall, heir to his father's Broadway Stage Line fortune and owner of the state-of-the-art auxiliary schooner *Atlantic,* wanted to win the Kaiser's Cup and shanghaied Charlie Barr to do it for him. It proved an excruciating relationship for both.

He was elected to the New York Yacht Club less than a month after his gala twenty-first birthday party—more than a year before he graduated from Ivy League Columbia. But his club membership marked his real graduation: into the rarefied aeries of men of unlimited means. He never set foot in a classroom again. He ravenously pursued the pleasures of club life. In New York he belonged to not only the New York Yacht Club but also to Manhattan's exclusive Union Club, as well as the Larchmont Yacht Club on Long Island Sound. At his Connecticut country estate Marina, in fashionable Bridgeport, he belonged to the posh Brooklawn Country Club and the Algonquin Club. Membership in these elite Skull-and-Bones-like societies of the ultrarich was really the whole basis of Marshall's identity. They provided a ready-bought answer to the questions that vexed Marshall most: "Who am I?" and perhaps more vitally to him, the outside question "Who are you?" Other than club memberships, Marshall's only answer to those questions was "Son of Jesse Marshall, who ran a fleet of horse cabs" or the equally pallid "Columbia, class of 1891." Beyond those answers, he had nothing.

He couldn't really tell anyone that his wife, Jessica, favorite granddaughter of showman P. T. Barnum, died in 1897, shortly after giving birth to their only child, Wilson Marshall Jr. He couldn't tell them that her death had devastated him, that he saw her every day in the eyes of his eight-year-old son. He couldn't tell them that half of him died when she did and that since age twenty-eight he had lived in her shadow.

He retreated to the sanctuary of club life, where no such questions were asked and where a plush bonhomie reigned. It was a place where fireplaces always burned cheerfully, the martinis were always achingly cold, and conversation was always affable. His ultimate sanctuary, however, floated under the burgee of the New York Yacht Club—a sleek, auxiliary schooner he christened *Atlantic*. All the troubles in the world couldn't catch up to him in *Atlantic*. He'd commissioned American marine architect William

Atlantic—like Charlie Barr—fed off the wind. Under full sail, she made a spectacular appearance—"slicing through the waves," wrote a reporter, "with gigantic power portrayed in every swing of her long, shearing hull."

Gardner to design him a grand, fast, seagoing gentlemen's club of his own in 1903. Gardner produced a steel-hulled, teak-decked, three-masted schooner with a low freeboard and sweeping sheer. She was, by no means, a large auxiliary by the measure of the New York Yacht Club at the time—184 feet length overall and 139 feet at the waterline with a waspish beam of 30 feet—but for her size she was among the most expensive. In today's dollars she cost Marshall $30 million.

She boasted a marble-floored reception lobby, dining saloon with table seating for ten, an 18-by-30-foot grand saloon with three Tiffany skylights, a palatial owner's suite, four posh guest staterooms, and three porcelain-tiled bathrooms with hot and cold running water. The cabins were paneled in mahogany and bird's-eye maple. The carpeted saloon was luxuriously appointed with rosewood card tables, oxblood leather chairs and ottomans, and a huge sideboard displaying legions of monogrammed china and silver salvers.

Forward of the guest accommodations were a pantry, hotel-size galley, and cabins for eight ship's officers with their own mess room. The forecastle had berths and mess tables for twenty-four crewmen. Below the berthing deck were cold storage rooms, provision rooms, engine and boiler rooms, sail lockers, and storerooms. Marshall outfitted her with all the latest conveniences. Instead of oil or kerosene lamps, she had a generator powering Edison's incandescent electrical lights that burned bright and without fumes at the flip of a switch. Instead of zinc-lined iceboxes, she featured a whopping 800 cubic feet of electrically powered refrigeration. Marshall, who didn't want to wait on wind or tide, had her equipped with a 400-horsepower steam engine of the latest, most powerful triple-expansion design. With a feathering, low-drag propeller, she could economically steam at 10 knots; with throttles full out, she could sprint at 17. That was quite fast for auxiliaries at the time: equivalent to battleship or ocean liner speed. But under sail—nearly 22,000 square feet of canvas—she truly took wing. In her first sea trials she averaged 18 knots: when reaching she logged almost 20.

Gardner had fashioned Marshall a state-of-the-art, luxury wind machine. But from what Lem Miller told him, Charlie was concerned that she might prove another *Reliance*—a boat with too much of everything. She had exceeding tall but slender racing masts: the foremast topped out at 125 feet (12½ stories), the main-mast at 132 feet, and the mizzenmast at a dizzying 137 feet. That amounted to a lot of tall, intricately stayed timber overhead. While she was heavily sparred for strong winds, her rigging was light. Julius Hawthorne, a contemporary yachting correspondent, thought the rig too light for the punishing ocean race ahead. *"Atlantic,"* he declared unequivocally, "is *not* an Atlantic boat." For her length and girth she also was a comparative lightweight, her net tonnage just 206 tons. The smaller *Sunbeam* (170 feet LOA) and *Thistle* (150 feet LOA) had net registered tonnages of 228 and 235, respectively.

Gardner designed her as a centerboard schooner, so Marshall could take her cruising into shallow sounds and anchorages on the

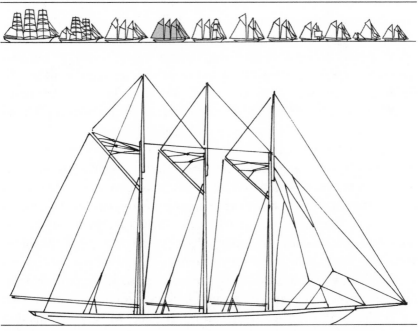

The three-masted *Atlantic,* carrying over 18,000 square feet of canvas, logged over 18 knots in her initial sea trials in 1903. In the 1905 ocean race, Barr would push her to more than 20.

U.S. East Coast and the Caribbean. When lowered, her 25½-foot-long iron centerboard dug 15 feet deep in the water, making her an exceptionally stiff sailer; when raised, she could skate over bars and banks. In coastal races her centerboard design had proven both seaworthy and fast: fast enough for Lem Miller to capture the Cape May, Brenton's Reef, and Astor Cups the previous year.

But two weeks before Charlie Barr was shanghaied into skippering *Atlantic,* Marshall had her hauled out of the water at Morse's Ironworks at fifty-seventh Street in southern Brooklyn. He ordered her centerboard removed and refitted with a lead keel of 70 tons. His friends at the New York Yacht Club convinced him to make the change for the ocean race. It was, to say the least, a drastic change, like performing elective spinal surgery on a top-seeded marathon runner six weeks before the starting gun. It was apparently a messily expedited operation. *Yachtsman* magazine reported that *Atlantic*'s "inside ballast was transferred to her keel, a couple of inches of oak being first bolted on under the iron plating, after which the lead was added to the depth of a foot amidships, tapering into the fairline of the keel forward." Nobody knew if this operation would be a success. The only way to tell was to put her through sea trials, under all variations of sail, and under all conditions. But there was no time for proper trials. In fact, Marshall's incessant meddling with almost every detail of the boat left Charlie almost no time to prepare her for sea.

Barr had never experienced such a three-ring circus. He was accustomed to the methodical, almost religious way boats were fitted out in the Herreshoffs' Rhode Island yard. Arriving at Morse's Ironworks forty-eight hours after taking the job to sail *Atlantic* in the race, he found chaos. Hauled out of the water, the newly keeled boat was assailed by an army of workmen in slings, scraping, scouring, repainting, and then varnishing her black steel hull. Another army was engaged in removing her propeller, riveting steel plates over the screw aperture, and blocking her empty centerboard slot with wood. Another army was on its knees topside, burnishing decks and brightwork, while yet another army swarmed aloft splicing rigging and replacing spars. In their midst, laborers were carrying aboard the all-new suit of sails Marshall had ordered. The work of each army was under the direction of half a dozen different experts Marshall had hired to go over *Atlantic* keel to truck. Barr was left almost nothing to say about these critical matters. The work had been ordered before he'd been hired and was being rushed to completion. The experts reported more or less to Marshall and only perfunctorily to him. Making sense of the cumulative effect of the 1,001 changes being made on the boat, however, was left entirely to Barr. He was in the yard twelve hours a day and often more.

Crewing the boat was largely Marshall's plan, too. With the exception of his nephew John Barr Jr.—an experienced racing skipper who he'd brought as his first mate—Barr was stuck with *Atlantic*'s existing crew. Marshall had already engaged them for the 1905 yachting season, so would get their services in the transatlantic race essentially for free. So far as the ship's petty officers and seamen went, that was not a bad thing. Most of them were Lem Miller's handpicked boys. They knew *Atlantic*, each other, and the business of yacht racing thoroughly. Whether or not they resented Barr for taking Miller's place, he didn't ask. He knew any orders given Lem's boys would be sharply executed.

It was the number of supernumeraries Marshall insisted on taking along that made Barr uneasy. There'd be *two* captains aboard: himself and Captain Edward Pagel, whom Marshall had hired to take charge of *Atlantic* in Europe after the race. With the owner aboard that was just plain bad medicine, sure to invite opinion and comment on his every action. In a transatlantic race—where there'd be split seconds to make decisions, but days to second-guess them— that kind of thing could be fatal.

Since Marshall planned an extended cruise in European waters after the race, he also insisted on taking *Atlantic*'s full engine room complement: chief engineer William Waldron, assistant engineer Aubrey Falconer, and two firemen. These hands were useless to Barr in a sailing race. By the race rules, *Atlantic*'s propeller had been removed and the shaft sealed.

He didn't begrudge the two cooks Marshall enlisted. Having been a ship's cook himself, he knew the labor of feeding forty-eight men three times day. But the chief cook, William Whitecross, was a fancy chef, not a ship's cook. He could no doubt whip up French sauces, soups, and roux with intimidating dexterity and turn out galantines and soufflés in a storm. But he was another superfluous hand, shipped for nothing more than to grace the owner's table. The work of feeding *Atlantic*'s officers and crewmen would devolve on second cook Robert Mitchell. Barr did what he could to help. He shipped an abundance of bottled beer, bread, and sandwich makings for the crew. Mitchell and the men on deck would not have time for much more. Marshall, on the other hand, sent aboard a full three weeks' provisions for his guests. The supply of gastronomic delights amounted to some 650 pounds: fresh meats, fish, shellfish, vegetables, hothouse fruits, and a cellar of fine champagne, vintage Bordeaux, Madeira, and dusty finos.

The four stewards embarked to attend Marshall and his six guests went beyond Charlie's comprehension. Uniformed in fancy white mess jackets, they had no purpose aboard except to pour, serve, and clean up for the afterguard. That was *twice* as many stewards as Morton Plant had shipped to pamper his guests in *Ingomar* cruising in Europe the year before, but Marshall wouldn't hear of taking fewer.

In all—counting Marshall, his guests, Captain Pagel, the engine room gang, cooks and stewards—Barr was saddled with eighteen so-called idlers, hands that stood no watches and didn't work ship. That amounted to well over a third of *Atlantic*'s whole complement. It was crazy to carry that number in an ocean race. It left Barr with only enough room to ship two mates, two quartermasters, a boatswain, and twenty-four able-bodied seamen. *Hamburg,* a smaller, two-masted schooner, much less complicated to sail than three-masted *Atlantic,* shipped twenty-three seamen. Miller, on tiny *Ailsa,* had eighteen deckhands. By any measure, Charlie was seriously shorthanded. What's more, other than his nephew, he was sailing with men he didn't know.

Marshall also was adamant about maintaining his comforts. On both *Hamburg* and *Ailsa,* saloons and guest cabins, which typically provided the fastest, most unencumbered access to deck, had been sensibly converted to sail lockers for the race, so canvas could be changed quickly. Marshall, despite the fact that he was refitting

Atlantic for a transatlantic race, left the owner's areas belowdecks rigged for a pleasure cruise. *Atlantic*'s elegant grand saloon would *not* be turned into a sail locker. Neither would any of her posh staterooms. They were to remain the domain of himself and his guests. Captain Barr and the crew would use the existing sail lockers. It might take a bit more time and effort, but his party wouldn't be disturbed. The arrangement, Marshall told Barr, had never posed any problem for Captain Miller.

The smoldering fuse between the two men reached the point of explosion over the ship's boats. Normally the vessel carried four large, elegant launches and cutters from davits but—rigging *Atlantic* for an ocean race—Barr sent them ashore. There was simply no room to ship them on deck. He had already crowded it with critical spare booms, spars, and topmasts. Lashed amidships on each side of the main hatch, extending nearly the length of the boat, was a spare mizzenboom 79 feet long; spare spinnaker boom 76 feet long; and spare main and forebooms 35 feet long each. Spare spars—the mizzen gaff spar was more than 50 feet long—and square-sail and topsail yards added to the heap. Concerned about losing *Atlantic*'s slender, tapering topmasts in a blow, Barr carried replacements for them on deck, too, as well as a 31-foot-long spare bowsprit. He'd also draped heavy mats of manila parceling on the rails forward and aft, to protect the jib and mainsheets from being chaffed to shreds in heavy weather. He draped more amidships to prevent chaffing the staysail and topsail sheets. When he'd finished, it was hard for *Atlantic*'s crew to negotiate the deck.

The next day, however, he found that the overloaded deck was piled anew with boats. Two deep and beamy patent lifeboats—exclusively for Marshall and his guests—had been lashed down just forward of the main companionway. On the afterdeck, nested in two stacks, were six dories for the crew. All these boats were anathema to Barr. They were racing, after all, and boats were of no practical use. If foundering in a storm—the only excuse for taking them—none could be gotten off without swamping or capsizing. If any did, only the passengers' lifeboats stood a chance in the open sea: the shallow-draft, low-freeboard dories for the crew were cosmetics. But it was another of Marshall's orders. The boats—like Captain Pagel, the engineers, and stewards—were going. Barr and his crew would simply have to work around them.

That was it for Charlie Barr. He quit. One week before the start of the race. He left *Atlantic* and took the train home to New London, Connecticut, and his wife. Wilson Marshall was incensed. The *New York Herald* headlined: "AMERICA'S CUP WINNER QUITS *ATLANTIC.*" The *Boston Globe* gave the reason: "Captain Barr loves a free hand and it is said that the fact that he does not have it on the *Atlantic* resulted in his 'yanking his dunnage.'" In jaw-dropping understatement, the *New York Sun* observed: "There seems to be some dissatisfaction on board this boat, which does not help her chances of winning. The chief trouble seems to be 'too many cooks' and Captain Barr has not had full charge." A *New York Times* reporter, who visited the boat a day before Barr jumped ship, put a finer point on the affair: "The *Atlantic* was [anchored] alone at the Hook. Her owner and guests were not aboard. Captain Barr walked the deck in no amiable mood. He has been spoiling for a chance to take the boat out under full sail for 10 days' past. He is in the peculiar position of starting in an international race without an opportunity to familiarize himself with his ship, and will be handicapped by the fact decidedly. Her owner has been *grooming* the vessel ever since Barr has had her."

All that was quite true: Marshall had ordered *Atlantic* hauled out of the water no less than three times since Barr had taken command. He kept her in the yards so long, lavishing every dollar he could spend to prepare her for his transatlantic adventure, that he gave Barr little or no chance to sail her. The *New York Herald* put it more succinctly: "Charlie Barr is plainly in an ill humor about something, and it develops that this is due to his lack of luck in getting a trial spin."

The public embarrassment to Marshall and the New York Yacht Club was too great to last long. The club's senior, cooler heads intervened. Within twenty-four hours, Barr was back aboard *Atlantic,* with a free rein to use the time before the start of the race to test the effects of her new keel and ballast change, new sails and spars, and tune her trim and rig accordingly. Wilson Marshall was to remain ashore until the eve of the start. Charlie had won the showdown, but relations between the two men chilled to the freezing point.

When the *New York Herald*'s press boat found *Atlantic* anchoring in the Lower Bay, following one of her first real offshore trials after Barr's return, the reporter aboard told him he was glad to see him back. Barr didn't reply. The reporter asked if he now thought he would win. "'Win?'" the reporter recollected Barr saying "in a surprised way as he stopped pacing the deck for a moment. 'Win? Well, I don't know. Goin' to try anyway, you know.' Then he shoved his hands deeper than ever into his pockets and walked on."

Nobody had ever seen Charlie Barr unhappier on the eve of a race.

CHAPTER 21

A World in Waiting

*There comes to the whole public the realization that three of
the great nations of the world are in for a fight—to be sure, a
friendly fight—but nevertheless a stern battle of wits and
skill for the nautical supremacy of the sea.*
                              —*New York Evening Sun,*
                                 May 2, 1905

On the eve of the race, Kaiser Wilhelm and his propaganda officers must have been delighted at the news from New York. Sporting considerations aside, the ocean race had come down to exactly
what the *Evening Sun* described and exactly what they wanted: an
international battle for the supremacy of the sea. It was a figurative
battle, of course, but the *Sun* was in error calling it a friendly fight.
National maritime pride was running sky-high; all three nations
were locked in cutthroat competition for control of the critically
important North Atlantic shipping trade; and all three were
engaged in an out-and-out naval arms race. There was too much
realpolitik capital at stake in the supposedly gentlemanly Kaiser's
Cup yachting contest for anyone to ignore—capital the winning
country could, quite literally, take to the bank along with the honor
of proving its flag the fastest on the high seas. It was just the kind
of worldwide publicity Wilhelm craved and precisely the spin on the

event he'd hoped for. It quickly proved anything but a friendly competition.

The arrival of the British and German yachts in New York caused consternation in the American press. The size of Lord Crawford's *Valhalla*, seen firsthand, took everyone's breath away. Swinging at anchor, the sides of her 245-foot-long steel hull towered house-high above the waters of the Hudson River. Her three masts soared 14 to 15 stories abovedecks, so high their tops were lost to reporters' view in the fog. Her mainsail yard alone was 75 feet long, nearly the waterline length of American schooner *Fleur de Lys*. Her tonnage was more than *twice* that of the next largest entry in the race, the American bark *Apache*. All that plus the fact she was the sole full-rigged ship in the race—capable of spreading more than 55 sails, two to three times as many as any of the other contestants— struck many of them as unfair. "She looks anything *but* a racing yacht," complained the *New York Herald*. Flying the white ensign of the Royal Navy, a privilege accorded only to vessels of Britain's exclusive Royal Yacht Squadron, she looked in fact every bit what she was: the empire's heavyweight and the Royal Navy's surrogate in the race.

Valhalla had been designed to run oceans. She was big enough (648 tons, net registered) to weather the roughest seas and keep running long after smaller yachts were compelled to heave-to. Her size and strength made her a strong favorite in the ocean race.

Hamburg—which materialized ghostlike out of the fog in New York's Lower Harbor and anchored off the quarantine station at St. George, Staten Island—was greeted with outright suspicion. Painted all-black, the 158-foot schooner, its two enormous masts raked back at an angle, looked sinister. Though press boats clustered around her, Adolf Tietjens, the kaiser's representative aboard, remained below and declined to talk to reporters. In fact, the *New York Herald* noted an "almost entire exclusion of visitors, even visitors on business, from the *Hamburg* since her arrival." Like a cragside Bavarian castle, she stood dark and aloof in New York Harbor.

The American papers freely reported what they did know, however. Tietjens was a director of the Hamburg-America Line, whose fast steamers were designated auxiliaries—armed merchant cruisers—of the German Imperial Navy in event of war. He was accompanied by his son Captain-Lieutenant John Tietjens of the German Imperial Navy. All of *Hamburg*'s crew—from her commanding officer, Captain-Lieutenant Edward Peters, and two mates, down to twenty-three seamen, two cooks, and two stewards—were regulars

Hamburg's officers and crew (Captain Peters center), photographed by the *New York American* before the start of the race, weren't merchant seamen, like those of other yachts in the race—but regulars in the German Imperial Navy.

in the German Imperial Navy. The yacht itself was principally employed as a training ship for officer candidates in the German Imperial Navy. The fact of things was plain: the Kaiser's navy, not the Hamburg Yacht Club, had arrived to do battle with Britain and America.

When Lord Brassey and *Sunbeam* anchored in New York, all hell broke loose. The New York Chamber of Commerce hosted a luncheon banquet in his honor. He proceeded to seize the stage and eat the scenery. Addressing the richest men in America, Brassey painted the upcoming race in the darkest anti-German terms imaginable. "Is it not our [U.S. and U.K.] policy to keep together?" he asked the crowd. "Great change is at work," he said, reminding everyone of the fast-tilting balance of naval power, "and in those changes the interests of our two countries are involved." That got the businessmens' attention. His next statement had them squirming on their wallets. "As traders and producers," he warned America's foremost traders and producers, "we cannot suffer ourselves to be excluded from markets to which the steamship is now only beginning to give access. We ask only for an open door."

Brassey, of course, was asking nothing of the kind. He was preaching to the converted and unambiguously telling them that doors to trade swung both ways and that it would be best to shut them before anybody but immediate company got to share the spoils. He put some very sharp teeth on the point: "To a request so reasonable, backed by two navies which, combined, are invincible, who should say to us nay?" It was abundantly clear who he was talking about. That in itself was plowing the ground for an international incident.

But Brassey didn't stop there. God help him, he elevated the race to nothing less than a contest between Anglo-American or German world hegemony. "The unity of all *English-speaking* men," he concluded, vilifying Germans by omission, "is the only sure guarantee for *peace,* for equal *justice* among nations, for the general *happiness* of mankind." There was thunderous applause, followed by three cheers. Brassey had been in politics long enough to know fully what he was saying. The fact that he'd chosen to say it at the most public function imaginable made it echo all the way to the Second Reich.

At the same time, Jamie Bennett's jingoistic *New York Herald* openly questioned whether any German-run race would be fair. The kaiser's Kiel Regatta, held the summer before, had been plagued by egregious rule violations in favor of German yachts. In one race the American schooner *Ingomar,* under command of Charlie Barr, had lost a commanding lead over *Hamburg* because the course was changed *after* the race had been half sailed. In at least two other races, the German yacht *Meteor*—Wilhelm himself at the helm— blatantly ignored the rules of the road yet wasn't penalized. The *Herald* minced no words about it: "The rules of the road are as old as the ages and are known from the China seas to the North Pole," it wrote, "except, apparently, in Baltic yachting circles. Are the par- ticipants in the forthcoming ocean race—a serious undertaking, by the way—to meet with such *monkeyshines?*"

Publicly, the German-run race committee and the imperial Ger- man government behind it had no response to such barbed com- ments. Privately, the kaiser's chief of foreign affairs, Baron von Holstein, seethed. Americans, a cheap aristocracy of the dollar, accusing His Royal Highness, the emperor of Germany and king of Prussia, of *monkeyshines?* He coldly dismissed such imprecations with a simian characterization of his own: "I'm unable to under- stand how they [Americans] made the transition from walking on four legs to two," he told a colleague, "except probably someone indicated there was more money to be made walking that way." The German press pilloried American and British contestants alike as lily-livered millionaires; content to let hirelings, who were largely not American or British, face the *Herrenvolk* of the Fatherland.

A letter to the *New York Sun* fired an equally damning broad- side back at the Germans: "While with my ship at Kiel," wrote wealthy American yachtsman Albert Robbins, "I carefully noted the ways of the native [German] yachtsmen and the art of navigation seemed to find its greatest activity in the handling of beer schooners in the rathskeller of the Imperial German Yacht Club." He was dis- gusted at "the spectacle of German army officers, yachtingly inclined, prancing on a yacht's quarterdeck, arrayed in epaulettes and clank- ing swords . . . looking like pirates." He asked an old German sail- ing master, an accomplished offshore man, what he thought about it. "We used to have wooden ships with iron sailors," the master told him, "and now we have iron ships with wooden sailors." Robbins disabused him of any such notion: "I didn't like to tell the old man he must be dreaming if he remembered any really good German seamen. There *never were any.*"

All this international mudslinging raised patriotic passions to a fever pitch. "Interest in this great international contest," noted the *New York Evening Sun,* "is widening far beyond the scope of yacht club discussion." Indeed, the Kaiser's Cup was all anyone could talk about.

On the eve of the start, there wasn't a boat left for charter in all of New York. The entire Dalzell tugboat fleet, fourteen vessels, was engaged in towing and servicing the racers. All the tugs of the Moran Towing Company and the Mutual Line were under contract. The New York Yacht Club's commodore Frederick G. Bourne Esq., head of the Singer Sewing Machine Company, hired the tug *Edward Berwin* to carry a private party to witness the start. The tug *Runyon* was hired by friends of Wilson Marshall to give a send-off to *Atlantic,* the tug *Unique* by intimates of Robert Tod to cheer on *Thistle,* and the tug *Mutual* by the Seawanhaka Yacht Club in Oyster Bay, New York, to see off its entry, *Hildegarde.* Chartering a tugboat to go "down the bay" became the rage, and soon the tugs *Nonpareil. Fireproof, Manhattan, Admiral Dewey, Filibuster, John Nichols, David Dearborn, Robert Palmer, Lawrence,* and *R. B. Little* were all spoken for. The New York Athletic Club booked the tug *Catherine Moran* and the New York Racquet and Tennis Club booked the tug *Unity.* The Harlem Democratic Club snapped up the tugboat *M. Trimmins,* and the New York Produce Exchange had to settle for the lighter *America.*

For its private party, the New York Yacht Club chartered the Iron Steamboat Company's sixteen-hundred-passenger liner *Cygnus,* but she proved too small to accommodate all the club's guests. The overflow—more than four hundred—necessitated chartering a second liner. The steamer *Sirius* was booked by the Atlantic Yacht Club to ship six hundred of its members and guests, including those of the Indian Harbor Yacht Club in Greenwich, Connecticut, down the bay for a gala *bon voyage* event.

For the public who could afford it, tickets could be had on the steamers *Cerebus, Taurus,* and *Cepheus.* On the latter, tickets cost more because the hottest musical group in New York was aboard—the ragtime Old Guard Band, which was anything *but* old guard. Ragtime was the rap music of its day, assessed by a modern-day music critic in the *New York Times* as a "sometimes morally compromised, often vulgar, always vital form of popular music, perhaps closer in its articulation to hip-hop than the jazz that was its immediate descendant." At the time, the New York press took a dim view of it, noting that women of the white middle class were so titillated by its beat that they shamelessly did the "pie-dance" and "cake walk." On all the public vessels, concessionaires hawked the fast foods of the day: raw oysters; pickled pigs' feet; pickled eggs; ox tongues; sauerkraut; and the latest novelty, "hot dogs." There were barrels of ale, lager beer, hard cider, and according to the bill of fare "some wines," but not many and nothing fancy: the public at the time didn't drink wine. Hard liquor was sold by the drink.

A listing "Parties on Private Yachts" filled three columns in the *New York Times.* Besides hosting a Scottish earl (Crawford) and an English baron (Brassey), the royalty-ravenous members of the New York Yacht Club gobbled up two German barons and a German count (with wonderfully impressive names such as Baron von Bussche-Haddenhausen and Count de Limburg-Stirum). They also bagged half a dozen honorables in the British peerage and two British knights.

They competed with each other to invite foreign ambassadors and American politicians. U.S. Secretary of the Navy Paul Morton, a trophy guest, proved something of an embarrassment: he'd been incriminated in a rebates scandal stemming from his second job, as a vice president of the Atchison, Topeka, & Santa Fe Railroad, and was under investigation (he was forced to resign less than a month later). The secretary of the U.S. Parks Department and the current and past mayors of New York all accepted New York Yacht Club invitations. After these were spoken for, members scrambled for "uniforms": the British and German naval and military attachés, the captain of the battleship USS *Alabama,* and four U.S. cruiser commanders. At the same time, they fell all over themselves to get "old money" New York society—Barclays, Barlows, and Beekmans, Livingstons and Lorillards, Schermerhorns and Schuylers and Van Rensselaers—to their soirees. When the old money list had been mined, a gold rush commenced to get "new money" names: Astors, Goelets and Goulds, Harrimans and Huntingtons, Roosevelts and countless Vanderbilts.

Owners of competing American yachts were not to be outdone. They, too, filled their boats with the rich and the famous. Dr. Stimson had a best-selling author of sea tales, James B. Connolly, aboard his *Fleur de Lys*. George Lauder Jr. took four of his multimillionaire friends and popular Spanish-American and Philippine War hero Dr. Henry C. Rowland aboard *Endymion*. Edward Coleman's guests on *Hildegard* included the heir to the Diamond Match, fortune, an insurance tycoon, and the surgeon general of Pennsylvania. Aboard *Thistle*, the astute Robert Tod Esq. took two worldrenowned physicians and Poultney Bigelow, influential publisher of *Outing* magazine: the former might prove useful during the race and the latter at the finish, since Bigelow was an outspoken proponent of ocean racing and one of the few Americans whom Kaiser Wilhelm truly considered a friend. Neophyte yacht owner Edmond Randolph Jr. took six fellow, hard-partying American multimillionaire heirs with him on his big *Apache,* including American railroad heir Joseph Harriman. Aboard the equally big *Utowana,* solitary, studious Allison Armour took only two close friends, both wealthy heirs like himself. One of them, Jordan L. Mott Jr., heir to Mott Ironworks, held a golden monopoly, supplying the most lackluster of products—almost all of America's plumbing fixtures.

Unsurprisingly, the A-list for private yacht parties floated under the burgee of the New York Yacht Club. The biggest, most palatial vessels on the club's list were moored at its pier on East Twenty-third Street on the East River. Railroad heir Howard Gould's steam yacht *Niagara* was typical. She was 247 feet long, cost the equivalent of $15 million today to build, and cost a staggering $3.75 million in today's dollars to operate annually. Her crew numbered sixty-five, not including chefs, stewards, maids, and laundresses. She boasted a 36-foot-wide Renaissance Revival drawing room warmed by ornate seacoal fireplaces, a mahoghany paneled library with a "church-size pipe organ," a recreation room equipped with an "orchestrion" (a turn-of-the-twentieth-century music synthesizer), and a photographic darkroom—complete with photographer.

Equally big and opulent was oil millionaire Henry Huddleston Rogers' steam yacht *Kanawha,* belonging to Frank Gould (another of freebooting financier Jay Gould's heirs), the steam yacht *Helenita* and Frederick Gallatin's steam yacht *Riviera.* Also at the club's East Twenty-third Street station were the palatial yachts *Oneida, Privateer, Levanter, Elsa II, Aloha,* and *Tuscarora,* all hosting more or less continuous luncheons, teas, and dinner parties.

The topic of discussion dominating these high-society events, however, wasn't the race, yachting, international politics, or anything of the kind. It was all about the mysterious guest aboard the Kaiser's schooner *Hamburg.* It sounds downright vaudevillian, but the one question all New York society was asking itself—somehow with a straight face—was "Who is Sigmund Picconnelli?"

A tall but stout, clean-shaven young man of that dreadfully dissonant name was reported to be a second guest aboard *Hamburg.* Reporters at once observed he was given far more than guest treatment. He got royal treatment. A *New York Herald* correspondent noted he was "treated with unusual courtesy, of whom extreme reticence was observed by all on the ship and ignorance professed by all Germans of official position ashore." He was also kept out of sight. In photographs, however, the *Herald* stressed the young man bore a "remarkable resemblance to Prince Adalbert, son of the German Emperor." Curiosity ran wild.

When Adolf Tietjens stepped ashore with the young man one rainy night on their way to dinner, an army of reporters was waiting. Tietjens was asked to give a list of *Hamburg*'s passengers and replied: "I have my son with me. He is a naval officer whom the Emperor graciously allowed to come." "Are there any others?" he was asked. "Yes, there is another young man," he answered nonchalantly. Reporters, knowing twenty-year old Prince Adalbert was a lieutenant in the Imperial Navy, shouted; "Is he a naval officer also?" "No," Tietjens said emphatically. In chorus, the reporters shouted, "What's his name?" "You may say he is Mr. Picconnelli," replied Tietjens. "Call him an Italian merchant."

The press immediately turned their questions upon the smooth-faced, affably smiling Mr. Picconnelli. He said nothing, bowed politely, and was relieved from replying by Captain Peters, *Hamburg*'s skipper, who shielded him from reporters. As Tietjens and Picconnelli were whisked away by horsecab, Peters called reports of Prince Adalbert's being aboard as "absurd." Pressed for details about Picconnelli, he would say only "He is a friend."

This, of course, merely deepened the mystery. So did a letter two days later in the *Berlin Zeitun*. It read: "On board the *Hamburg* will be found a passenger who has been requested by the Emperor to make a detailed report of the race and its conclusion." The letter was signed "Triton," which the *New York Herald* identified as "the *nom de plume* of a high German naval officer" who frequently used unofficial channels to deniably, but credibly, communicate official actions. Berlin was sending a message in the clear for anyone listening.

The man was certainly no Italian merchant or friend. He was heard to speak only occasionally, but when he did, he showed a very thorough knowledge of the yacht and her working, and his words were received as orders by officers and crew alike. He roamed the *Hamburg* like a cat, seldom leaving her, even when she was hauled out of the water to have her bottom scraped and painted. Whenever reporters appeared, he vanished belowdecks. "So far as can be learned," reported the *Herald*'s correspondent, "he has not yet spoken to a stranger." Indeed, he never did.

The mystery was further compounded. As *Hamburg* prepared to sail, S. Picconnelli was listed—as the rules required—in the vessel's manifest as an owner's guest in the transatlantic race. But a day before the start, sharp-eyed New York reporters followed him ashore, where he furtively made his way to the pier where the elegant German liner *Kaiser Wilhelm der Grosse* was docked. He registered under the name Oberleutnant Gliser of the German Imperial Army. For a lowly first lieutenant, he had very deep pockets: he was booked as a first-class passenger. That convinced many skeptics that the young man could only be Prince Adalbert, until a confounding wire was received from the *New York Herald*'s Berlin correspondent: "There is not the slightest truth in the rumor that Prince Adalbert is going to sail in the transatlantic race," the correspondent informed his editors, "He is here quietly amusing himself sailing the *Samoa II* in the Wansee."

That hardly doused the still-burning questions, Who the devil, then, *is* Picconnelli or Gliser or whatever his handlers call him? Why is he aboard *Hamburg* in the first place? Why is he afforded deference and secrecy unwarranted by an Italian merchant or low-ranking army officer? And—as perplexingly—why had he suddenly left? It seemed almost certain that Kaiser Wilhelm would have wanted an observer of his own aboard ship to report on the race. Officially Tietjens fit this bill, but he was, after all, part of the Hamburg Yacht Club's sycophantic syndicate, eager to tell the kaiser only good news. Yet it is emphatically certain that Picconnelli or whoever he was left the *Hamburg* before the starting gun was fired and never observed the race at all. So what had he been sent all the way from Germany to do?

Recent news reports strongly suggested an answer. In the three months before the race, there had been an unprecedented number of unsolved dockyard explosions and fires in New York—accidents that destroyed no fewer than four New York Yacht Club vessels.

On Valentine's Day, a massive fire consumed two big steam auxiliary yachts at the Fifteenth Street Basin in Hoboken, New Jersey. Both—coincidentally or not—happened to belong to Frederick G. Bourne, commodore of the New York Yacht Club. Both were docked at the end of a long pier, their hulls fast in midwinter ice. Only a lone night watchman was on duty. The blaze erupted after midnight aboard *Delaware,* a very fast, 253 foot, George L. Watson–designed schooner and a potential contender for the Kaiser's Cup. When firefighters arrived they quickly discovered their hoses too short to stretch from shoreside hydrants to the end of the pier. Using axes and picaroons, they tried chopping through the ice at the stems of the vessels in an attempt to drag them back within range of the hoses, but the ice was too thick and the flames spread too fast. By that time *Delaware* was a fireball and Bourne's equally fast, 160-foot schooner *Colonia,* another potential Cup contender, was ablaze. When a firefighting tug finally arrived, it was too late. *Delaware* had burned right down to her waterline. *Colonia* sank at the pier. Both were written off as complete wrecks. Insurers estimated Bourne's loss at $550,000—equivalent to more than $10 million today.

Fewer than two months later—on the morning of April 6—Tebo's Basin at Twenty-third Street in Brooklyn, a favorite pier of wealthy yacht owners, was rocked by a tremendous explosion. It occurred on the 125-foot, state-of-the-art, gasoline-powered auxiliary schooner *Grisle,* proud possession of John T. Pratt, heir to his father's Standard Oil fortune. Lashed alongside her was Brooklyn millionaire Alfred Richard's big steam yacht *Mendora,* and on the same pier railroad heir Cornelius Vanderbilt's *Tarantula* and oil millionaire H. H. Rogers' *Kanawha*—two of the biggest yachts on the New York Yacht Club list.

"No one knows the cause of the explosion," reported the *Herald,* but somehow the filled and securely capped port gasoline tank of the *Grisle* went off like a bomb. The captain, first mate, a ship joiner, and a plumber were blown sky-high, cartwheeling like flaming torches and thudding on deck with third-degree burns and shrapnel-like wounds from the burst steel fuel tank. The mushrooming fireball set *Mendora* ablaze at once and licked down the pier for *Tarantula* and *Kanawha.* Both vessels chopped their docking lines and were hauled back from the flames. *Mendora*'s crew cut her lines with *Grisle,* but *Mendora*'s port side was already a wall of fire, fast raging up the rigging. By the time the fireboat *Seth Low* extinguished the flames, the two yachts were smoldering ruins.

It could have been far worse. Tebo's Basin was tightly packed with yachts of the New York Yacht Club, fitting out early in the season, primarily for the Kaiser's Cup race. Tons of coal, open cans of paint and varnish, barrels of smoldering tar, acetylene tanks, and gas lines were on their decks. A calculated explosion in their midst—especially aboard the only volatile-gasoline-fueled yacht in the yard—could reasonably be expected to wreak havoc. Two mysterious, multiple ship disasters, at two locations, all involving New York Yacht Club vessels, so shortly before the race, raised eyebrows. And not just in New York.

Cablegrams flashed the news to Berlin. *Hamburg,* preparing to sail to the States for the race, received a last-minute, unannounced, and very important guest. Tietjens certainly knew who he was, yet went to extraordinary lengths not to reveal it. In his log on the outward voyage he identified him only as a "gentleman." In New York, Tietjens publicly identified him with a name and an occupation no one in his right mind—with the possible exception of New York society—took seriously. *Who* he was didn't really concern the public, after all. *What* he was doing, on the other hand, had already been made plain by "Triton" in the *Berlin Zeitung.* He stuck to the *Hamburg* like glue the entire time she was in New York: especially when she was in dry dock and most vulnerable. He left her barely twenty-four hours before the start of the race, only after she was safely anchored in Lower New York Bay. And he took passage straight as an arrow back to Germany aboard the fastest German liner on the North Atlantic when his job was done. All that, in light of the disasters involving New York Yacht Club vessels, strongly suggests he was someone sent to make absolutely certain no such acts of God—or more likely sabotage—befell the Kaiser's *Hamburg* prior to the race. A high-ranking naval demolitions expert, given *carte blanche* by Wilhelm, would have fit the bill nicely. Whatever the case, *Hamburg* wasn't troubled with any accidents. The juicy intrigue surrounding Prussian princes and shadowy saboteurs sent public interest in the upcoming race sky-high.

"Ocean racing is now the yachtsman's mania," reported the *New York Herald.* "The same fever is raging among landsmen. In clubs and in private places, the every hour discussion has some reference to the contest at hand for the German Emperor's Cup. The air is brine laden, and endorsement or criticism of the sailors and sportsmen who are ready to compete in the long, maybe wild, race across the Atlantic is heard upon every side." Hundreds of yachtsmen journeyed by carriage—the very richest by White or Stanley steam automobiles—to the yards of the Morse Iron Works in Brooklyn to look over the contestants. The torrent of spectators soon became a flood, with "thousands of enthusiasts visiting the docks where the boats are receiving their final grooming." Crowds descended on Morse's to see *Atlantic, Hamburg, Sunbeam,* and *Apache* in dry dock; flocked to Tebo's Basin to view *Endymion;* went to Manning's Yard to look at little *Fleur de Lys;* out to City Island to see *Ailsa,* or took the ferry across the Hudson to Tietjen

& Lang's boatyard in Hoboken to gaze at the giants *Valhalla* and *Utowana.*

Few in the crowd were idle sightseers. Betting on the race was epidemic. In the yachting haunts of the rich, "unusual interest in the race is evidenced by many wagers," wrote the *New York Herald.* Sadly, these weren't recorded for posterity, but they must have been typical of those placed by American millionaires at the time. In 1905 Standard Oil tycoon John D. Rockefeller, who was notoriously parsimonious, bet—and lost—$27,537 (equivalent to more than $525,000 today) on a round of golf. A contemporary, John Warne Gates, who made his fortune holding a monopoly on the manufacture of barbed wire, bet $40,000 (that's $760,000 today) on a single coin toss. He won. He became known as "Bet-a-Million Gates," wagering—and usually winning—on everything from horse races ($600,000 on his horse Royal Flush) and bridge games ($10 a point) to what one flabbergasted observer reported as "the progress of raindrops trickling down a train window." Another contemporary, William Collins Whitney, who'd lined his pockets financing New York City's street railway system, wasn't so lucky. While waiting for his wife to dress for dinner at Saratoga, he lost $385,000 ($7.3 million today) at the gaming tables.

The Kaiser's Cup race, which had been touted for months and was near and dear to ultrarich American yachtsmen, undoubtedly resulted in far higher stakes than these. Unfortunately, the only one we know of is a private wager, almost certainly one of the smallest. New York Yacht Club member Chester Paulmann bet $10,000 (equivalent to $190,000 today) on *Atlantic* to win. Gloucester fishing Captain B. H. Hardy, who must have been rooting for fellow Gloucesterman Tommie Bohlin in *Fleur de Lys,* promptly covered the bet.

Outside yachting circles, the public furiously laid wagers, too. Well-to-do New York businessmen—those who could afford champagne and fine cigars in select bars such as the Hoffman House, its walls adorned with paintings of nude water nymphs by noted French artist William Bouguereau—bet from $100 to as much as $1,000 ($1,900 to $19,000 today). New York's shopkeepers, clerks, machinists, and workers were alive to their chance as well.

In thousands of neighborhood saloons such as McSorley's Old Ale House on East Seventh Street—its motto "Good ale, raw onions, and no ladies"—men plunked down $1, $5, and $10 wagers ($19, $95, and $190 today). The problem in all this betting was that New York's bookmakers were positively stymied and hopelessly divided about how to figure the odds.

The eleven contestants varied dizzyingly in size: from 208 feet at the waterline to a mere 86, and from 648 to 86 tons net registered. They included about every rig imaginable: a three-masted ship, a three-masted bark, a three-masted topsail schooner, a pair of three-masted schooners, five two-masted schooners, and a yawl. Depending on which way the wind blew—and for how long—any of these rigs had its advantages and its disadvantages. Winds from behind favored the square-rigged ship, bark, and topsail schooner. Winds from abeam (the side) favored three- and two-masted schooners. Headwinds favored the yawl.

Too much or too little wind, however, could turn those assumptions on their heads. Heavy winds and weather—even from a favorable direction—could be expected to slow the smaller, lighter, low-built schooners, while the larger, heavily-built square-riggers could crash ahead. The five biggest vessels, on the other hand, were all steam auxiliaries, which, though stripped of their propellers for the race, remained burdened with tons of machinery that could slow them in light winds. Then again, wind, weather, and seas could change a hundred times or more during the race. Gales and storms could cripple leaders and turn laggards into front-runners. The North Atlantic was notorious for that. The bookies had only to look at the 1866, 1870, and 1887 races.

The course each yacht might shape once offshore was, of course, a carefully guarded secret. But the oddsmakers knew there were only really two practical, great circle courses for the racers to steer. Maddeningly, neither offered a clear advantage over the other.

The so-called northern route offered the most direct way to the finish—almost a straight line over the globe from Nantucket Shoals off Massachusetts to the Lizard lighthouse at the westernmost entrance to the English Channel. As the most direct line from New York to England, it was also the shortest: a distance of approxi-

mately 2,875 nautical miles. Under favorable conditions it promised to be the fastest. It was the route Bully Samuels had followed
in *Henrietta* in the 1866 ocean race.

But conditions along the northern route were notoriously
uncertain and unfavorable. For the first 1,200 miles out of New
York, it coursed dangerously near the North American mainland:
passing just 150 miles off the elbow of Cape Cod, within 120
miles of Cape Sable, Nova Scotia, within 60 miles of Sable Island,
and within 70 miles of Cape Race, Newfoundland. A half day's gale
blowing in from sea could set a boat aground on any of these treacherous headlands. They were legendary boneyards for passing ships.

Steering the northern route also took a boat straight across the
perpetually foggy and stormy Grand Banks. Cold Arctic currents
and the warm Gulf Stream meshed together there like gears, ther-
mally powering a perpetual fog-making machine. Two weeks of
blinding fog a month wasn't unusual. Cold and warm air masses
from the North American mainland and the North Atlantic, respectively, collided more or less constantly over the Banks, too, stirring
a cauldron of fast-moving, violent storm fronts. In any kind of a
blow, the comparatively shallow waters covering the Banks erupted
into very heavy, dangerous seas very swiftly.

Clear of the Banks, the route over the roof of the North Atlantic
coursed more and more northerly, from 45 to above 50 degrees latitude. In those latitudes, especially in spring, ice could be expected
almost anywhere. But the greatest concentration—the normal range
of the Arctic ice drift—routinely blocked the northern route like a
floating cordillera. From Greenland, icebergs drifted as far south as
40 degrees latitude and reached from the Grand Banks in the west
as far east as 35 degrees longitude out into the mid-Atlantic. That represented an ice field roughly 1,500 miles long and 1,200 miles wide.

If the northern route was like crossing the icy, exposed roof of
the North Atlantic, the southern route was like running around it
under the eaves. It avoided the hazards of the shorter, direct passage
by following a longer, indirect course—one of roughly 3, 100 nautical miles versus 2,875. From New York it ran southeast for some
300 miles and then turned almost due east for 1,200 miles. This
quickly took a vessel into deep water, out beyond the often bois-

terous weather and seas characteristic of the continental shelf, and put it on a course roughly parallel with the North American mainland but well clear of its capes, islands, sandbanks, and shoals. It cleared the southern extremities of the foggy, stormy Grand Banks and the normal range of the ice drift before making any real northing. At roughly 50 degrees longitude—seamen called it "the Comer"—mariners abruptly altered course northward, for the English Channel.

All that—theoretically, at least—made the southern route safer. It put most foul weather and ice a good 10 degrees to the north. The prevailing wind and the current of the Gulf Stream gave eastbound vessels a speed boost. It had been universally adopted by the shipping lines as the principal steamer track across the North Atlantic. In fact, the lines had divided it into a two-lane, east–west ocean highway, running steamers between New York and the Channel on parallel courses some 60 miles apart to avoid collisions. At the time of the race, however, it was probably the busiest, most dangerously congested sea lane in the world.

Figuring the wildly different variables of eleven boats, following different courses, in a hundred different stripes of weather led the oddsmakers nowhere. They latched onto one of the only things they really knew for certain: the mettle of the skipper of each boat. Betting odds reflected that. "Among the leading yachtsmen whose daily walks are in the financial district," the New York Herald reported, "there have been betting books heard of and the odds presented have been something like these figures: Atlantic 4 to 1; Endymion 5 to 1; Ailsa 5 to 1; Hildegarde 6 to 1; Hamburg 6 to 1; Valhalla 8 to 1; Apache 8 to 1; Utowana 8 to 1; Fleur de Lys 8 to 1; Thistle 10 to 1; Sunbeam 12 to 1" Plainly, oddsmakers figured the men to watch were Barr on Atlantic, closely followed by Loesch on Endymion, Miller on Ailsa then Marsters on Hildegarde and Peters on Hamburg. Ironically, the odds on the three largest boats in the race (Valhalla, Apache, and Utowana) and the smallest (Fleur de Lys) were identical. Sheer size dictated consideration of the "big boys"; the weight of Captain Tommie Bohlin's reputation alone made tiny Fleur's chances equal to theirs. Amateur skipper Tod's Thistle and elderly Lord Brassey's equally elderly Sunbeam weren't given much of a chance at all. In addition to betting on who would win, there was betting if the winner would break *Endymion*'s 1900 transatlantic record from Sandy Hook to the Needles—thirteen days, twenty hours, and thirty-six minutes—and if so, by how much. Speculation varied widely. The papers noted that a new record was generally expected—from twelve to a remarkable nine days.

The one authority everyone seized on to make some kind of sense of this jumbled field of seagoing thoroughbreds was an eighty-two-year-old man in Brooklyn. Newspaper reporters stood in line at 134 Clinton Street to interview Bully Samuels. The *New York Herald*'s correspondent was surprised to learn that he was still alive and even more startled to see that "despite his many years, his pale grey eyes are still bright and clear and his brain is as active as it was when his name and that of his renowned clipper were known wherever the flag of this country waved." Indeed, Samuels was as excited about the race as a schoolboy.

When asked his views on the contest, he could scarcely contain himself "Unevenly matched and starting without time allowance," he said, shaking his head, "it will be hard picking. But if the winds are strong, the biggest should win." He qualified that at once: "I don't say that the biggest *will,* but say it *should* because of greater sail power." At the same time, he pointed out that with the exception of two-year-old *Atlantic,* the five biggest vessels in the race also were the oldest. *Sunbeam* was thirty-one, *Apache* fifteen, *Utowana* fourteen, and *Valhalla* thirteen—rather antiquated designs compared with *Hamburg,* and *Endymion,* both five-year-olds, and *Thistle,* which was four. Samuels commented on the age difference. "I suppose these newer boats will do better than the old ones," he said. "The new ones have the long overhand aft and that gives them a better purchase." By that he meant that the long, overhanging stems and bows of the newer boats—designed to ride out of the water to minimize water resistance and maintain speed in light winds—were also expressly designed to engage the seas when heeled over in heavier winds, effectively lengthening the boat's waterline, stiffening it in a strong breeze, and materially increasing its speed. It was a neat design trick that offered the best of both worlds, at least in short America's Cup races and brief offshore contests.

Out in the mid-Atlantic, however, Samuels thought such designs downright dangerous.

"I don't consider them as safe as the older boats," he told the *Herald* reporter. "In a gale of wind, I'll take the older type." When asked why, he replied automatically, "The long overhang is well enough for smooth water, but when you get out in a seaway"—he slammed his hand down on his knee—"the slap is hard, yes, hard. They've got to be pretty stout, otherwise the jar will hurt." And Samuels was an authority on how hard the North Atlantic could hit and how lethally it could hurt. "I doubt if these new boats will fare as well as we did in the 1866 race," he said, "and we didn't fare well then, the *Fleetwing* losing six of her crew overboard."

Nobody had to look farther than New York Harbor to see what Samuels meant. The battered British schooner *Laconia* had just arrived after a 163-day North Atlantic horror story. A big, three-masted, oceangoing schooner, she'd sailed from St. John, New Brunswick, before Thanksgiving 1904, bound for New York with a cargo of timber. It was a pedestrian voyage, one she'd made countless times before: an offshore run of 700 miles or so, expected to take a week to ten days. She sailed on November 3, 1904. Three days later, off the Georges Bank, she was struck by a violent storm with terrific winds and seas that stripped away her sails, ship's boats, and deck cargo. She broached, lost all three masts, flooded, and was driven helplessly out to sea. For the next forty-six days, pumps barely keeping her afloat, the North Atlantic gang-raped her by turns. By her captain's account, she was "hit by seventeen hurricanes [more likely strong gales or storms] and more than a dozen times on the verge of sinking." For twenty-six days after that, the North Atlantic slapped her east into midocean, dragged her north, back-slapped her west, and savagely kicked her south. She drifted comatose until she finally grounded off Barbados—2,000 miles from her intended destination—the crew so emaciated and exhausted they were hospitalized for two months. When the vessel, refloated and repaired, finally appeared in New York, it seemed like a real-life *Flying Dutchman* had arrived.

The ill omen electrified the public. Every sea trial of the competing boats was watched with redoubled interest. When it was announced that Robert Tod was taking *Thistle* on an offshore speed run from New York Harbor to Hampton Roads, Virginia, crowds turned out. High drama quickly turned to high comedy. Beating against the wind down the main shipping channel in a squall, Tod ran hard aground on the point of Sandy Hook before getting out of the lower bay. Red-faced, Tod and his crew worked her off with a kedge anchor and returned to port. The mishap of the Atlantic Yacht Club's premier Corinthian sailor greatly amused the public, though not half as much as the members of the New York Yacht Club.

When Captain Tommie Bohlin and his Gloucestermen took underdog *Fleur de Lys* out to stretch every inch of her canvas, however, there was a patriotic pride that bordered on reverence. It came not from wealthy yacht owners but from people who owned almost nothing at all. Bohlin and his crew weren't expecting it. They were busy hauling up and trimming sail. But when *Fleur*, "spars groaning under the strain, drove past Sandy Hook," as the *New York World* reported, "the soldiers in front of the barracks gave 'Three times three!' for the little American yacht." A few minutes afterward, she shot past the fishing boats off Seabright. The moment the fishermen recognized her, the *World*'s correspondent said they quit their trawls and nets, lined the rails, and "yelled their lusty 'Aye, ayes!' as Bohlin's fisherman crew swept by."

The huge British *Valhalla* made no trial sails at all. She remained at anchor in the Hudson River off West Forty-fourth Street, yards perfectly square, canvas all in gaskets and snugly covered, boat booms swung out and steam launches at the pendants, as if she hadn't a care in the world. She was perfectly situated for Lord Crawford's purposes. He was but blocks away, at the New York Yacht Club, where he was a daily visitor: spending hours inspecting the great collection of yacht models in the Model Room, or buried in the stacks of the library. If he wasn't there, he was at the Collectors' Club on West Twenty-sixth Street, where his U.S. stamp collection was on display.

Lord Brassey practically abandoned *Sunbeam* to attend to a full schedule of events ashore—social, economic, philanthropic, and political—waving the Union Jack and preaching Anglo-American

solidarity at each of them. He somehow made time to stump dys-
peptically around every yacht in the race but one. Asked to take a
look around the *Atlantic,* which at the time was in the same dry
dock as *Sunbeam* and "not more than five steps away," according
a reporter, "he did not have the curiosity to do so." When pressed,
he snapped, "No, I do not care to walk around her. I don't like these
big rigs." Apparently Anglo-American solidarity, ended with looking at the most favored yacht in the race.

He did give *Sunbeam*'s crew a final liberty that day. In the
afternoon they visited New York's newest, most fantastic attraction:
the Hippodrome, on Sixth Avenue between Forty-third and Forty-
fourth Streets. The fifty-two-hundred-seat entertainment palace,
ablaze with more newfangled electric lights than anyplace in the
world at the time, would rightfully be called "the spark that would
forever light Times Square." Its eye-popping stage shows combined vaudeville, pantomime, circus, and popular music. In the
spring of 1905 it was selling out two double-feature shows six days
a week. Brassey's men were treated to "A Yankee Circus on Mars"
and "A Society Circus," the latter producing the greatest laughter
and applause. That evening—rather disappointingly, one suspects—
Brassey sent them to Madison Square Garden to watch a gymnas-
tics tournament of the Military Athletic League.

Tietjens and Captain Peters gave *Hamburg*'s crew liberty, too,
but on a very short leash. In charge of what the papers called
"a branch pilot," meaning one of *Hamburg*'s senior petty officers
assigned as chaperon, they were packed off to the new amusement
park out on Coney Island for the day—far from any midtown
Manhattan temptations. By dark they were all back aboard
Hamburg.

Charlie Barr's men didn't get any liberty at all. Prior to the start,
the *New York Times* reported "There was not a busier body than
Captain Barr. He was over and about on the *Atlantic,* overlooking
the men as they worked on her spars and rigging and got things
ready." He remained as sour as vinegar. Asked why his crew was
hard at work while others were at play he replied, "We don't have
time to loaf "

On Saturday night, May 13—four days before the scheduled

start of the race—meatpacking heir Allison Armour quit his luxurious yacht *Utowana* and came ashore to host the most prestigious and rigidly exclusive soiree of all: a banquet for the eleven yacht owners competing for the Kaiser's Cup. It was to be the last occasion on which the eleven men would meet in America before setting sail.

The event took place in the Palm Room at legendary Delmonico's restaurant—the sanctum sanctorum of America's very, very rich. Delmonico's was renowned for its elegance, sublimely fresh foods (delivered daily from its own farm in Brooklyn), and culinary innovation. Lobster Newburg and lobster Thermidor (named for the eleventh month of the French Revolutionary calendar), exquisitely time-consuming, complex, and expensive dishes, were creations of Delmonico's kitchen. So, too, were Delmonico-cut steak, flaming baked Alaska, and eggs Benedict. The latter was concocted for an American yachting millionaire with a hangover who snappishly ordered "buttered toast, poached eggs, crisp bacon, and a hooker of hollandaise." That was lunch-counter cuisine, and Delmonico's prodigiously proud chefs had no intention of serving it, substituting newfangled English muffins for toast and Canadian ham for bacon. Like most dishes they turned their hand to, it proved an immediate sensation.

Delmonico's also was prized for its discretion. Men of great wealth at the time usually dined with other men of great wealth. Wives were seldom, if ever, taken to public restaurants. Mistresses were another matter entirely, and men of great wealth typically had several. According to a contemporary food historian, the *maître d'* at Delmonico's was trusted to keep "a notebook in his pocket, so that he would not mistakenly place two members of the same family in the same dining room at the same time."

More than anything else, however, the restaurant was known for extravagant expense. "To dine at Delmonico's," noted a contemporary observer, "two things are requisite—money and French. Of the latter little will answer. But the more you have of the former, the better off you are." Indeed, the restaurant's menu listed "346 entries in French, running from lamb's kidneys in champagne sauce and artichokes *à la poivrade* . . . to 29 variations on beef, 27 on veal,

14 on poultry and 48 fish specialties, among them salmon with caper sauce and mussels stewed or *aux fines herbes*." Amid the hundreds of wines on its list, there were no fewer than 58 select vintages, a bottle of which could cost more than a single-family house. A staggering array of desserts was accompanied by a litany of coffees, teas, punches, and 24 ethereal liqueurs. That was the *normal* bill of fare. Armour's farewell banquet for the Kaiser's Cup owners trumped it in spades.

Before the diners were seated, however, a just-received telegram from Kaiser Wilhelm was read aloud. On the eve of such an auspicious event, for an emperor who could afford to transmit volumes, it was miserly and brief. "Best greetings to yacht-owners and Starting Committee," it read. "Hoping race will be a success and wishing good and speedy cruises—Wilhelm I.R." That was all.

CHAPTER 22

Starting Gun

Remember the Hamburg *is a dangerous boat and keep your eye on the German yacht.*

—William Gardner,
designer of *Atlantic*

The start of the race dawned as damp, chill, and foggy as the day before and altogether depressing for Adolph Tietjens, the kaiser's representative on the afterdeck of *Hamburg*. There was virtually no wind, only a faint breeze, straight out of the east and smelling of rain. He had a bad cold. The acrid smoke of the tug *W. A. Sherman*, towing her to the starting line, made him nauseous. The previous day's postponement and the morning's conditions made him jumpy. Unless the fog lifted, it meant another interminable delay, about which no one—least of all the kaiser—would be happy. Tietjens had not eaten the big breakfast the ship's cook had prepared. And now he had a boat of drunks shouting at him.

It turned out to be the tug *Catherine Moran*, filled with men of the New York Athletic Club—most of them three sheets to the wind, though it was hours until noon. On her afterdeck stood Humphrey's famed Seventh Regiment Band. A moment later the strains of "Die Wacht am Rhein" were heard in honor of the Germans. *Hamburg*'s white-uniformed crew, drawn up on deck and wearing rakish, new red tam-o'-shanters, came smartly to attention. Captain Peters dipped his colors in salute. At once the band changed tunes, playing "Ach du lieber Augustin" to the New York Athletic Club's slurred chorus. It was a prep school boys' kind of joke.

Tietjens had a moment of deep satisfaction shortly afterward, however, as they were towed out from Sandy Hook. The opulent, new British Cunard leviathan *Caronia*—all 674 feet of her—remained hard and fast on Flynn's Knoll, where she'd grounded outward bound in the fog the previous afternoon. She lay outside the northern side of the main shipping channel, twice her length (more than ¼ mile) from deep water, bow pointed north, almost at right angles to her proper course. She had a list of about 10 degrees to starboard, and the outgoing tide was fast leaving her like a beached whale.

By comparison, Tietjens gleefully noted in his log that "the North German Lloyd steamer *Kaiser Wilhelm der Grosse* succeeded in starting her trip from New York, at the same time, in the same conditions, without accident and on time." Since Tietjens's log was to be turned over to the emperor upon the conclusion of the race, this may look like good, old-fashioned brownnosing. But the fact of the thing wasn't lost on Tietjens or anyone else. *Kaiser Wilhelm der Grosse,* the biggest and fastest ship in the world—German-designed and built by Germans in a German shipyard—was the civilian parallel to what His Highness sought in his rapidly building navy. "It is little less than remarkable," the British press wrote of her, "that a nation which in the eighties was more or less dependent on this country for construction of her mail ships, should have so rapidly developed her shipbuilding talents that she now produces a vessel which is the largest in the world and which in point of speed promises to be equal to any steamship yet afloat."

Now *Kaiser Wilhelm der Grosse*—as Tietjens proudly informed the kaiser—was well started on her way across the Atlantic at 23 knots, while *Caronia* was stuck on a mudbank, reduced to what the *New York Herald* called "a first class grandstand," her thirty-three hundred passengers thronging the officers' bridge, promenade decks, and steerage rails. So much for the rubbish Lord Brassey had been spouting to the press about the nautical supremacy of English-speaking peoples. The lie was exposed there on Flynn's Knoll for the world to see. What made the incident all the more deliciously embarrassing was the fact that Lady Brassey was among the passengers stranded aboard *Caronia*. As *Hamburg* was towed past her, Tietjens couldn't resist joking; "There's the fastest boat. Six tugs can't move her."

The infernal press tug *Eugene Moran* fell in alongside *Hamburg* shortly afterward, bristling with men barking through megaphones and snapping with cameras. The same infernal questions erupted: "Where's the prince?" and "Is Adalbert aboard?" This time however, they were larded with new ones: "Where's Mr. Picconnelli?" and "What do you know about Lieutenant Gliser?" Since none of the questions was addressed to him by name, Tietjens said nothing. Captain Peters, busy getting under way, had no time for any more such nonsense. In his quarterdeck voice he shouted back; "A friend came over with us, he is not coming back with us—now bear off!"

As the tug fell away, a *New York Times* reporter yelled, "Herr Tietjens, who do you think will win?" The Hamburg-America Line chief elegantly raised his hat. "We may win and we may not," he replied, "We *will* sail." It rang with Germanic pride and not unintentionally, one thinks, echoed Kaiser Wilhelm's sentiments to a precisely calculated millimeter and microsecond. It was the last official word spoken from *Hamburg* before the race. Tietjens could only hope the American press quoted him properly.

Lord Brassey didn't learn of *Caronia*'s "mishap," as he called it in his log, until *Sunbeam* was towed past her on the way to the starting line. It was surely as disheartening a sight to him as it was uplifting to the Germans. The latest, most advanced ship from British yards was sticking out of the mud in Lower New York Bay like a derelict piling, with legions of marooned passengers—his wife included—perched on her thicker than seagulls. He wasted few words on it, however. "Passed *Caronia,* Cunard Line," he tersely noted, "with Lady Brassey and Mrs. Pakenham [wife of Colonel Pakenham, one of his guests on *Sunbeam*] on board, aground."

He was busy shaking out every inch of canvas that might give *Sunbeam* an advantage at the start. This amounted to a prodigious and varied cloud for the venerable three-masted topsail schooner. In his log he hurriedly scribbled that he "set all plain [lower] sail, large outer jib, fore topsail, top-gallant sail, main topmast staysail, balloon mizzen topmast-staysail and mizzen topsail." That was pretty close to the maximum 8,333 square feet of canvas she could carry. It was an announcement—if any was needed—that *Sunbeam*'s owner was deadly serious about the business ahead.

Candace Stimson found herself the unwanted center of attention as *Fleur de Lys* was moving to the line. She was, in fact, the one oddity afloat when everybody wanted to see: the first woman ever to hazard the dangers of a transatlantic race and, perhaps more interesting to the general public, the sole woman—unmarried woman, mind you—in the whole 359-man contest. Even the various ships' mascots in the race—an alley cat on *Hildegarde* and a crowing gamecock on *Endymion*—were male. Yet of all the men heading to sea that morning—which among owners and guests alone included thirty-six multimillionaires (billionaires by today's calculation), nine renowned physicians, three noted journalists, and three high-ranking military officers—none sparked as much interest as the lone Miss Stimson. Why, the press wondered in print, was she going? What part would she play? How did she feel? They got no answers from Candace Stimson. She'd politely but resoundingly refused interviews; which only started the New York press asking why in the world she didn't want to talk.

She was, to be sure, in a very ticklish spot for an aging debutante in 1905. Proper ladies of her station—and she was very much part of New York society—simply did not join a stag yachting party, even if it was glorified by a Kaiser's Cup. The fact that she was going with her father didn't ameliorate matters. For some 3,000 miles, day and night, for weeks, she'd be living with fourteen unrelated men— twelve of whom were common fishermen—in exquisitely close quarters, where privacy would be all but impossible and familiarity all but unavoidable. That had the dowagers of Fifth Avenue wagging their heads more than the equally dread possibility of her losing her life altogether. Even if her father's little yacht won, their reasoning went, Candace Stimson could only lose her reputation and any hopes for marriage ruined.

The male yacht club oligarchies involved in the race were no more keen to see her on her way to the starting line. Other than her sex, she was really no different from many of the guests aboard other yachts that morning: another child of inherited wealth and privilege. Yet her sex alone made her a liability. In their thinking, if a woman finished the race—win or lose—it rather materially diluted the whole manly achievement. If she were injured or killed, they would be crucified for allowing her to enter.

Most sailors in the race looked on her as an ill omen, plain and simple. It was a common superstition among seamen at the time. Women and priests were thought to be unlucky passengers on board ship. Priests, because of their black robes and job consigning dead sailors to the deep, presaged death aboard. Women, for some reason, were thought to make the sea angry and presaged gales and storms. In the latter case, the sailors' superstition would prove quite right.

There was really only one constituency who supported Candace Stimson. It was the least likely, most uncompromising one of all: Captain Bohlin and his eleven Gloucestermen. They'd watched her on deck during the *Fleur de Lys*'s sea trials—trials so severe and punishing they left the crew exhausted, but Miss Stimson somehow exuberant. She was certainly no idler. She knew every sail, stay, shroud, halyard, and sheet of the boat; could helm her competently, even in the roughest conditions; and delighted most in driving her fast. She might be a rich man's daughter, but none like they'd ever seen. There was blue water in this blue blood. She showed no fear, only eagerness, about sharing the brutal North Atlantic ordeal the men fully realized lay ahead for the little schooner. More than that, she remembered all their names and, however lowly their station, invariably prefaced them with a respectful "Mr." All those attributes—plus the fact that she was petite, pretty, and announced her presence with fragrance—were more than enough to smite even Gloucestermen. The hard-bitten, sour-smelling fishermen closed ranks around her like brothers. Candace Stimson didn't have to say more. To anybody.

Before the start, a reporter for the *New York American* glimpsed her on the afterdeck of *Fleur de Lys* through his binoculars. She was wearing "a blue mackintosh, a sable boa around her neck, a soft white felt storm hat on her head and a huge bunch of American Beauty roses in her arms," some of which the reporter couldn't help noting "were buttonholed in her lapel man-style." It was a last, parting shot from the press that there was surely something unfeminine about a woman competing in a man's race. The dislike was mutual. According to the same reporter, the moment Candace Stimson saw the press tug *Eugene Moran* approach "with a score of cameras levelled at her—before her picture could be taken—she disappeared down the companionway."

She didn't reappear on deck until the tug was ½ mile away. When she did, the mackintosh, sable boa, and roses were gone. Only the storm hat remained. Like the rest of the *Fleur*'s crew, she was wearing oilskins.

Charlie Barr had spent the morning taking on and stowing 5 tons of pig lead. He still wasn't satisfied with *Atlantic*'s ballast. In fact, he was fuming about it. The instant the race had been postponed the day before, he'd sent an urgent message for extra ballast to be brought down to Sandy Hook at first light. Because of dense morning fog, the tug *Nonpareil* didn't arrive with it until 10:00 A.M.— barely an hour before *Atlantic* was scheduled to be towed out to the starting line.

Unluckily, she showed up at exactly the same time as the tug *Runyon*, come to top off *Atlantic*'s water tanks. Barr found himself engaged in a Chinese fire drill: speaking to two thrashing tugs alongside while simultaneously directing three working parties—one getting under way; one filling water tanks; and another, formed in a bucket brigade, furiously passing some two hundred 50-pound lead ingots below. It must have been professionally mortifying for him, making such obvious preparations in front of everybody at the last minute. What's more, thanks to Marshall, he had only twenty-four able-bodied seamen to do it all. Shipping and stowing the all-important ballast and water took priority, leaving but a handful of men to ready *Atlantic* for sea.

In the midst of this studiously directed confusion, the ship's crisply attired chief steward, Theodore Bell, stepped forward and offered his services. He and his fellow African Americans—stewards G. E. Perry, James White, and Percival Marucheau—weren't sailors. They were aboard strictly to serve Marshall and his six guests. But they knew a halyard from a sheet and a hawser from an anchor chain and could haul either just as well, if not better, than any other men. As the tugs cast off, all four white-jacketed stewards were seen smartly hauling up *Atlantic*'s huge, heavy mainsail.

The moment *Hamburg* cleared Sandy Hook, the fetch of the easterly breeze blowing in from the sea rolled back the morning fog. It revealed a sight that took Tietjens' breath away. In *Hamburg*'s wake, the entire racing fleet was moving in solemn, majestic procession out toward Sandy Hook Lightship. He'd never seen anything like it. No one had. Ten of the largest, fastest, and undoubtedly most opulent yachts ever built in line ahead. They dwarfed the tugs towing them. With their towering, raked masts; jutting bowsprits; long, lean, sweeping hulls; and clipper bows, they looked to Tietjens like "a fleet of greyhounds" emerging from the mist to do battle.

Looming immediately astern of *Hamburg* was the tug *John Bouker*, towing the enormous, white-hulled *Valhalla*, followed by the white-hulled topsail schooner *Sunbeam*—both flying the White Ensign of the Royal Navy and signature of the Royal Yacht Squadron. Then came Commodore Tod's jaunty, green-topped schooner *Thistle*, under the Atlantic Yacht Club's burgee, in tow of the tug *Unity*. Little *Ailsa*, flying the burgee of the New York Yacht Club, was next, towed by the tugboat *Fred Dalzell*, and behind her the tug towing the Corinthian Yacht Club of Philadelphia's white-hulled schooner *Hildegarde*. In her wake, the tug *Fireproof* hauled the Indian Harbor Yacht Club's sleek, black-hulled schooner *Endymion*, holder of the transatlantic record. The black-hulled, three-masted schooner *Utowana* followed in tow of another Moran tug; then the black-hulled, three-masted schooner *Atlantic* in tow of *Nonpareil*,—the New York Yacht Club burgee snapping over both ships. After them came the tug *DeWitt Ivins* towing the New York Yacht Club's big, black-hulled bark *Apache.*

The only yacht not under tow was the smallest in the race. Dr. Stimson's *Fleur de Lys,* struck by a mud scow in the fog the day before, had been hastily repaired and was back showing 40 feet of new, unpainted bulwarks and planking on her side. Captain Bohlin, the Gloucester fishing skipper, eschewed tugs and had decided to sail her out to the starting line despite the headwind. Through binoculars, Tietjens watched one of her crewman climb high aloft to snap on a topsail sheet. He had on his rubber boots. Tietjens was momentarily lost in admiration. Fishermen, he marveled—the only sailors in the world who kept their rubber boots on even when going up to the masthead. It was very theatrical—typically American—but pointless in the end. Tacking to and fro, *Fleur de Lys* soon fell so far behind that she accepted a tow from one of the chartered spectator tugs.

Led by *Hamburg,* the stately column proceeded 6 miles out to sea to Sandy Hook Lightship, a white, rust-smeared "No. 51" painted on her red topsides. The ship's prominent lighthouse mast would mark the western end of the starting line. The tug *Vigilant,* its deckhouse charred from the fire the day before, with the race committee and judges aboard, chugged ½ mile due east of her and dropped anchor. At once she hoisted the burgee of the Imperial Yacht Club at Kiel: a pointed white pennant with two broad black bands—one perpendicular, one horizontal, the imperial crown of Germany superposed at their point of crossing. It was to be—start to finish—very much the Kaiser's race.

This made the starting line due east and west and, as the wind was about due east, meant that all the yachts, even the square-riggers *Valhalla, Sunbeam,* and *Apache,* could fairly cross the line by the wind. Yet the ½ mile of open water separating the committee boat from the lightship made a frighteningly narrow gateway for eleven large competing yachts to pass. The usual formula for establishing the length of a starting line is to multiply the combined length of all the vessels in the racing fleet at least one and a quarter times. In total, the Kaiser's Cup racers measured 1,800 feet, so a starting line ½ mile long was only 250 yards more than the bare minimum.

Indeed, some firsthand observers claimed it was only ¼ mile long. Whichever the case, in the light headwind, the square-riggers—which coincidentally included the two big British entries and America's largest yacht, oceangoing vessels that were real threats in an ocean race—would be hard pressed to find seaway enough to thread such a needle. Whether this was the intent of the German-run race committee boat, of course, no one knows. Knowing it was the Kaiser's race, however, raises the question.

A fearsome jumble of fore-and-aft boats proceeded well eastward of the committee boat before dropping their towlines, to be able to run back with the wind when the starting signal was given. This pack included the yawl *Ailsa* and not fewer than six schooners (*Hildegarde, Hamburg, Utowana, Endymion, Atlantic,* and *Thistle*). The bigger square-rigged vessels—*Valhalla, Apache,* and *Sunbeam*—hovered northward of the starting line. Tiny *Fleur de Lys,* among the last to grudgingly accept a towline and first to cast it off, lay somewhat west of them. Sails began to go up at once on all the racers. Swarms of sailors hauled on the halyards; others scrambled aloft, shaking out canvas fold on fold until the tall vessels were cloaked in clouds of white. Tietjens watched the sails on the square-riggers—allowed to use steam power to hoist them—go up "as if someone had pushed a button." He wondered what would happen when they all made for the short line at once.

Hamburg was maneuvering to the leeward of the committee boat when—precisely at 12:00 P.M.—a jet of smoke broke from her port side and the roar of the warning gun sounded over the water. Every racing captain in the American fleet suddenly headed up to the line. Tietjens supposed they couldn't help it. They were, after all, professional racing skippers unable to rid themselves of the impression that this was an offshore jaunt of 30 miles to windward and return—not a race of 3,000 miles or more. Their pride had them all jockeying for the best position to attack the line. They quickly crowded out *Hamburg*. Once they'd found their place, they killed their headway and awaited the preparatory gun.

It sounded at 12:10 P.M. For an interminable five minutes longer, the whole fleet hung fire—luffing motionless, drifting, or nudging nearer the line. The easterly gentle 6-to-7-knot breeze held steady, seas smooth, waves 2 feet high, with only an occasional, lopping crest. The skies remained completely overcast, heavy with low-lying clouds threatening rain. The quiet was pronounced. Tietjens could plainly see the owners and guests on the afterdecks of other yachts, all of them wrapped in overcoats, some smoking, some looking through binoculars. All of them waiting.

When the starting gun boomed at 12:15 P.M., it felt like a door slamming in Tietjens's face. With *Hamburg* scarcely under way, two American boats, *Ailsa* and *Hildegarde,* were already atop the starting line. The suddeness of it had the *New York Sun*'s reporter mixing metaphors to keep up: they were "running nose to nose like hounds in leash, both ripping through the tumble of waves as smoothly as knives would rip silk." They crested the starting line side by side, "their bowsprits rising and falling on the same seas, so that nobody except those stationed on the committee boat could tell which was in the lead." In fact, *Ailsa*'s stem had passed but 16 feet over the line when *Hildegarde*'s bowsprit surged over it, too. Some observers said they crossed simultaneously. The judges on *Vigilant* clocked *Ailsa* over the line a razor-thin five seconds ahead of *Hildegarde*—just twenty-nine seconds after the starting gun.

That was all the time it took for Lem Miller to show his stern to the whole racing fleet: in front of the world press and every major yacht owner and skipper in America and abroad—especially Wilson Marshall and Charlie Barr. He surely would have relished the *New York Daily Tribune*'s estimation: "The fact that *Ailsa* outmaneuvered *Atlantic* in the start is a distinct feather in the cap of Lem Miller, Captain Barr's old mate, who was captain of the *Atlantic* last. It is also indicative of the underground rivalry which marks the contesting boats." There was nothing, in fact, underground about the animosity between the hired guns skippering the American yachts. At the line, they attacked each other like berserk Celts.

Atlantic, under all plain sail with Barr at the helm, charged over the line only thirty-one seconds after *Ailsa*. The big three-masted schooner was making surprising speed in the 7-knot breeze. A reporter on the press boat wrote she came "slicing through the waves, with gigantic power portrayed in every swing of her long, shearing hull." Rounding the committee boat, Barr set his sights on

The start of the 1905 Kaiser's Cup race, off Sandy Hook, New Jersey. The shortness of the starting line is evident in the crowd of yachts endeavoring to cross it.

Ailsa, dogging her wake, only three ship lengths (552 feet) behind her. Remarkably—sixty seconds after the gun—three American fore-and-aft schooners were over the line. A *fourth* American schooner, *Endymion,* swept over it a minute later.

Tietjens was stunned. *Hamburg,* dubbed by the press "the most dangerous boat in the race," was not looking dangerous in the least. She was fifth over the line—a disappointing two and a half minutes after the gun. Hot in pursuit, just thirty seconds behind her, was a *fifth* American schooner: amateur skipper Robert Tod's green-painted *Thistle.*

Cornering around the committee boat, Captain Peters ordered *Hamburg* "squared out rap full"—coming as close to the light headwind as he dared, yet somehow still managing to keep all sails full, without as much as a wrinkle in them. As she came around, Tietjens saw that only about ¼ mile separated *Hamburg* from front-running *Ailsa* to windward, with *Hildegarde, Atlantic,* and *Endymion* in between. It was remarkably close: five big yachts hammering east by southeast, close-hauled on the port tack, in an area no bigger than three football fields. No one had expected it to be so close.

Hanging on *Ailsa*'s lee quarter was gray-whiskered Captain Marsters and *Hildegarde*. Behind her was Captain Barr and *Atlantic,* chased by barrel-chested Captain Loesch at the wheel of transatlantic record-holder *Endymion*. Peters had *Hamburg* at *Endymion*'s heels as *Thistle* nipped at *Hamburg*'s. To Tietjens, however—who, after all, would have to make a personal report to the kaiser—it didn't look at all close. It looked like unfolding disaster. The professional American racing skippers were fast pulling away. Not that Captain Peters seemed to take undue notice. In fact, he didn't seem to be doing much of anything beyond murmuring orders and constantly looking aloft. Tietjens glassed the yachts in front and immediately behind. From the halyards of each wagged the American flag.

For the contestants still behind the starting line, the view was infinitely worse. Some twelve minutes after the gun, three late-starters closed on it at once. Crowding toward the ½-mile-wide bottleneck between the committee boat and Sandy Hook Lightship, they were more or less on a collision course. Bespectacled Captain Bohlin, who'd had last-minute trouble with a stuck foresail halyard on *Fleur de Lys,* was making up for lost time. He drove the little fore-and-aft schooner, close-hauled on a port tack, straight from the northwestern end of the starting line toward the race committee tug *Vigilant* at the eastern end. This took her right in front of the big, oncoming three-masted schooner *Utowana* and the even bigger ship *Valhalla*.

Lord Crawford, on the afterdeck of his *Valhalla,* watched the whole thing unfold with remarkable detachment. He was perched in the mizzen shrouds, dressed as he habitually was at sea: misshapen white commander's cap on his head, in his bright yellow oilskin slicker with comfortable, threadbare carpet slippers on his feet. Captain Caws had the 648-ton, 245-foot-long square-rigger under twenty-two sails—far less than the fifty or more she could carry, but all that could be kept filled when essentially beating to windward in the gentle easterly breeze. Yet with her massive forward momentum building, she was moving toward the line like a juggernaut from the north. On an almost parallel course, slightly eastward of her and with all plain sail set, was Allison Armour's 267-ton, 190-foot-long three-masted schooner *Utowana*. All three vessels—*Fleur de Lys*, *Utowana* and *Valhalla*—descended on *Vigilant*.

Bohlin, whose smaller boat could sail faster and closer to the wind, reached it first; passing shaving-close to its stern, barely inside the line. The bigger boats, aiming for the same mark, either miscalculated or were thrown off course avoiding *Fleur de Lys*. Just ahead of *Valhalla*, Crawford saw *Utowana* heading squarely for the press tug *Eugene Moran*—off the bow of the committee boat and clearly outside the starting line. Captain J. H. Crawford, skipper of *Utowana*, came running forward along her deck, howling, "Back out o' there, *Moran!* Get out or we'll be into you! Get her *out* of the way!" As the tug reversed engines and tried to back away, *Utowana* came "bowling on," according to a reporter, "with water shearing from her bow in cascades." It was very nearly a disastrous collision. *Utowana* cleaved so close to the backpedaling *Moran* that her bow wave broke over the heavy mats on the tug's bow.

Crawford's detachment dissolved when he realized that *Valhalla* was practically in *Utowana*'s wake. She was so close behind, in fact, that the reporter on the *Moran* described her "like a big sheep following a little one." There was no stopping her. The *Moran* escaped being run down a second time only because Captain Caws veered easterly, into the wind, to avoid her. They came stupendously—grazingly—close. The shadows of *Valhalla*'s long yards swept over the escaping tug like a predatory bird. The big ship's boiling wake left the tug bouncing like a cork. By passing on the wrong side of the committee boat, however, both *Utowana* and *Valhalla* had fouled the starting line. A shrieking whistle on *Vigilant* sounded a loud and long note, recalling them to come around and cross the line properly. For a vessel the size of *Valhalla*, with the wind as light as it was, that could take hours. For the time being, Lord Crawford was—in a most embarrassing fashion—out of the race.

All the milling boats, smoke, whistles, and recall signals at the starting line forced Lord Brassey and *Sunbeam* to keep clear of the chaos for five full minutes. When *Sunbeam* finally rounded the committee boat at a sedate 4 knots, she was the next-to-last yacht over the line—seventeen minutes after the gun. By that time the kaiser's *Hamburg*—the one boat he most wanted to catch and that in his log he parenthetically identified as "ex-Rainbow" to indicate its British parentage—was already 2 miles out to sea.

He was not in the least concerned about that. He was a circumnavigator, used to long passages. The little fore-and-afters across the line in such a frenzy would soon effervesce. Once fairly offshore and running free, the stoutly built square-riggers would have their say. *Valhalla's* blundering, on the other hand, was vexing. Before the race he'd called her "a true mistress of the seas," and now she was shamefacedly doubling back to the starting line. Figured with *Caronia's* grounding, it made for a terrible show of British seamanship and the flag.

The big square-rigged American bark *Apache* was the last yacht over the line. Nobody could understand why until its neophyte owner, Wall Street heir Edmond Randolph—intoxicated by excite-

The American bark *Apache* was the last yacht over the starting line. By some accounts, her owner was drunk.

ment or drink—swung his hat at the judges on the committee boat. "Don't worry," he shouted, "we'll get there!"

All eyes on *Hamburg*, however, were looking ahead. Tietjens watched Captain Peters methodically run up on *Endymion*. Within an hour of the start, the larger, heavier German schooner overtook and passed her. Soon after, she hissed past *Hildegarde*. At about 2:30 P.M. Peters came up leeward of *Ailsa* and passed her in turn. Tietjens was ecstatic—at least as far as the ranking director of the Hamburg-America Line and the kaiser's personal representative could allow himself to be. He offered a cigar to Captain Peters, who replied he would smoke it later; he had his hands full at the moment.

The only vessel left in front of *Hamburg*, about 2 miles distant, was the fleeting *Atlantic*. She was making very good speed—Tietjens estimated 10 knots. With a longer waterline than *Hamburg*, spreading canvas on three masts to *Hamburg*'s two, she looked uncatchable. But Peters quickly ran up on her. At times, in fact, he ran up so close behind her that her patent log (paid out from her stern to measure her speed) almost touched *Hamburg*'s foaming stem. Throughout the afternoon, Peters charged up even with *Atlantic* and plunged ahead a few lengths, only to see Barr bring the big three-master back abeam of him and spur it a few lengths into the lead again.

By 3:30 P.M. the easy wind out of the east had strengthened to a "fresh breeze," meaning 17 to 21 knots. The seas were making up in pounding, close-ranked 4-to-8-foot-waves. Spray drenched everything on deck as both schooners hammered to windward in a flat-out board-by-board (tack-by-tack) race. At 4:30 P.M., with the ships still locked together, *Hamburg*'s jib topsail suddenly split with a resounding boom. Peters immediately hauled it down and ran up another. But in the time it took to do it, Barr and *Atlantic* skated away.

Half an hour later, Tietjens was astonished to see *Atlantic*—well ahead—suddenly shorten sail. She hauled down *her* jib topsail, followed by her main and mizzen staysails, steered closer to the wind, and slowed to a pedestrian 5.5 knots. He couldn't understand it. But the lack of time Charlie Barr had before the race to get to know *Atlantic* had showed itself for one fateful moment. Fairly, the canvas Barr hauled down, according to yachting correspondent Julian Hawthorne, who watched, "could not be kept full on the wind and was better on deck." Captain Peters, on the other hand, had skippered *Hamburg* for three years and knew without thinking what canvas she best carried racing to windward. He pressed on every inch.

At about 5:30 P.M. *Hamburg* descended on the big, black-hulled *Atlantic* like an owl upon larger prey. At 6:00 P.M. *Hamburg* neatly crossed her wake and hauled abeam of her—a scant 50 yards to windward. At that distance, everybody on the deck of either ship could plainly see and hear everything going on aboard the other. Yet other than grating winches, creaking sheets and the thrashing of their wakes, there was absolute, stony silence. Neither crew cheered. Neither captain spoke to the other vessel. *Hamburg*—whose designer, George L. Watson, never produced a slow boat and acknowledged *Hamburg* to be one of the fastest large racing yachts he ever turned out—grazed past the bigger American auxiliary yacht and left *Atlantic* behind on her starboard quarter. The figures on her deck grew smaller and smaller. The ensign of the German Imperial Navy snapped at them.

At 9:15 P.M., through his binoculars, Tietjens could see only the pinprick sidelights of the *Atlantic* quickly sinking on the western horizon. At about the same time, however, the fresh breeze abruptly died to a puffy 4 knots and a dense fog set in. Yet as *Hamburg* vanished into the mists on the first day's run of the long 3,000-mile struggle from Sandy Hook to the Lizard, Tietjens and everybody else aboard was exuberant. "*Hamburg* is leading," he penned in his log, "that is the principal thing—to the great surprise of the Americans."

Indeed, when NYYC member Edward C. Bennett's steam yacht *Oneida*—which had followed the racers farthest out to sea—returned to New York with the news, the Americans were shocked. *Hamburg* had come from behind like a dagger and deftly disposed of four of the fastest boats in America, in conditions more favorable to the American boats than herself. The fact that she had "a good lead" over *Atlantic* at nightfall was ominous.

More ominous was the fact that the Germans—whom American yachtsmen had publicly lampooned for their "lubberliness"—had whipped the best professional yacht skippers and crews money could buy. It is no great leap of imagination to divine the conversation in the cigar-smoke-filled Model Room at the New York Yacht Club that evening. Loesch was at the helm of the yacht holding the transatlantic record, for God's sake. The headwind and conditions had all favored Miller's *Ailsa*. And what, in God's name, was wrong with Charlie Barr and *Atlantic?* The three-time America's Cup winner, at the wheel of the fastest, odds-on favorite in the race, outsailed by a lieutenant-captain in the German navy aboard a secondhand yacht? Others no doubt hazarded the opinion that a close start meant nothing in an ocean race of 3,000 miles. No doubt they were just as quickly silenced by the admonition to remember the 1877 race—when but an hour and a half separated the winner from the loser. The news doused the enthusiasm of the NYYC like a cold slop of sea.

When the news was cabled to Berlin, there was jubilation.

CHAPTER 23

In for a Fight

HAMBURG *LEADS IN OCEAN RACE*:
German Yacht Ahead of the Atlantic *at Night-Fall and Going Fast.*

—*New York Herald,*
May 19, 1905

Charlie Barr hated to admit it. Admitting it to Wilson Marshall made it worse. But there was no way around the fact of the thing: Captain Peters had plainly surprised and outsailed him. He knew *Hamburg* was a fast boat, but he hadn't realized how good Peters and his German navy crew was. The outward passage to the States had finely salted them. They'd worked the schooner like they were grown part of it; fluidly, instinctively taking advantage of every condition that suited her. It was clear that they knew how to get the utmost out of *Hamburg* on the wind. They'd damned well shown him, and Lem, Jimmy Loesch, and Marsters, too. Running free in the open ocean, it was a sure bet they knew how to make her go a helluva lot faster. Charlie, on the other hand, was still getting to know *Atlantic,* and he wasn't happy about doing it in a transatlantic race.

Nobody aboard was happy that first night at sea. The cooks and stewards, anticipating a winning start, had laid on a lavish supper for the afterguard, but Marshall and his guests didn't have any appetite for celebration. Most of the food went unappreciated, though there was a lot of serious grumbling, drinking, and cigar smoking in *Atlantic*'s grand saloon. After dark, the white-painted New York Yacht Club steam schooner *Oneida* ghosted alongside with the news everybody dreaded but already knew. *Hamburg* was in the van, some 10 miles ahead when last sighted and coursing handsomely eastward. The first watch (8:00 P.M. to midnight) got double work. Besides making sail changes and working ship, Barr had them laboriously restowing the 5 tons of pig lead hurriedly shipped that morning until he was satisfied. The weather deteriorated hourly: intermittent downpours, ever-diminishing wind, and thickening fog that finally set up into a perfect porridge. Barr was obliged to continuously sound *Atlantic*'s fog signal—one echoing sound bomb followed by horn blasts in a 4-3-1 sequence.

At about midnight the wind died almost completely. Barr could barely maintain steerageway. At 1:00 A.M. he tacked *Atlantic* to northward, looking for wind. At 1:45 A.M. he tacked ship back to southward but could find no breeze. This peripatetic exercise went on all night yet led to nothing. By 4:00 A.M. Charlie disgustedly logged *Atlantic*'s speed at ½ knot (0.57 mile per hour)—for all purposes dead in the water, her empty sails slatting back and forth lifelessly.

At first light Marshall and his guests—whose eight hours' sleep had been made impossible by the incessant fog signals—appeared on deck again. They were red-eyed and grumpy, fresh-washed and shaved; all of them in just-pressed dark-blue officers' uniforms and caps except for Marshall, who wore a white-covered commodore's cap. There was little for them to see but flapping canvas and mastheads that vanished into the same fog that obscured every point of the compass.

Marshall's first question, naturally, was how far *Atlantic* had progressed since he and his entourage had retired the night before. "Eleven miles," Barr answered, "with the wind a lot to say about it." Marshall didn't like that, didn't like it at all. It was, without doubt, the slowest eight-hour run he'd ever heard his always fast yacht log. In a transatlantic race that pace—a snail-like average

Select Courses/Daily Fixes

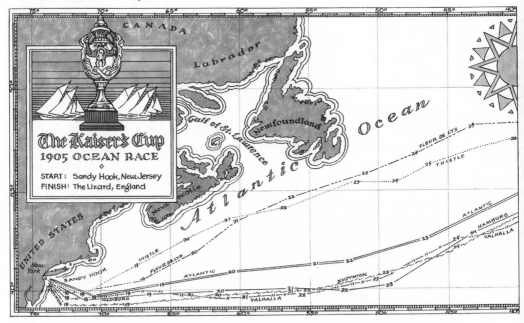

speed of fewer than 50 feet per minute—was disgraceful. Light wind or no wind, he expected more from the renowned and expensive Charlie Barr. He'd spent a fortune on him and refitting *Atlantic*. All he knew positively that morning was that he wasn't getting what he'd paid for. His boat had been beaten at the starting line, beaten in the offshore run that followed, and now was going nowhere at all. He had to endure the chaffing of his guests who, expecting a ride on Pegasus, found themselves hitched to a mule. He left Captain Barr with the admonishment that "we shall have to do much better" and retreated belowdecks. The stewards were serving up a four-course breakfast.

Barr and the morning watch didn't get anything to eat. At about 6:00 A.M. the wind abruptly returned. It shredded the fog, hauled around from the east to the northwest, and made up into a strong breeze (22 to 27 knots or 25 to 31 miles per hour). Barr quietly ordered his nephew, First Mate John Barr, to strike the baby topsail, hoist the bigger No. 1 jib topsail in its place, and haul up the big main topsail and mizzen staysail, too. Under these and all plain

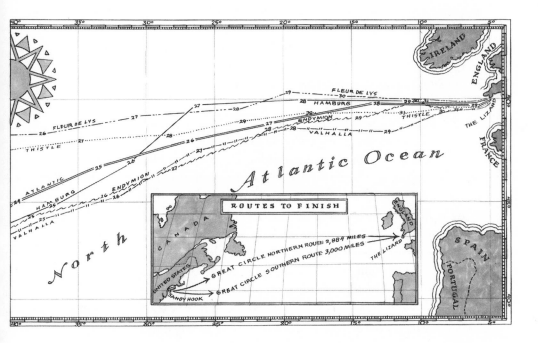

sail, steering east by south, *Atlantic* heeled over sharply and jumped forward at 9 knots (10.35 miles per hour). By 10:00 A.M. she was coursing along at 11¼ knots (12.9 miles per hour) and by noon she was fuming ahead at 13½ knots (15.5 miles per hour).

Marshall and his guests left their luncheon to come up and see. As they did, the lookouts on watch called out a sail on the lee beam, only 3 miles distant. All binoculars on deck fixed on her. It was a two-masted schooner. She was flying day signal flags—international code letters RMVH. It was Captain Peters and *Hamburg*.

Adolph Tietjens had retired to his cabin shortly after he'd seen the last lights of *Atlantic* fade on the western horizon the night before. He'd slept wonderfully, either lulled by *Hamburg*'s lead or the pacific seas. At 4:30 A.M., however, he was nearly hurled out of his bunk. He heard the thunder of boots as all hands turned out on deck. When he got topside, *Hamburg* was dead in the water, nose to a snapping 21-knot northwesterly wind.

He could not imagine what was the matter—until the ship's

massive mainboom swung out of the darkness and nearly took his head off. Hermann Vollmers, the first mate, shouted that one of three new wire straps attaching the mainsheet to the boom had snapped. The strain on the other two proved too much: they'd snapped like pistol shots. The boom, still full-sailed, lashed lethally just 4 feet above the deck.

Captain Peters had no choice but to heave to. Both watches worked furiously to capture the flailing boom and repair the damage. It took an hour for the men to fix. During that time, *Hamburg* went nowhere. As soon as the job was done, however, the wind vanished and an impenetrable fog descended. For the next six hours *Hamburg* wallowed in a gentle swell—blind.

At about noon, the fog lifted long enough for Peters to shoot a sight. *Hamburg* had logged 142 miles since the start of the race. Considering the headwinds of the day before and the time taken to repair the mainsheet that night, this was cause for congratulations. It did not last long. Through patchy fog, the watch was startled to sight *two* schooner yachts: one 3 miles astern to leeward and another—square abeam—3 miles to windward and drawing ahead. Maddeningly, the shifting fog made it impossible to identify either vessel.

Tietjens put his binoculars back in their case. He didn't need them to see that the accident had cost *Hamburg* the lead.

Charlie Barr could plainly see and identify *Hamburg,* yet completely missed sighting any other yacht. At any rate, his eyes were riveted on *Hamburg.* He couldn't figure out what she'd done with the lead she'd held the night before. Perhaps she'd lost the dying easterly wind before *Atlantic,* or perhaps *Atlantic* had caught the northwesterly wind first, or—most likely—she'd had some kind of trouble. It didn't matter. He was abeam of her, had the weather gauge, a spanking breeze off his quarter, and in short order put *Atlantic* into warp drive. In addition to all lower sail, he hauled up her light racing sails—everything from balloon staysails to her huge spinnaker. Under this mountain of overstretched canvas, all *Atlantic*'s plain sails trimmed flat, he had *Hamburg* astern in the haze by 1:00 P.M. By 5:00 P.M. she had vanished from sight.

Marshall and his guests commenced celebrating at once. Barr

didn't join them. The night was fine, almost cloudless, moonlit, polestar shining bright, sea smooth and *Atlantic* coursing ahead at 10 knots. When the middle watch (12:00 A.M. to 4:00 A.M.) came on duty, he remained on deck. Below in the saloon, he heard the rattle of ice in buckets, popping corks, and laughter. It was still going on when he went to his cabin to catch a few hours' sleep.

The morning after proved a sobering one for Marshall and his guests. The wind had shifted again and gotten up smartly—blowing straight out of the west, almost dead astern—at 17 to 21 knots. This was by no means *Atlantic*'s fastest or most comfortable point of sail. Before following seas, the boat plowed ahead at 10 to 12 knots, rolling heavily, often wildly at times. For anyone with a pounding hangover, this amounted to agony. Barr seemed to enjoy inflicting it, hauling up more and more canvas. "Running free, gentlemen," he told those of the afterguard who ventured on deck.

The North Atlantic quickly and loudly reminded everyone who was running things. At 9:00 A.M. the wind split and carried off the main topsail with an awful screech. The crew fetched a spare from the sail locker, bent it to its heavy gaff, and hauled it up again—just as *Atlantic*'s huge, wind-stretched spinnaker exploded, torn into a dozen fragments. Barr didn't risk running up its replacement, but he wasn't about to let it slow him down either. Instead he ran up *Atlantic*'s big squaresail and raffee to take its place. An hour later, the rolling got so bad Barr was forced to take in *Atlantic*'s mainsail to prevent its being slatted to pieces. But every stitch of canvas that could be kept full was kept aloft.

For the rest of the day this caused Marshall and his guests a good deal of seasickness accompanied by serious secondthoughts. They'd experienced the damage and the discomfort the ocean could inflict on a *good* morning. What the coming days might bring was probably more than they wanted to think about. The great adventure of a transatlantic race suddenly seemed less an adventure and more a hair-whitening trial than they imagined. It did not seem that way to Charlie Barr. He was just getting warmed up.

At dawn on May 19, Tietjens felt better. *Hamburg* had reeled off more than 50 miles since midnight, making over 8 knots in variable winds and fog. The wind had hauled around to the west and freshened, the sky was crystal clear, and there was brilliant sunshine. Whatever vessel was ahead of them couldn't be far ahead, and Tietjens fully expected to see it on the eastern horizon. Instead daylight revealed a yacht to the *west,* square astern of *Hamburg,* just 2 miles distant and steadily moving up. It was the *last* yacht, other than *Atlantic,* Tietjens wanted to see. It was American captain Loesch and the *Endymion,* holders of the transatlantic record.

He came up very fast, his big spinnaker and balloon jib set, while *Hamburg* was under only her plain sails. On first sighting the American, Peters hauled up his light racing sails, too. But by 11:00 A.M. Loesch had closed the gap and the two yachts were neck-and-neck.

By noon the wind and the sea increased to the point that Loesch hauled down his spinnaker and set his squaresail instead. At once Peters followed suit. Under this canvas, however, Loesch soon passed *Hamburg,* ½ mile to windward, and throughout the afternoon gradually increased his lead to 1 mile, then 2, then 3. Crestfallen, Tietjens watched her race away. Nothing Captain Peters did closed the lengthening gap between them.

But at 1:00 P.M., to everyone's shock, *Endymion*'s taut-trimmed squaresail and raffee suddenly collapsed. The long foresail yard carrying both big sails snapped in half—as if a perfectly aimed round shot had hit it. She slowed immediately, seamen teeming up her shrouds like ants. Captain Peters didn't hesitate an instant taking advantage of her distress. Despite the 17-to-21-knot breeze blowing, he ordered *Hamburg*'s huge spinnaker hauled up again. Bowling ahead, at times making 13 knots, he ran up to *Endymion* as she was making repairs and passed her.

As he did, he saw Loesch furiously running up his spinnaker again and his light racing sails, too. Both yachts fumed forward almost due east, on parallel courses, averaging 12 knots apiece. All night the two were close enough to clearly see each other's lights. All night Peters managed to hold the lead.

At daylight, however, with a light westerly breeze of 7 to 10 knots blowing, *Endymion* was still there, shadowing *Hamburg*'s easterly course, not more than 1 mile behind. By 9:00 A.M. Captain

Loesch overtook her and knifed ahead on *Hamburg*'s starboard side. For the next five hours he doggedly lengthened his lead, leaving *Hamburg* 7 miles astern. At about 4:30 P.M. the wind veered to the southwest, blew harder, and brought squalls and pouring rain. Loesch hauled down his light racing sails. Peters didn't. With "all headsails drawing nicely," *Hamburg* logged 12 knots, then 13, then 13½ knots, and swiftly overtook *Endymion.* "Left *Endymion* in grand style," Peters wrote in his log, "and before dusk she was nearly out of sight." Tietjens relievedly noted; "Before twilight set in, lost sight of *Endymion* astern."

They had now neatly dispatched Captain Loesch. It only remained to catch and do the same to Captain Barr.

Charlie Barr wasn't worried about *Hamburg* or any other yacht in the eastbound racing fleet that night. He was too worried about the westbound steamers that had been coming at him like missiles all day.

The first near-miss happened at 1:30 P.M. Riding a strong westerly wind, *Atlantic* was steering east by south, logging almost 13 knots (15 miles per hour) and enduring an incredibly bumpy ride. She was bucking a heavy head sea (an easterly swell running contrary to the westerly wind) and "plunging badly," as Barr put it. Water was taken aboard forward, and the decks washed fore and aft. Glimpsing anything in such churning seas was difficult. Lookouts in the shrouds had barely shouted "Ship ho!" when a steamship burst out of the swells just 800 yards broad off the port bow. On her smoking funnel Barr could clearly see the insignia of the Red Star Line, one of J. P. Morgan's shipping companies. She cleaved past at 18 knots in one direction as *Atlantic* knifed at 13 knots in the opposite direction. The encounter happened so fast and lasted so briefly that, though Barr exchanged signals with her, he couldn't get her name before both vessels lost sight of each other in the jumbled seas. The adrenaline rush of the incident lingered far longer.

Four hours later, almost dead ahead, some 1,700 yards away, a larger steamship came charging out of the easterly swell. She showed four masts, a tall funnel, a towering white superstructure, and was fuming straight toward them at an estimated 16 knots. Barr immediately ordered *Atlantic*'s helmsman to bear off and signaled his identity and course to the oncoming steamer. In the time it took her to reply, her full dimensions became frighteningly evident: more than 600-feet long, 8 stories high and more than 13,000 tons. It was the American passenger liner *Minnehaha,* a notoriously unlucky ship no seaman wanted to get near. On her maiden voyage in 1900 she'd rammed and sunk the tug *American* before she'd cleared New York Harbor (her luck never improved: in 1910 she grounded in the Scilly Isles and in 1917 she was torpedoed by a German U-boat and sank in four minutes with virtually all hands). To Barr's amazement she altered her course to come near enough to *Atlantic* to allow the passengers lining her rails to get a good look at one of the Kaiser's Cup racers.

At dusk, an hour and a half later, Barr was almost run down by the westbound Dutch steamer *La Campania.*

After dark, severe squalls, followed by rains so heavy it was at times impossible to see the bow from the stern, much less oncoming ships, forced him to shorten sail and slow down. By 9:00 P.M., however, the heavy weather had passed over, and Barr hoisted all sail again—racing into the inky darkness at speeds of up to a fantastic 19 knots (almost 22 miles per hour). It was the first time Barr had experienced what *Atlantic* could really do. He'd never experienced anything like it, even on *Reliance. Atlantic* was feeding on the wind and, even at 19 knots, was hungry for more. It was exhilarating, of course, but a very risky thing to do at night, so near the westbound steamer track. Barr ignored that. He had a favorable, stiff southwest wind, bad weather behind him, and *Atlantic* was reeling off knots. He drove her east by south as fast as she could go.

About an hour later, however, the lookout in the port bow reported engine noises. Nobody else could hear it. An instant later a blinding white masthead light split the dark like a lighthouse, only 1,000 yards abeam. A second, blinding masthead light showed an instant later, followed by a red-eyed port running light. All at once—echoing like an oncoming freight train—came the syncopated sound of throbbing engines. Within a minute, a wall of yellow porthole and promenade deck lights rose into full view off *Atlantic*'s port side. Faintly, but distinctly, the watch heard an orchestra, laughter, and conversation.

Charlie didn't need binoculars to make out "a large, two-funneled White Star steamer, bound west." She was closing at more than 20 knots. Quite clearly she didn't see *Atlantic*'s Coston lights. Barr frantically transmitted his identity, course, and speed by signal lamp but got no acknowledgment. The liner—orchestra playing gaily—ripped past without altering course, scarcely ½ mile away, without ever seeing *Atlantic*. In her wake she left only acrid coal fumes.

When the middle watch (12:00 A.M. to 4:00 A.M.) took over, Barr remained on deck. Far from slowing down, he ordered *Atlantic*'s big squaresail hoisted and continued racing into the void.

After leaving *Endymion* in her wake at dusk on May 20, *Hamburg* was abandoned by the wind. On the afternoon of May 21, it was calm. By 8:30 P.M. Tiejens wrote there was "not sufficient wind to fill the sails, which were flapping in the swell." Peters fumed in his log, "A miserable day for racing." On May 22 it was no better. In the morning the wind was northerly and very light. In the afternoon it went dead calm, the seas flat.

Hamburg, however, found herself surrounded by a new peril: a vast school of whales, some spouting, some slumbering on the surface, like a barnacle-covered boulder field all around. Tietjens had no idea what kind of whales they were, except "exceeding large." Whether that meant 100-foot-long, 150-ton blue whales or 60-foot-long, 50-ton sperm whales, or 40-ton right whales or 30-ton bottlenose whales was rather immaterial. Crashing into any of these sleeping leviathans could easily stove-in the wood-planked *Hamburg*. The danger quickly passed. Swimming languidly east, the whales soon left the kaiser's windless yacht in their wakes.

On the morning of May 22 Lord Crawford never felt better. He usually did when he was at sea. His asthma seemed to go away. The business of taking observations and plotting *Valhalla*'s position was endlessly engrossing. Driving the square-rigged ship in mid-ocean under a freshening southwest breeze was invigorating. But the view from deck at 10:00 A.M. was a positive tonic. On the eastern horizon he could see the American schooner *Endymion* and the yawl *Ailsa*.

It was enough to make him forget the mortifying embarrassment of fouling the starting line in front of the whole world. Coming about and returning to cross the line again had cost *Valhalla* almost two hours, during which every yacht but *Utowana,* which also fouled the line, had disappeared from sight. But the incident had served to boil and settle Captain Caws and his sixty-man crew into a pot of very strong brew. The first day (noon-to-noon) out of Sandy Hook, fighting unfavorable headwinds and fog, they'd managed to claw out 136 miles of easting. The next day, conditions little better, they logged 162; the next, 225; and the fourth day, 256 miles at a very fast average speed of 10.6 knots. *Valhalla*'s new sails drew tight as boards. Crawford's homemade electronic position plotter worked like a charm.

When *Endymion* and *Ailsa* fetched into sight on the morning of the fifth day, Crawford ordered an issue of grog for all hands. They'd certainly earned it. The speedy *Ailsa* had been the first boat over the starting line and the sleek transatlantic recordholder *Endymion* the fourth. Overtaking them both—on the same fine morning—convinced Crawford and every man aboard *Valhalla* that they were not only very much back in the race but also very close to seizing the lead.

By afternoon, however, the southwest breeze diminished from fresh to faint and the big *Valhalla* slowed like a locomotive running out of steam. The far lighter, smaller American yachts grew smaller and smaller on the eastern horizon. At dusk they had disappeared entirely.

Charlie Barr and *Atlantic* fared worse than the whale-serenaded *Hamburg* on May 22. Variable, confused winds weakened from light to very light and occasionally dead calm. In the twenty-four-hour run ending at noon that day, *Atlantic* had logged a miserable 112 nautical miles—by far her worst day's run, fully 48 miles *less* than *Hamburg* during the same period. Neither yacht knew it, but they were steering near-parallel courses about 120 miles apart.

Atlantic, to the north and steering a somewhat shorter great circle route, found the wind—and danger—first.

In his log that day, Barr paid as much attention to the air and the water temperature as he did to the wind and the barometer. North of 40 degrees latitude, he took the former religiously—every hour upon the hour, in fact. It was a primitive way to predict the presence of ice, but the only one at the time and, for all its short-comings, an effective one. At 10:00 A.M. on May 22 the air temperature was a relatively balmy 63°F and the sea 57°F. By 10:00 P.M. both had plummeted more than 20 degrees. The night air registered a raw 37°F and the black water a deadly 35°F.

In water below 40°F, a person can lose consciousness in as few as fifteen minutes as their core body temperature—and life—quite literally hemorrhage away in the cold. Nobody called it hypothermia in 1905. The educated called it exposure. Seamen called it "cold locker." *Atlantic*'s Scandinavian crew called it "gone to Ran." In Viking mythology Ran was the wife of Aegir, god of the icy northern ocean: red-haired and notoriously bad-tempered, she snared the souls of dead sailors in her net like fish. In paralyzing cold water, nothing could save a man overboard from her.

Everyone knew full well that they were closing with ice. It was late May, which, counterintuitively, is the height of the iceberg season in the North Atlantic. Warming spring temperatures freed bergs in hundreds from Greenland waters to ride southward on the Labrador Current and disperse widely over the Grand Banks off Newfoundland like a minefield. And that night *Atlantic* was within 100 miles of the southern reaches of the Banks.

Steering his racing course, Barr had no choice but to pass through the area as quickly as possible. There was no fast route around it. Keeping farther south wouldn't lessen the risk. Prior to the race, the U.S. Hydrographic Office had reported "a great deal of ice as far south this year as the 39th parallel, pushed there by heavy Northers." Going farther north would only make it worse. There was nothing for him to do but hold his course and sail 700 miles easterly, straight through the range of the ice drift.

Shortly after 10:00 P.M., that night, buttoned tight with doubled lookouts, Atlantic was making 11 knots under a light southeast

The complex standing and running rigging of a three-masted schooner is plain in this deck shot of *Atlantic.* Working this web of sheets, lines, and halyards—in pitch darkness, subzero temperatures, and 45-foot seas—was incredibly dangerous. With the mountain of canvas Charlie Barr carried, it was terrifying.

breeze, on a calm sea. Barr had instructed the watch to keep a sharp eye out for breakaway chunks of icebergs called "growlers." Fewer than 16 feet long and showing only 3 feet out of the water, these didn't seem to pose much of a threat to the 184-foot, steel hulled *Atlantic.* But at night, even in a calm sea, they were next to impossible to spot until you were on top of one. Since only a ninth of the total mass of such ice is visible above water level, that meant almost 30 feet lurked unseen below the surface—which was twice as deep as *Atlantic*'s keel. Striking one of these growlers—essentially midocean rocks—at 11 knots could be catastrophic. The three-masted schooner displaced 206 tons, roughly the equivalent of four loaded railroad coal cars. Moving at 13 miles per hour, even a glancing blow with an immovable object—as Barr knew only too well from his collision with the Nantucket Light Ship in the steel-hulled *Navahoe*—could ruin a vessel's rigging, shear off rivets, open leaks, and put her out of the race. A head-on collision could split her like a can opener.

Barr and the rest of the watch was consequently scanning the sea for low-lying growlers. No one was prepared for what suddenly materialized out of the darkness on the port bow less than 1 mile away. It was a mountain of ice bigger than the ship. Barr reckoned it at more than 200 feet long, its clifflike sides dwarfing *Atlantic*'s tallest 137-foot mizzenmast. It glowed gray-green in the darkness, as if electrified from within. In midocean it filled the night air with the sweet smell of fresh, not salt, water.

Marshall and his guests trooped on deck to see the thing. Though Charlie altered course to keep it at 1 mile's distance, they argued it was nearer. Some of them wondered aloud if it might make sense to slow down a little. It was pitch dark, after all, a murky haze rising off the water, and there could very well be even bigger bergs nearby. Eleven knots seemed a bit fast to go ripping through an ice field. Wouldn't it be prudent to reduce canvas? All this second-guessing was done within Barr's hearing.

Whether or not it influenced him, he made a show that it did. He promptly hauled down *Atlantic*'s mizzen topsail and jib topsail, which seemed to satisfy Marshall and his guests. But the canvas he reduced was slatting so badly in the light southeast by south breeze, Barr was going to haul it down anyway. At midnight—the afterguard sound asleep—Barr had both sails and more back up and was racing along at almost 12 knots in a freshening breeze. At 3:00 A.M., still on deck, he was making 12¾ knots. And at 5:00 A.M. he was logging 13¾ knots—icebergs, the Hydrographic Office, and *Atlantic*'s afterguard be damned.

The day dawned freezing cold and startlingly clear. Everyone on deck saw it and shouted at once. Five miles to the north, two pyramids of sail showed plainly on the horizon. It looked for all the world like a big two-masted schooner—and the biggest two-masted schooner in the race was none other than *Hamburg*. Marshall and his entourage clambered on deck looking anything but pleased. With binoculars and telescopes they examined it and pronounced it could only be the German yacht. Barr himself couldn't tell, but one of his two weathered Scandinavian quartermasters—either Ole Bogstrand or Edward Osmonsen—quickly identified it for what it was: an iceberg. A monstrous one, the biggest they'd ever seen.

It was, in fact, one of the biggest icebergs anybody had seen in a century. Today's International Ice Patrol classifies a large iceberg as one more than 670 feet long and more than 240 feet high. They're extremely rare; only about 3 percent of icebergs that big survive to drift into the North Atlantic. Looming off *Atlantic*'s port bow however, was an iceberg ½ mile long and almost 300 feet high. The sight of it—fully as long as three of today's Enterprise-class aircraft carriers and as tall as a 30-story skyscraper—chilled everybody. One of Marshall's guests wrote that "with the sun sparkling upon it, it made a beautiful sight." He was the only one who thought so.

Barr grimly logged its position: 42° 20' north and 48° 30' west. Without radio, of course, he couldn't notify anyone about it. Only the American bark *Apache,* last over the starting line and somewhere far behind and following God only knew what course, carried a Marconi wireless radio set. The best Barr could hope for was the off-chance to signal the danger to an eastbound or westbound steamer by flag or by lamp. He could not have imagined that almost exactly seven years later—in virtually the same place (41° 46' north and 50° 12' west)—RMS *Titanic,* westbound at 22 knots with 2,207 souls aboard, would strike a much smaller, medium-sized iceberg (51 to 150 feet high and 201 to 400 feet long) a glancing blow. He could scarcely have imagined it could sink such a liner in just two hours and forty minutes, with the loss of more than 1,500 passengers and crew.

He could never have imagined that one of those passengers would be a man he knew quite well: amiable American millionaire and New York Yacht Club member John Jacob Astor IV. Astor had not sought a place in the lifeboats. His corpse was found, frozen erect in his life belt, in a blue suit with $2,500 in his pockets. Barr could never, ever, have conceived that one of the men standing next to him that morning—Frederick M. Hoyt, one of Marshall's millionaire guests—would be one of the survivors. Hoyt joined his wife in a lifeboat reserved for women and children. He was among the few first-class male passengers to escape.

Wilson Marshall no longer wanted to slow down. Not in broad daylight, with icebergs dwarfing his boat. Certainly not after that day's noon sight. For the last six days he'd watched the twenty-four-hour runs Barr inked in the log like an investor watching a favorite stock fall. Six days out of Sandy Hook, *Atlantic* had logged only 1,242 nautical miles, a lackluster average of 207 miles a day. She was approximately 500 miles southeast of Newfoundland, not yet in midocean and considerably less than halfway to the finish line. If Captain Barr continued at that rate it would take another nine days—more than fifteen days altogether—to raise the Lizard. That was nowhere near breaking *Endymion*'s transatlantic record and damned unlikely to win the race. Clearly *Atlantic* had to go faster, and he wasn't shy about saying so.

Barr was busy doing just that, hauling down and recutting canvas, a slow process Marshall found vexing. *Atlantic*'s topsails were badly stretched out of shape, "the mizzentopsail looking like a bag," according to a guest aboard. The unbending of old and bending of new canvas took hours, every minute of which made Marshall itch. When Barr finally scratched, the big three-masted schooner took everyone's breath away. Reaching before a strong south-southeast wind, she rocketed ahead. For the next twenty-four hours, under full sail, she logged an *average* speed of more than 14 knots. At the end of the day she'd logged a mind-boggling 341 nautical miles—more than any other yacht had ever made in a single day's transatlantic run. For a time it left Marshall and his guests speechless and Charlie Barr free to race without interference.

Tietjens was on deck at first light on May 23, cold and with a knot in his stomach. *Hamburg*, 993 miles out from Sandy Hook, had passed north of 40 degrees latitude during the night—into the realm of lurking ice. The U.S. Hydrographic Office had been explicit in warning the racers to keep a sharp lookout for it. Yet that morning it was almost impossible to see anything. The wind had returned, blowing lightly out of the southeast, with a "very fine, almost exquisite rain." Massed all around were low-hanging fog-banks. Captain Peters lowered his balloon sails and slowed down. At 8:00 A.M. the fog to the north thinned briefly. Off the port bow to the northeast stood a jagged spire of ice 200 feet high, roughly the height of the Statue of Liberty back in New York. A berg that size extended ¼ mile below the surface and extended out only God knew how far. In the gloom, Captain Peters gave it a wide berth.

As the noon sight was being taken with difficulty, another big berg loomed out of the mist—dead ahead and no more than 1 mile away. *Hamburg*'s helm was put over smartly, and she neatly coursed out of the way. The suddenness and almost total silence of the near-collision jarred Tietjens. "The surface of the sea was as on a pond," he wrote, "and although we were making 8 or 9 knots, there was no trace of air current on the water." Within moments *Hamburg*'s helmsman was steering through a fog-draped minefield of smaller but equally lethal ice floes. Tietjens watched horrified as the helm dodged them; many passing as few as 10 yards away. Peters was, too: he shortened sail and slowed down even more. Tiptoeing through fog and ice, *Hamburg* logged only 160 miles.

Though he didn't know it when he took his noon sight on May 23, Lord Brassey had driven his venerable, much-disparaged *Sunbeam* to within striking distance of the kaiser's *Hamburg*. Six days out of Sandy Hook, she was well over a third of the way to the Lizard. For the oldest, slowest vessel in the race and next to last over the starting line, that represented some very fine sailing. And the sixty-nine-year-old Brassey had done almost all of it.

The log shows he was on deck with virtually every change of the watch. Every watch change he ordered "all possible sail" carried, including studding sails. This boosted *Sunbeam*'s normal sailing speed of 8 knots to 10 knots and, at times, a full 12 knots. Brassey's navigation put her in the fringe of the eastward-running Gulf Stream, which alone added 20 miles a day or more to her progress.

The wear and tear of sustaining that pace, however, had begun to show on *Sunbeam*. "Press of sail," Brassey logged on May 23, "has discovered here and there weak fittings, more suitable for the Solent [protected waters] than for racing across the Atlantic." He oversaw the repair of these personally. He showed no wear and tear himself. He was hoping for heavier weather: stronger winds to the southward and westward, with some fall in the barometer. Whether anyone else aboard hoped for bad weather is doubtful. Brassey noted it: "Evening prayers at 4:00 p.m., according to custom. Well attended."

At dusk that evening, *Hamburg* emerged from the freezing fog at the easternmost edge of the ice field. The horizon ahead stretched clear, as far as the eye could see. Wind, water, air temperature, and barometer rose abruptly. Captain Peters clapped on sail. He steered east by south, speeding away at 13 knots and then 14 knots. In his log Tietjens relievedly wrote: "The ice now lies behind us." Surely the worst of the voyage was, too.

But at about 6:00 P.M. a two-funnel, four-masted gray steamer flying the Belgian flag appeared out of the last, dying light in the west. She ran up behind them at 15 knots. She flashed *Hamburg* a gut-punching signal: "PASSED ABREAST ENDYMION AT 5:30 P.M. GREENWICH TIME, AILSA AT 6:37." By Captain Peters' rough calculations, that meant *Endymion* was only 17.5 miles behind and *Ailsa*—with her damnable German skipper Miller—barely 12 miles behind. Despite the ice field, the American bloodhounds were fast closing. Peters estimated Loesch and *Endymion* three hours and thirty minutes astern; Miller and *Ailsa,* just two hours and twenty-three minutes away.

Tietjens couldn't understand how they'd managed it, except by running right through the ice field. Given the extent and the density of the ice he'd seen, that took incredible nerve. Though he didn't know it, in forty-eight hours the seven leading yachts in the race encountered no fewer than fourteen icebergs, a phenomenal number. They covered a swath of ocean as big as Arizona.

To the north, in falling wind and dense fog at dawn on May 24, *Hildegarde* found herself ghosting through a midocean cordillera of icebergs, no less than four of them looming sinisterly in the mists. Captain Marsters logged that two were small and two "large." On the same day, also on the northern route, *Fleur de Lys* and *Thistle* also ran afoul of ice. *Fleur de Lys,* blinded by fog, narrowly avoided what Captain Bohlin called a "small iceberg, fifty-feet high & 200-feet long," only to encounter what he called a "good-sized iceberg" dead ahead. *Thistle,* coursing through the murk, discovered herself in a sea serrated with drift ice and had to throw her helm clear over to miss hitting what Captain Tod described as an "almost invisible iceberg about 40 or 50 feet long and 5 or 6 feet out of the water."

Along the southern route, conditions were no better. *Hamburg* and *Atlantic* each encountered two large bergs. *Endymion* sliced past an icy monolith just "off the port bow," according to Captain Loesch, "estimated about 200' high." Captain Miller in *Ailsa* sighted two icebergs that day and swerved to avoid a collision. In fog and darkness, with a sharp lookout the only warning device, it was little short of amazing that no catastrophe occurred.

There was no time to think about that. Captain Peters had all hands furiously hauling up light racing canvas. Heeling hard over, *Hamburg* soon was coursing away from her pursuers, at times making a wake-thrashing 15 knots.

Wireless reports from the eastbound Belgian steamer were picked up by other vessels, wired to shore stations, and quickly cabled around the world. In Britain the *Times* announced "Germany's Yacht Now to the Fore." In America the *New York Herald* trumpeted "*Hamburg* Showing the Way" and the *New York Times* "*Hamburg* Leading." The *Boston Herald* flashed the news in a triple-decked headline: "*HAMBURG* FIRST. *Ailsa* 13 Miles Astern. *Endymion, Atlantic,* and *Fleur de Lys* Next."

CHAPTER 24

"*You Hired Me to Win*"

The snotgreen sea. The scrotum-tightening sea.
—James Joyce

It struck *Fleur de Lys* first. She was about 500 miles due east of Cape St. John's, Newfoundland, driving into the mid-Atlantic. She and three other racers—*Hildegarde, Thistle,* and *Apache*—had split off from the rest of the fleet a day out of Sandy Hook, bound for the shorter but rougher northern great circle route across the ocean. Bohlin had fished those waters his whole life and knew the one thing he could count on catching there was wind and plenty of it. But seven days out of Sandy Hook, he still hadn't found the wind. He'd found plenty of fog all week, especially on the notoriously steaming Grand Banks, where ice-cold currents from the north and warm winds from just about any other direction raised it in clouds, and he logged visibility "no farther than a man can spit." *Fleur* had run only 1,060 miles in that time, at a dismal average speed of 6 knots, despite the Gloucestermen doing all they could to prod her faster.

They were passing to the north of the Flemish Cap, easternmost thumb on the outstretched palm of the Newfoundland fishing banks, just after midnight on May 25. The light southeast breeze carrying them suddenly vanished, the way a ship's cat did when

Daily Runs & Positions

NAME OF YACHT		May 18 Noon	May 19 Noon	May 20 Noon	May 21 Noon	May 22 Noon	May 23 Noon	May 24 Noon	May 25 Noon	May 26 Noon
ATLANTIC	Lat.	39°40'	40°14'	40°45'	41°09'	41°24'	42°30'	44°57'	46°33'	47°58'
	Dist.	165	222	229	271	112	243	341	282	279
	Long.	70°24'	65°37'	60°38'	54°40'	52°12'	46°37'	39°50'	33°30'	26°48'
HAMBURG	Lat.	39°39'	39°48'	39°54'	39°49'	39°53'	40°25'	42°38'	44°54'	47°15'
	Dist.	142	216	219	247	169	160	303	306	272
	Long.	71°01'	66°20'	61°35'	56°13'	52°42'	49°19'	43°21'	37°03'	31°31'
VALHALLA	Lat.	39°19'	39°20'	39°40'	39°42'	39°54'	40°44'	42°18'	44°00'	45°25'
	Dist.	136	162	225	256	184	240	287	310	289
	Long.	72°30'	68°18'	63°56'	59°04'	55°19'	50°25'	44°39'	37°58'	32°12'
ENDYMION	Lat.	39°44'	39°46'	39°45'	39°58'	40°00'	40°40'	41°59'	44°06'	45°26'
	Dist.	150	200	214	243	59	253	246	291	246
	Long.	70°39'	66°20'	61°41'	56°22'	55°05'	49°39'	44°27'	38°31'	33°02'
HILDEGARD	Lat.	39°32'	40°15'	41°29'	43°00'	44°38'	47°05'	48°20'	48°30'	48°28'
	Dist.	202	225	192	230	167	232	187	134	203
	Long.	70°00'	66°22'	62°30'	58°22'	55°14'	50°44'	46°28'	43°09'	37°11'
SUNBEAM	Lat.	39°32'	39°35	40°12'	40°24'	40°24'	41°12'	42°57'	45°30'	46°42'
	Dist.	112	198	230	227	117	243	272	282	270
	Long.	71°18'	67°32'	62°49'	58°50'	55°20'	50°04'	44°28'	38°58'	33°05'
FLEUR DELYS	Lat.	39°56'	40°28'	41°45'	43°21'	44°36'	45°50'	46°45'	48°10'	48°17'
	Dist.	140	180	182	170	183	242	146	205	242
	Long.	70°54'	67°03'	63°21'	60°13'	56°21'	50°55'	47°40'	43°25'	37°35'
AILSA	Lat.	39°44'	39°38'	39°20'	39°32'	39°40'	40°35'	41°50'	43°52'	45°00'
	Dist.	98	229	192	204	144	264	256	251	226
	Long.	71°48'	67°17'	63°20'	58°46'	55°20'	49°36'	44°12'	39°12'	34°00'
UTOWANA	Lat.	39°27'	39°28'	39°25'	39°24'	39°13'	40°16'	41°05'	43°31'	44°39'
	Dist.	112	180	184	236	171	233	180	292	233
	Long.	71°48'	67°55'	63°56'	58°50'	55°11'	50°17'	46°29'	40°45'	35°40'
THISTLE	Lat.	39°50'	41°07'	42°15'	43°15'	44°01'	45°23'	45°30'	46°10'	47°20'
	Dist.	128	180	172	167	183	240	122	105	262
	Long.	71°18'	67°38'	64°10'	60°50'	56°50'	51°33'	48°45'	46°20'	40°25'
APACHE	Lat.	39°50'	40°38'	41°31'	42°43'	43°37'	44°44'	45°07'	45°15'	46°01'
	Dist.	138	158	149	170	145	184	68	73	125
	Long.	72°00'	68°43'	65°38'	62°09'	59°03'	55°05'	53°35'	51°53	49°07'

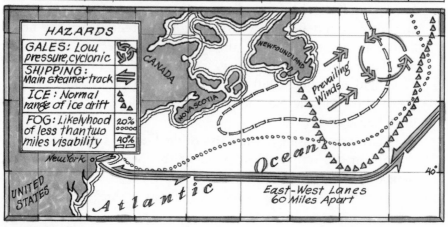

HAZARDS

GALES: Low pressure, cyclonic

SHIPPING: Main steamer track

ICE: Normal range of ice drift

FOG: Likelyhood of less than two miles visability — 20% — 40%

CANADA

NEWFOUNDLAND

NOVA SCOTIA

Prevailing Winds

New York

UNITED STATES

Atlantic Ocean

East-West Lanes 60 Miles Apart

40°

May 27 Noon	May 28 Noon	May 29 Noon	May 30 Noon	May 31 Noon	June 1 Noon	June 2 Noon	June 3 Noon	June 4 Noon	June 5 Noon	Dist. sailed	Avg. per hour
48°36' 243 20°53'	49°52' 309 13°06'	49°48 282 05°59'	to Lizard 35 miles							3013	10.32
49°26' 253 26°09'	49°54' 292 18°41'	49°59' 312 10°35'	49°46' 161 06°13'	to Lizard 41 miles						3093	9.84
47°28' 278 26°06'	48°33' 280 19°19'	48°55' 278 12°35'	49°35' 156 08°50'	to Lizard 142 miles						3223	9.51
46°42' 274 27°00'	48°44' 264 21°11'	48°59' 266 14°27'	49°07' 148 10°44'	49°32 133 07°24'	to Lizard 90 miles					3077	9.04
49°02' 263 30°32'	49°33' 298 23°36'	49°54' 205 17°22'	49°44' 154 13°23'	49°44' 202 08°09'	to Lizard 115 miles					3009	8.82
47°48' 250 27°06'	48°22' 246 21°00'	48°35' 242 14°52'	48°51' 120 12°00'	49°39' 146 08°30'	to Lizard 138 miles					3093	9.03
49°02' 271 30°52'	49°23' 293 23°26'	50°23' 183 19°38'	50°18' 172 15°10'	49°50 222 09°23'	to Lizard 165 miles					2996	8.67
46°11' 162 30°43'	47°29' 243 25°06'	48°45' 218 20°00'	49°20' 136 16°15'	49°30' 250 09°46'	to Lizard 148 miles					3013	8.70
46°50' 286 29°37'	47°57' 233 24°12'	48°55' 205 19°18'	49°18' 114 16°28'	49°40' 253 10°03'	to Lizard 189 miles					3101	8.91
47°57' 234 34°50'	48°13' 260 28°15'	48°50' 210 22°54'	49°02' 202 17°57'	49°21' 289 10°45'	to Lizard 226 miles					2980	8.39
46°25' 69 47°34'	47°39' 170 43°44'	48°20' 160 39°52'	49°50' 193 35°32'	49°47' 222 29°41'	50°24' 240 25°30'	50°33' 270 16°	50°05' 190 11°36'	49°42' 127 08°19'	to lizard 121 mi.	2972	6.62

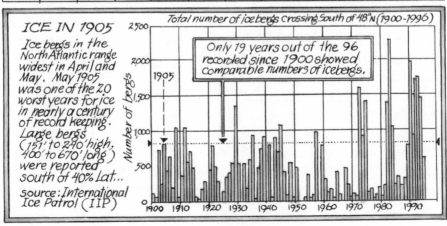

ICE IN 1905

Ice bergs in the North Atlantic range widest in April and May. May 1905 was one of the 20 worst years for ice in nearly a century of record keeping. Large bergs (151' to 240' high, 400' to 670' long) were reported south of 40° Lat...

source: International Ice Patrol (IIP)

Total number of icebergs crossing South of 48°N (1900-1996)

Only 19 years out of the 96 recorded since 1900 showed comparable numbers of icebergs.

1905

Number of bergs

2,500 · 2,000 · 1,900 · 1,000 · 500 · 0

1900 · 1910 · 1920 · 1930 · 1940 · 1950 · 1960 · 1970 · 1980 · 1990

frightened. In its place, a fresh breeze (17 to 21 knots) commenced blowing out of the northeast. To fishermen like Bohlin and his crew, it stank: like seasick vomit, bilge water, kerosene lamps. Any easterly wind in those latitudes generally brought heavy weather—and hell with it. Generally, the harder it blew, the bigger the hell it was bringing and the faster it would arrive. This one came in screaming. It intensified hourly: strengthening at first into a strong northeast wind (22 to 27 knots) that raised seas into rank after rank of drenching, oncoming 13-foot waves, then morphing into a near gale that moaned through the rigging at 28 to 33 knots and brought 20-foot breakers out of the darkness.

By 3:00 A.M. it was blowing at force 9: a violent gale of 41 to 47 knots (47 to 54 miles per hour): strong enough to flatten fences, strip shingles off roofs and branches from trees; driving waves 2½ stories high at *Fleur*, and turning the night white with spindrift. Bohlin fought it, stubbornly reefing but not hauling down canvas, attempting to hold as close to his racing course as he could. But little *Fleur* was soon taking such a brutal pounding that even Tommie Bohlin finally threw in his hand. Conditions had to be life-threatening for him to do that. A wall back at Gloucester City Hall was inscribed, like a war memorial, with names of Gloucestermen lost in battle with the sea. On average, thirty-two new townsmen's names, painfully fresh, went up on the wall every year. None of them, pridefully, were any of Bohlin's crews. He drove men and boats to their ultimate limits, but—like Bully Samuels—knew in the soles of his boots when those limits had been reached. He hauled down the mainsail, set the outer jib and trysail, and hove to to wait out the storm.

The gale raged all day. And the next day. And the day after. It never attacked from the same direction. It hauled from the northeast to the north and then to north-northwest. Bohlin didn't remain hove to for long. As soon as the wind hauled around to the northwest on the twenty-sixth—though still blowing a gale-force 34 to 40 knots, with 22-foot following seas—he steelily upped the mainsail and foresail again. Kiting along, rolling and plunging, *Fleur* logged 242 miles that day, averaging 10 knots, her best speed so far. But it was a very rough, dangerous ride. Little *Fleur*—the shortest, narrowest, lightest vessel in the race, with less keel under her than any other—took a bone-rattling beating from the following seas. Whatever her mettle, it must have painfully tried Candace Stimson as well as her father and his guests. Bohlin had to continually steer *Fleur* north of his course to keep the mainsail from jibing and the boat from broaching.

It got much worse on May 27. The northwest wind strengthened again from a gale to a strong gale; howling at a sustained 47 knots, with gusts exceeding 55 knots. "Sea is very heavy," Bohlin scribbled in his noon log entry. "The main boom goes into the slings often, for half its length. Lee side often full above the main ropes. Helmsman has been lashed [to the wheel] now two days." Shortly after noon, the wind carried away *Fleur*'s jib tackle and jib. At dusk it ripped the big foresail off its boom. At 9:00 P.M. the following seas were running so high they began breaking over *Fleur*'s port quarter and sweeping the decks.

The eyes of *Fleur*'s six-man watch were naturally drawn in that direction. A fellow working ship in a North Atlantic gale couldn't help but look back to see when the next homicidal wave would hit, so he could catch a proper handhold, brace himself for the impact, and hang on for dear life. Not with "Cap'n Tommie" bronco-busting before the wind, under double-reefed sail, at up to 14 knots.

The boat was under the crest of the huge wave surging in off the port beam—not the stern quarter—before anyone fairly saw it. It smashed into the main rigging like a landslide, knocking *Fleur* on her beam ends, and burying the boat in black water. All four seamen on watch forward were washed aft to the mainsheet, gouged by every chock, cleat, and hatchway on deck and knocked senseless. They were stopped from washing overboard only because they were hurled square into the quartermaster and the first mate lashed to the helm.

Bohlin was on deck before *Fleur* recovered, stepping on bodies to grab the wheel. All hands—including the cook and the steward—scrambled on deck to bring the boat under control. Dr. Stimson and his male guests—author James Connelly and Elliot Tuckerman—dragged the injured below. All six men were in shock, retching salt water and bleeding profusely. Candace Stimson draped them in comforters she ripped from the bunks of the guest staterooms. Her father, who was one of the finest trauma surgeons of his day, went to work, his daughter assisting. One seaman was coughing blood: most of the ribs on the right side of his chest were broken. Two had multiple cuts and gashes, some requiring up to thirty stitches apiece to close. The other three had severe lacerations and contusions. Dr. Stimson patched them up, made his way topside on the rolling, wave-washed deck, and shouted Bohlin the news: six hands down, half of *Fleur*'s crew.

It did not seem to alarm him. His salt-frosted spectacles shined. "Hell, Doctor," he shouted back, "their wives whip 'em worse than that at home." With *Fleur* back under control, hammering before the gale under reefed sail and still logging 12 knots or more, he was in his element. His Gloucestermen would bounce back. Until they did, Dr. Stimson told him, he and his guests would stand their watches.

Candace Stimson stood hers at the yacht's helm.

The same violent mid-Atlantic storm struck all six leading yachts in the race on May 25. It didn't matter if they were sailing the northern or the southern route—the storm system boiled up big enough to engulf both. Viewed from one of today's weather satellites, it would have covered a triangular expanse of ocean roughly 600 nautical miles on its sides and 350 nautical miles at its base—an area the size of Texas.

Some 360 miles southeast of *Fleur de Lys*, down on the southern route, it hit Captain Loesch and *Endymion* with a particular vengeance that Thursday. It couldn't have hit at a worse time. He was fast-closing with what was surely the leading yacht in the race. The day before—at 10:30 A.M.—the westbound American steamer *Oceanic* had signaled him: "SIGHTED *HAMBURG* ONE HOUR AGO." He'd been hot after her ever since, expecting to see the German yacht at any moment. As conditions worsened on May 25—deteriorating from a near-gale to a gale and then to a furious, strong gale—he continued to carry all canvas that could be kept aloft. At noon that day he was 1,656 miles from Sandy Hook, well over halfway to the finish line by his course, despite the jury-rigged square-sail yard that had broken on May 18 and a full day of absolutely no wind on May 22, when the boat logged but 59 miles. Under double-reefed mainsails and foresails, rolling in very heavy seas, he was still driving *Endymion* at more than 12 knots. He was not about to let Captain Peters get away.

On the morning of May 26, gale winds gusting at more than 50 knots ripped *Endymion*'s jib stay from the foremast and carried her jib off like a kite. Repairing it took four hours. Three hours later a gust split the fore topsail like the sword of Gideon. Evidently, it made hash of it: it took the crew seven hours to stitch it back together and set it again. For the next sixteen hours the gale took *Endymion* apart piece by piece. In the dead of night it tore her raffee to shreds. Repairing and resetting it in the dark took three hours. As soon as it was fair up, the gale ripped it back down. Loesch had it repaired and rehoisted, only to watch the wind tear it into pieces again. Stubbornly, he ordered it mended and hauled up a *third* time. There was an ear-splitting crack and a screeching rip. The gale spared the patchworked raffee but stripped the laboriously repaired fore topsail from mast and gaff and carried it off for good. With no spare, Loesch flintily hoisted a jib topsail in its place.

By the night of May 27, still driving before the gale, *Endymion* was hurting. The spliced square-sail yard groaned and wailed with the sorely patched, overstretched raffee. It was an even bet which would give way first. The jib topsail, cut in half to substitute for the missing foretopsail, looked and acted as neither. The reattached jib stay stretched to the breaking point and vibrated with the sound of hornets' nests. Huge following seas rolled, pitched, and yawed the boat. Both watches had been on deck more or less continually for more than forty-eight hours and were soaked, shivering cold, and dangerously tired.

Loesch sent half the crew below to their bunks. He remained on deck with the rest. The weather and all the repairs bore watching. Despite the hammer blows, *Endymion*'s easting had improved remarkably. In two days riding the gale and the worst it could do, she'd logged 520 nautical miles, averaging a speed of almost 11 knots per hour. He couldn't ask more of the boat or the crew. He was, however, prepared to order whatever it took to win.

The same gale overtook *Hamburg*. At noon on May 25 she was approximately 100 miles northeast of *Endymion*, having crossed ahead and shaved north of her course after *Oceanic* sighted her the day before. Before a strong south-southwest wind (22 to 27 knots), Captain Peters had her under all lower sails, big fore square sail, all topsails, forestaysail, jib and jib topsail. She was booming along at 14½ knots. She was 1,762 miles out of Sandy Hook and 1,300 miles from the finish by her course. Things couldn't have been more perfect. Then the rising wind set the shrouds singing. By 2:00 P.M. it had turned into an Inquisitional chorus, the kind calculated to drown out the screams of burning heretics.

Blowing a near-gale with fast-massing, following 20-foot seas, Peters was forced to haul down the square sail, both topsails, and the jib topsail. By 4:00 P.M. he'd put three reefs in the mainsail. At 7:30 P.M., in a full gale blowing at 33 to 40 knots, he took in the forestaysail and put two reefs in the foresail. The wholesale shortening of canvas hardly slowed *Hamburg*. Showing only a triple-reefed mainsail and a double-reefed foresail, the storm carried her northeast like a leaf at nearly 13 knots.

The rolling, yawing, and pitching were so severe it took two men to control the wheel and keep her from broaching. Seas whipsawed and pounded the boat all night long. The noise was absolutely deafening. Tietjens got no sleep. Sharing the same cabin, his captain-lieutenant son, who'd served on destroyers in the North Sea, somehow slept like a baby.

There was no dawn on May 26, only dungeonlike dimness, echoing with wind. It was raining hard, gale howling from west by south, and the boat steering very badly before heavy, ugly, breaking seas. Peters ordered the boom of the triple-reefed mainsail lowered 4 feet. It took some pressure off the helm, helping to keep her before the wind, but in the awful rolling, half the boom often was underwater. Waves were breaking on deck. An oil bag suspended over the weather bow didn't stop them. The waves swept *Hamburg* freely fore and aft. The punishment went on all day. At

10:00 P.M. that night, the ship's barometer had dropped to 29.18—the lowest Tietjens had seen in his life. The gale raged unabated at 40 knots, massive following seas relentlessly slamming the boat to the northeast.

At noon on May 27, *Hamburg* had been blown from 45 to nearly 50 degrees latitude—far north of her course.

Beginning at 3:00 A.M. on May 24, Charlie Barr watched *Atlantic's* barometer go into freefall. In twenty-four hours it dropped from a steady 30.23 (fair weather) to 29.75 (severe storm imminent). It continued down every hour after that. Barr logged it: 29.73, 29.72, 29.71, 29.68, 29.66, 29.64, 29.63, 29.60, 29.58, 29.55, 29.52, 29.51. As fast as it dropped, the winds and the seas increased until it was blowing a force 9 gale out of the Southwest. At dawn on the 26 the seas were so rough it was necessary to deploy oil bags along *Atlantic's* weather rail to prevent the waves from breaking aboard and sweeping her.

No skipper did this unless he had to. It was a low-sided racing yacht's last defense against massive, peaked seas. Bags of heavy duck canvas, the size and shape of sides of beef, were stuffed with oakum and soaked in barrels of petroleum oil until sodden. They were stitched up, punched through with holes, and hung over the windward side of the ship. The heavier-than-water film of oil—hemorrhaging from the bags and trailing astern—smothered oncoming breakers. It was amazingly effective, as long as the oil lasted. In very high seas, two or sometimes three bags did the trick.

By noon on May 26, Barr had *four* oil bags over *Atlantic's* windward side, the barometer was down to 29.45, and waves were beginning to break on deck like incoming artillery. That isn't an exaggeration. *Atlantic,* running before the wind at 12 knots, was being overtaken by following seas up to 30 feet high. One of these breaking over her starboard quarter was quite enough to drop 50 tons of seawater onto her; roughly the equivalent of dropping four African elephants or one modern-day M1A battletank onto her deck. The impact was pulverizing. It knocked men off their feet, slammed the 2-inch-thick teak deck planking like a battering ram, and clanged the steel hull like an anvil. The wild snaproll afterward sent everything aboard crashing to leeward. The dizzying roll back up into the wind—to take more of the same—was sickening. The oil washed back over her made the decks and the rigging doubly treacherous to work.

By 4:00 P.M. conditions were so awful Barr hauled down every stitch of canvas but fore and mizzen trysails. Under these bare storm sails, he continued driving *Atlantic* before the gale at 11 knots, taking a brutal beating. Throughout the first watch that night (8:00 P.M. to 12:00 A.M.), he logged that the vessel "rolled violently." The world's foremost yacht racing skipper didn't use that kind of phrase lightly. If Barr called it violent, it was horrifically so. He made the same notation at the end of the middle watch (12:00 A.M. to 4:00 A.M.), again at the end of the morning watch (4:00 a.m. to 8:00 A.M.), and again at the end of the forenoon watch (8:00 A.M. to 12:00 P.M.). He never left the deck.

The crew had then been battling the gale for some thirty-three consecutive hours. They had made sixteen sail changes in that time; repaired and reset *Atlantic*'s raffee; rigged and tended four oil bags; worked pumps to rid the ship of water; and been knocked nine ways to Sunday standing watch in piledriving seas and spindrift so blinding they could scarcely see. They couldn't keep it up much longer. Despite oilskins and boots, they were soaked through and shaking. With the air temperature at 50°F and a 40-mile-per-hour gale raging, the wind-chill on deck was a subfreezing 26°F.

Wilson Marshall and his guests hadn't bargained on anything remotely like it. Belowdecks, where they'd been the entire time, everything was amplified and made worse by the fact that they couldn't see what was going on. They could hear the wind screaming at the resistance of *Atlantic*'s long masts and heavy spars. The breaking seas thudded against the thin deck above their heads like a besieging army pounding to get in. Leaks had sprung everywhere; jets of black water spurting in from boarded-over skylights and portholes parted seams and battened hatches and doors. The saloon was ankle-deep in sloshing sea. Almost all the hanging lamps had shattered and gone dark.

From behind—always from behind—echoed an incredible, incessant boom. It jacked the boat up by the stern, wrenched her almost on her beams ends, and plunged her downwave to a neck-snapping stop. Above all the terrible noises, it was the nonstop thrumming and vibration in the rigging—a devil's harp—that had Wilson Marshall shaking. The gale obviously wasn't moderating in the least. His prized *Atlantic* was being smashed. His guests were terrified. His crew was exhausted and at the breaking point. Yet Captain Barr continued to run her before the wind. It was all too much. The only reasonable thing to do was heave to and ride out the storm.

There are two starkly different accounts of what happened next. Marshall's was that Barr made his way below to see him as the gale intensified and said "Commodore, if we are going to lay to, we must do it now or not at all." Reportedly Marshall looked at him thunderstruck and said "Captain Barr, I am racing." Reputedly Barr's reply was "That is all I wanted to know, sir."

Everything screams against this account. It has Charlie Barr leaving the helm of *Atlantic* at the height of a full gale, something he had not done for two days. One can scarcely imagine him doing so unless he was ordered to, and even then reluctantly. It has Barr—the most accomplished racing skipper of the day, perhaps ever—deferring to a novice yachtsman whether or not to heave to in the middle of a transatlantic race. What's more, it has Marshall—who despite being the vessel's owner and former commodore of the Larchmont Yacht Club, was no more than a passenger aboard—insisting he's racing, which he certainly wasn't. He wasn't even on deck.

The more plausible account, revealed only after the race, has Marshall popping his head out of the companionway and shouting at Barr—in no uncertain or polite terms—to heave to at once. Anyone in his right mind would have done the same. Hanging in the hatchway, with *Atlantic* snap-rolling 45 degrees or more—in pitch dark, under breaking seas to windward and blinded by spray—Marshall would have been hard pressed to say anything more. Fifteen feet from his head, the lee rails of the boat were fully underwater and climbing the deck. Overheard the screech of canvas and screaming rigging was deafening. About the only intelligible utterance he could have made was an order to heave to. For Barr, lashed with his quartermaster to the wheel and fighting to hold her before the wind, it was the last straw. "You hired me to win this race," he shouted back, "and that is what I intend to do."

CHAPTER 25

"Are We First?"

The men on board very naturally began to wonder about the other boats, though it did not seem possible that anything could be ahead.

—Adolph Tietjens,
schooner *Hamburg*

Valhalla profited most from the heavy weather. As Crawford told the press before the start: "My vessel feeds on it." She did: gluttonously. From May 25—when the gale slammed the leading yachts in the race, until it blew itself out on May 27—the huge square-rigged ship logged 877 nautical miles. With twice the freeboard of the American and German racing schooners, more than twice their tonnage, and a far deeper keel—able to carry twice as many sails as any vessel in the race and carry them far longer in a blow—she crashed through the heavy seas and boomed up from behind every vessel on the southern route. In the next two days, she reeled off another 558 miles. Crawford couldn't have been more pleased with his palatial sailing machine. She was doing just what he'd commissioned her to do—run oceans.

At noon on May 29 she was running exceptionally well. She was 12 days and 2,925 miles from Sandy Hook, an outstanding run considering she'd lost the better part of a full day at the start of the race.

By Lord Crawford's electronic position plotter, she was only 298 miles from the finish line at the Lizard. That gave her a capital opportunity to carry the White Ensign of the Royal Navy over the finish line first.

It doubtless struck him as ironic, perhaps moronic, that the finish he was driving for—selected by the kaiser himself—was a marine graveyard, one of the most notorious on the English coast. It struck every participating yacht club and the whole press the same way. But the kaiser had a fascination for obscure points of geography when they suited his strategic purpose: Berlin-to-Baghdad railways, Moroccan ports on the Atlantic, harbors in northern China. He'd obviously chosen the finish for one reason and one alone: the Lizard was the southernmost point of mainland in all of Great Britain: the perfect location to wave his imperial flag in the face of the British lion at the earliest possible moment.

For sailing yachts ending a transatlantic race, however, it was a perfectly dreadful place—the kind ships fled *from,* not to. It was aptly named the Lizard, a fat peninsula jutting out from the coast of Cornwall, constantly shedding its rock scales from cliffs into the sea. Like the tongue of a lizard, its crags and jumbled boulder fields licked 1 mile or more out to sea, to the edge of the 20-fathom line (120 feet deep) and were barely visible except at low water. Its subordinate features—Beast Point, Foam Rock, Black Head, the Manacles Rocks—were well named. With prevailing onshore winds and currents, seas fetched up across the whole of the North Atlantic, and thick and boisterous weather, even well-skippered, bravely manned ships regularly met their doom there. In a typical year, as the returns of shipping losses in 1896–1897 showed, the wild Cornish coast claimed sixty vessels—the Lizard claiming the king's share.

The only friendly warnings to mariners were two lighthouses, with fixed lights, set atop the cliffs 200 feet above the sea. In fair weather they were visible for 21 miles. In foul weather a newfangled Marconi wireless station atop the cliffs warned away ocean liners, but that was of no use to the racing yachts. Only one was equipped with wireless apparatus.

Making the dangerous landfall even more perilous for onrushing racers was the layout of the finish line itself. The kaiser had dispatched the German light cruiser *Pfeil* (Arrow) to act as stakeboat and mark one end of the line; the Lizard lighthouse marked the other. *Pfeil* dropped her anchor due south of the lighthouse, 1 mile beyond the outermost rocks. Normally, a 1 mile-wide finish line, given the usual formula, was more than generous. But the Lizard wasn't normal, and a generously laid line there allowed no margin of error for a yacht under sail. The winning yacht—and all that followed— would have to steer unerringly through a comparatively short, completely unforgiving passage between *Pfeil* and the outermost rocks. Day or night, fair weather or foul.

If there were worse cards dealt to a finer gambler than Jimmie Loesch on the morning of May 29, it would have taken a saint to recognize them. At 4:00 A.M. *Endymion*'s ringtail—an extension of canvas fitted to the mainsail to eke more speed out of her before the gentle following wind—split and had to be hauled down. He set his light balloon sails, but the wind weakened so it was hard to keep them full. Between the time the gale struck on May 25 and noon on May 29, he'd somehow managed to drive the storm-tossed, badly damaged *Endymion* a distance of 1,435 nautical miles. That amounted to an average of some 287 miles a day, at an average speed of nearly 12 knots—very fast considering the weather and the condition of the boat.

But the day lost becalmed on May 22 and the havoc done to her sails and rigging since had told. So had six continuous days of hand-to-hand combat with raging North Atlantic seas: *Endymion*'s eighteen officers and crew were dead on their feet. Before a westerly breeze, under jury-rigged spars, patchworked canvas, and pieced-together rigging, with a jib for a foretopsail, they were still getting 10 knots out of her. Without more wind it looked doubtful that *Endymion* would beat her 1900 transatlantic record. Yet that didn't mean she couldn't win the race.

By the most direct course Loesch could figure, he was 371 miles to the finish. He laid on every stitch of canvas.

Spirits aboard *Hamburg* at noon on May 29 couldn't have been higher. The weather was splendidly clear and sunny, a spanking southwesterly breeze blowing moderate to fresh (11 to 21 knots), with easy seas. The noon sight confirmed the boat had logged its best twenty-four-hour run yet—312 nautical miles at an average speed of 13 knots. Tietjens's son, who in all but official title was *Hamburg*'s navigator, fixed their position. They were 2,891 miles out of Sandy Hook, about 140 miles southwest of Cape Clear, Ireland, boring straight for the Lizard, fewer than 200 miles away. Captain Peters had her ripping along under everything he could fill: big mainsails and foresails, all topsails, all staysails and jibs.

Tietjens was billowing along on the same heady air. They had not sighted a single vessel—steamer or racing yacht—in the four days since the gale hit. With the speed they'd been making, nobody could be ahead. If the wind held favorable, the finish line was less than a day's sailing away. *Hamburg* was on the verge not only of breaking *Endymion*'s 1900 transatlantic record but also shattering it. The latter had made the passage from Sandy Hook to the Needles by a course of 3,060 miles in thirteen days, twenty hours, and thirty-six minutes. That had beaten James Gordon Bennett's 1866 record in *Henrietta* by a mere one hour and nineteen minutes. Now it looked certain that *Hamburg* would smash *Endymion*'s record by as many as ten hours.

The prospect had *Hamburg*'s seamen puffing like gamecocks. For a German-crewed yacht, in its first transatlantic race, against the fastest, most professionally skippered racing yachts in the world, it was miraculous. Germans had taken up yacht racing only fifteen years before; the British and the Americans had dominated to sport for over sixty. All that—like the meteoric rise of Germany's merchant marine and navy—had been the kaiser's doing. No one but he, really, had believed Germans could do it: build a maritime power virtually overnight. And now a sun-bronzed German crew was bringing a German ship in to win the greatest ocean race the world had ever known.

By late afternoon, several westbound steamers were sighted. Most were too far off or going too fast to signal. At 3:00 P.M., however, one of them passed near enough for Captain Peters to inquire whether she'd met any other yachts. The crushing answer was:

"YES, A THREE-MASTED SCHOONER." The steamer was gone before Peters could ask anything more.

Tietjens penned the worst fears of everyone aboard in his log: "*Atlantic* ahead of us and not in sight."

Charlie Barr had been four days and four nights without sleep on the pitch-black morning of May 29. He was working the watch to wring every knot of speed out of *Atlantic*. He set the mainsails and mizzensails for the first time in four days, followed with topsails and topmast staysails, until the boat was reeling off 13 to 14 knots. Marshall was below in his bunk. The stewards brought up pots of piping hot coffee and thick sandwiches for the watch. It helped, but the crew was running on fumes.

Sunrise revealed a whitecapped sea and a moderate breeze from the south-southwest. At 7:40 A.M., winking off the lee bow, a lookout made out the Bishop's Rock lighthouse. That brought everyone on deck. Bishop's Rock marked the southwesternmost extremity of the Scilly Isles, a smattering of rocky islets and the traditional first landfall before making the English coast. Two hours later, Barr had it abeam. He snapped a quick sight and then took another to make sure. By his course—eleven days, sixteen hours, and twenty-one minutes after the starting gun—*Atlantic* was 2,978 miles from Sandy Hook. No yacht had ever made the ocean passage to Bishop's Rock light so fast. Marshall and his guests went to celebrating the moment they heard. The finish line at the Lizard was only 51 miles away.

But by 11:00 A.M. the moderate (11-to-16-knot) breeze fell away to a light breeze (4 to 6 knots). The whitecapped sea smoothed into wavelets, none breaking. At noon Barr set the enormous spinnaker and balloon topmast staysail to catch every puff of wind. An hour later the light breeze danced to westward and evaporated to light air (1 to 3 knots). The sea showed only ripples. At 2:00 P.M. a hard-running westward tide set against them. *Atlantic* slowed to the point she barely maintained headway.

It must have been maddening for Barr. He had no idea where *Hamburg* or any of the other racers were. He hadn't seen another vessel in almost six days. He hadn't sighted another competitor since passing *Hamburg* on May 18, some eleven days earlier. He had no earthly idea whether he was winning or losing the race. He knew only that *Atlantic* was sailing a record-setting passage. But if he could do it, Peters, Miller, Loesch, and Bohlin could do it, too. Any of them could have already crossed the finish line. There was no way of knowing.

At about 3:00 P.M. that afternoon, the wind abandoned him altogether. He was 25 miles short of the finish line.

The earl of Lonsdale, the kaiser's close friend and the man who'd suggested his purloining the great ocean race in the first place, didn't think much of the Lizard. It was miles from the nearest village. Other than the lighthouse and government wireless station, the only thing there was a small, musty-smelling seaside hotel. The English race committee charged with overseeing the finish—which included himself; British yachtsman Sir Edward Birbeck; and Captain Coerper, Germany's naval attaché in London, filled most of the cramped rooms. The rest were taken by American millionaire and New York Yacht Club member Charles Robinson, their counterpart on the American race committee. Robinson had witnessed the start of the race in New York, taken passage on a fast ocean liner to Plymouth, and was chauffeured out to the Lizard with his entourage in a luxury touring automobile filled with picnic baskets of delicacies from Fortnum & Mason's.

Lonsdale—with his butler, valet, and steamer trunks—arrived by carriage late on Sunday afternoon, May 28. No one expected any of the yachts to finish before then, and he had no wish to remain at the Lizard any longer than necessary. The committee pinned its charts all over the walls of the hotel lobby and made it their headquarters. Lookouts with powerful naval range-finding telescopes were posted atop the lighthouse towers. The wireless station was instructed to send runners with any messages from steamers about eastbound racers. Scores of newspapermen unable to find rooms pitched tents around the hotel and chartered local fishing boats to carry them out beyond *Pfeil* the following day.

That night the fog-shrouded hotel was noisy and overcrowded, the food was terrible and the blinding lights and horn blasts from the lighthouse made sleep impossible. In the morning the fog and the food were worse, but at least the throng of reporters was gone. Lonsdale read the *Times*, freshly ironed by his butler, and wondered how long he'd have to stay. Luncheon was improved over breakfast by the claret his butler produced. By afternoon, a bright sun had burned away the fog; a west wind from the sea blew gently, almost delicately; and the race committee in the hotel slumbered somnabulently. Their business—witnessing the finish and taking the times of arriving racers—wouldn't commence for days.

At about teatime a runner sprinted downhill from the lighthouse 500 yards away. A shiver of signal flags had just been run up on the *Pfeil*. She had the topmost sails of a yacht in view, bearing west by south and standing in toward the Lizard. Lonsdale couldn't believe it was one of the racers: they were a day away, at best. It had to be a pleasure yacht coming to view the finish, or a fishing schooner heading back to Falmouth with its catch. The rest of the race committee thought so, too. Still, they sent their boat—an oceangoing tug that the Admiralty had placed at their disposal—to steam out and see. Lonsdale, Sir Edward, and Captain Coerper sat down to tea, sherry, and cigars.

Charlie Barr couldn't keep his eyes open. The very light westerly breeze barely rippled the sea. It was hazy, sunny, hot. *Atlantic* undulated like a rocking chair. The boat was making 3 knots—a pedestrian pensioner's stroll. Everybody was on deck, looking east. At first the plume of smoke they spotted on the horizon seemed to be moving away. But soon it came sharply over and headed straight at them. It ran up at full speed: a Royal Navy tug, her spray-splashed bow crowded with yelling men.

As it thrashed alongside, Barr hoarsely called out, "Are we first?" The tug's skipper laughed and then shouted back, "No other yacht's finished!"

Atlantic's crew exploded in cheers. Marshall and his guests hurled their caps in the air. Barr's nephew—First Mate John Barr—jumped onto the back of Boatswain Harry Nelson. The ship's Viking Mafia—Second Mate Andrew Petersen and Quartermasters Ole Bogstrand and Edward Osmonsen—sent up a trilling berserkers' yell. The cooks—Chief Cook William Whitecross and Second Cook Robert Mitchell—banged pots and pans. The African American stewards—Chief Steward Theodore Bell and G. E. Perry, Percival Marucheau, and James White—stripped off and waved their white mess jackets. Charlie Barr didn't show any emotion. He hadn't crossed the finish line yet.

The special correspondent for the *New York Herald,* aboard the press boat off the Lizard, watched. "On the horizon far away we could just discern the top of an enormous cloud of canvas," he reported. "It was the *Atlantic.* There was no mistaking her. She came on, boomed out, with squaresail on her starboard side, every scrap of sail set, and drifted over the face of the sun." But the wind was so faint it was 8:30 P.M., nearly dark, before she approached *Pfeil.* The German cruiser hoisted *Atlantic*'s racing number and tersely signaled "Congratulate you." Barr signaled back a laconic "Thank you." He was so tired he couldn't think of anything more. And he was still—maddeningly—not over the line between *Pfeil* and the lighthouse. Some 3,011 miles out of Sandy Hook, wind almost gone, and stars showing, the finish lay another 2 miles off.

"Finally," reported the *Herald*'s correspondent, "there came a little puff of breeze and *Atlantic*'s bow reached the bar of the stake-boat *Pfeil.* At that moment, the big revolving three-million candle-power lamp in the Lizard lighthouse fell athwart her. The *Pfeil* discharged one of her biggest guns, declaring the *Atlantic* the winner." The first thing Barr did was take down his light sails. It was full dark, the menacing rocks of the Lizard square off the port beam. He left his nephew at the helm with orders to put as much seaway as possible between *Atlantic* and the rocks and to steer up the Channel straight for the Needles and the Isle of Wight.

He went below to his log and wrote: "9:16:19 P.M. Greenwich Mean Time crossed the finish line and received winning guns." In a wearily descending longhand, he inked the distance run: 3,013 nautical miles and "Time of passage Sandy Hook to Lizard: 12 days, 4 hours, 1 min. and 19 secs." Then—on the same page—he wrote it again and underlined it *twice,* as if he couldn't really believe it. It was the closest thing to a cheer that Charlie Barr could manage that night.

He was dead on his feet, of course. Worried sick about his wife and what he might learn when he arrived at Southampton. Once he got there, he had to refit the boat for the start of the Dover–Heligoland race on June 17, just over two weeks away. Then he had to take her to Kiel to fetch Mr. Marshall's trophy and run the regatta races there. Only when all that was done could he leave *Atlantic* and return to the States and his wife. He wasn't thinking about anything else.

Marshall was deliriously calculating everything his investment in *Atlantic* and "Wee Charlie" Barr had returned. They'd not only decisively won the Kaiser's Cup—surprising the English race committee at tea—they'd also smashed no fewer than *four* transatlantic yacht racing records. They'd beaten Bully Samuels' 1877 record for the longest, fastest 24-hour transatlantic run, logging 341 miles to his 328. *Atlantic*'s passage from Sandy Hook to Bishop's Rock in the Scilly Isles (11 days, 16 hours, 21 minutes) was the fastest ever. Her run from Sandy Hook to the Lizard (12 days, 4 hours, 1 minute) was the fastest ever. And her time from Sandy Hook to the Needles—13 days, 10 hours, 15 minutes—was the fastest ever recorded.

The magnitude of that margin can only be appreciated in context. In 1866, Bully Samuels had covered the Sandy Hook to Needles course in 13 days, 21 hours, and 45 minutes. No yacht beat that for 34 years. When Jimmy Loesch and *Endymion* finally did, they bettered it by just 1 hour and 29 minutes. Barr and *Atlantic* thumped that hollow. Maintaining an *average* speed of 10.32 knots—night and day, through light air, fog, ice, and ferocious gales—they eclipsed *Endymion*'s 1900 record by an incredible 10 hours and 21 minutes. To date, no monohull sailing yacht has beaten *Atlantic*'s Sandy Hook-to-Lizard transatlantic *racing* record.

Tietjens and *Hamburg* crossed the finish line exactly 22 hours and 5 minutes after *Atlantic,* backlit by a glorious, Wagnerian sunset at 7:27 P.M. on May 30. But a press boat from the Lizard, filled with American reporters, had come alongside hours before that with the awful news. Tietjens had nothing to say. The whole boat went silent. It was too stunning. At the line, they were 13 days, 2 hours, and 6 minutes out of Sandy Hook, having sailed a course of 3,093 nautical miles. By any calculation made before the race, that amounted to a recordbreaking transatlantic run and winning the Kaiser's Cup—but for the fact that *Atlantic* had already broken it and carried off the prize nearly a full day before.

The German sailors on *Pfeil*—brothers in ranks—lined the rails and gave them a far warmer reception than for the American yacht: three resounding cheers. But the thing was done. *Hamburg* had performed wonders. But she was second to perform them and too late. Like the rest of the yachts, she sent a copy of her log aboard the stakeboat, quit the dangerous waters around the Lizard, and continued up the English Channel to Cowes.

When she arrived at 3:30 p.m. on May 31, Tietjens found a telegram waiting for him. It was from the emperor. He braced himself and opened it. It read: "BERLIN CASTLE—MAY 31, 1905— 11:55 A.M.—CONGRATULATE YOU HEARTILY ON BRILLIANT WORK OF *HAMBURG* AND ON WELL-EARNED SECOND PRIZE—LET ME SOON HEAR DETAILS OF YOUR TRIP—ESPE- CIALLY ABOUT WHAT DIFFICULTIES YOU ENCOUNTERED FROM DRIFTING ICE—WILHELM, I.R." Ah, yes, drifting ice. That was the excuse the emperor expected from him.

Lord Crawford, squinting through his spectacles at the blinding Lizard light, swept over the line almost 24 hours after *Hamburg*. It was 8:08 P.M. on May 31, light darkening in the west. He and every man aboard *Valhalla* had long since been informed she was third to arrive.

The crew took it hard until the earl of Crawford went through the big ship, shaking every man's hand. He reminded them that they were the first British flag across the mark. Starting next to last from New York, they'd outsailed and overtaken eight of the fastest yachts in the world. They'd made Crawford's course of 3,169 nautical miles from Sandy Hook to the Lizard in 14 days, 2 hours, and 53 minutes—maintaining an average speed of 9.51 knots the entire time. It was, Crawford told them, "a wonderful showing."

Jimmy Loesch brought the battered *Endymion* over the line only 1 hour and 26 minutes later. Her luck remained rotten to the end. On the morning of May 31, under all light racing kites Loesch could

Endymion under
full sail in pleasant
conditions. By the
time she crossed
the finish line, she
was a wreck.

muster, a fresh south wind carried off her balloon jib topsail. Loesch
set a makeshift replacement: he was running out of spare sails.

When he crossed the finish it was 9:34 P.M., pitch black, and
there was nothing whatever to celebrate. He'd navigated a course
of 3,077 miles from Sandy Hook to the Lizard—shorter than either
Hamburg or *Valhalla*—but it was good for only a disappointing
fourth-place finish. The German emperor had offered prizes for the
first four winning yachts. For Loesch and *Endymion*'s owner,
George Lauder Jr., that amounted to a bitter, last-place cup. The
yacht itself—sails, rigging, and spars—was a jury-rigged wreck.

Captain Marsters and *Hildegarde* and Lord Brassey and *Sunbeam*
finished fifth and sixth, respectively, both crossing the line within
two hours of *Endymion*. Captain Bohlin and the Stimsons aboard
Fleur de Lys followed three hours later. Lem Miller and Stevenson
in *Ailsa* crossed the line fewer than two hours afterward, and Allison Armour and *Utowana* just 41 minutes later. This was a remarkably close series of finishes: seven vastly different yachts, sailing
northern and southern Great Circle routes, covering from 2,996 to
3,223 nautical miles—all crossing the finish line within *nine hours*
of one another. It was testament to the unbridaled competitiveness
of the skippers and the crews.

American Robert Tod and his green-painted *Thistle* finished on
June 1, too: in tenth place, almost eight hours after *Utowana.* But
Tod had the satisfaction of being the only owner to skipper and navigate his own yacht. In a showdown with the best mercenary captains in the world, the amateur Tod had struck a signal coup. Of all
of them, he'd sailed the shortest course across the Atlantic, which
would ordinarily have meant victory among boats of equal size, rig,
and speed. Caspar Whitney, editor of *Outing* magazine, in fact, uni-
laterally declared him the real winner of the race. "If these [ocean]
races stand for anything," he wrote, "they stand for tests of navigation and seamanship. Between Mr. Robert E. Tod who navigated
his own boat, *Thistle,* and Mr. Wilson Marshall, owner of the winning *Atlantic,* who employed a professional skipper at a big figure,
there is no doubt in my mind where the honors should rest." To
Whitney's thinking, Tod achieved the individual honors of the contest, irrespective of where his boat finished, because he had laid and
sailed the shortest course. Lacking handicaps and time allowances,
that was the only credible measure of winning. "If you come right
down to cold fact," Whitney wrote, "the only prize that has real sig-
nificance in ocean racing, is the one rewarding navigation."

He gave a scathing assessment of Wilson Marshall. "Mr. Marshall," he told his readers, "is no more entitled to be glorified for
Atlantic's winning than is Mr. Neumann, president of the N.Y. Central Railroad, when engine 999 is opened up for a sprint at the rate
of 77 m.p.h. by her skilled and nervy engineer. Mr. Marshall had
nothing more to do with *Atlantic*'s winning except to pay the bills."

Lord Lonsdale and the English race committee languished in the
cramped hotel at the Lizard for almost four days after *Thistle* finished, for any sign of the last of the contestants. The 198-foot, steel-
hulled, American bark *Apache,* second-largest yacht in the race,
hadn't been reported by any steamers, eastbound or westbound,
since leaving New York. With all the logs from arriving racers filled
with accounts of impenetrable fog, monstrous ice, and storms,
everyone gave her up for lost. When she finally appeared at the finish line on June 5 at 10:20 A.M.—last yacht to arrive—she had been
almost nineteen days out of Sandy Hook. It gave the race committee a helluva scare until they learned that, though steering the most

northerly route of all the racers, she'd been thoroughly becalmed on the Grand Banks for three full days: logging but 68, 73, and 69 nautical miles. During that time, wallowing at an average speed of 3 knots and less, her owner, Edmund Randolph, and his guests had been fishing.

After crossing the finish line, all the yachts continued past the dangerous rocks at the Lizard and skirted the wild Cornish coast up the English Channel. All of them came to anchor in the Solent, the waterway between Southampton and Cowes. It was the first time most of them had laid eyes on each other since leaving Sandy Hook. When they did, a remarkable thing happened.

As *Ailsa* sailed up Southampton water, a sailor aloft in the foremast of *Hildegarde* made her out and hailed the deck. "By the time we had got abreast of her," Stevenson wrote, "all hands had lined up along her starboard rail. Caps and yells filled the air till we had passed by and edged up on *Endymion,* who repeated the honor." Anchoring well up in the harbor alongside *Sunbeam,* the spontaneous salute was repeated and then echoed from every other racer in the fleet. It was heartfelt and universal. At that moment considerations of wealth, rank, and privilege evaporated. It was fellow sailors, after a hard-fought battle with the sea, welcoming one another home.

Lord Brassey pulled aboard as soon as *Ailsa* let go her anchor. He hoisted a silver flask, drank to the health of all souls aboard, and congratulated them "that everyone who'd left America in *Ailsa* was still on the earth's surface."

When little *Fleur de Lys* limped to her anchorage she looked a fright. Under patched rigging and sails stood Captain Bohlin, Dr. Stimson, Candace, and her bloodied, bandaged Gloucestermen. Half-smashed dories were stacked on deck, and her pumps were discharging water over the side. A British sailor in one of the first boats that pulled aboard whistled at the damage, then saw Miss Stimson on deck and respectfully took off his cap. "You must 'ave 'ad it something rough," he said. Candace Stimson smiled.

CHAPTER 26

The Empty Cup

A bolt of ribbon wins many battles.
—Napoleon

On June 22 at the Kiel Regatta, precisely as planned, Kaiser Wilhelm II presented the trophies for the great ocean race. But first, trailing an entourage of naval staff officers, he'd gone aboard *Atlantic* to see the American speedster for himself. Accompanied by Wilson Marshall, the only person with whom he deigned to speak, he inspected every part of the ship, from the deck to the boiler room. The visit, expected to last an hour, stretched into more than two. The kaiser said little, grunted approvingly often, and left.

Later that day, all the yacht owners attended a dinner aboard His Imperial Majesty's steam yacht *Hohenzollern*. An elevated dais, covered by an enormous awning, had been erected at the stern and plush carpeting laid over the deck. Eleven admirals of the German Imperial Navy, resplendent in full-dress uniform, were on board—each assigned to formally present a yacht owner to the emperor. Yacht owners, as customary, wore dark blue dress uniforms appropriate to their civilian club rank, Wilson Marshall and others in the trappings of commodores.

Stevenson watched the emperor emerge from a forward passageway. Stevenson saw "an imperious figure approaching with a sinewy stride, every few steps returning salutes. So swift was his walk that, before we knew it, Wilhelm II had passed by and assumed a position in the stern of the vessel, surrounded by the unveiled prizes." He was not wearing his blinding white *Gross-admiral*'s uniform; most likely because his German navy–crewed yacht had not won the race and association between the two was distasteful to him in the extreme. He would never publicly associate his navy being second to any. Instead, he wore his comfortable yachting costume: double-breasted, blue Cowes jacket, white shoes, white duck trousers, and white cap. Stevenson, who'd never seen him in person, was struck that "the fierce battle gleam that streams from all the published photographs of Wilhelm II is remarkable in real life by its absence."

It was exactly the effect the kaiser—who loved uniforms and reveled in wearing them—wished to achieve. That day he was not a warrior king. He was a gentleman yachtsman: patron saint of international ocean racing and peaceful competition on the high seas. All eyes and all cameras were on him.

Led by an admiral, Wilson Marshall and his guests filed up to the dais and were presented to the emperor. He firmly shook each man's hand and uttered a sentence or two of welcome to each. A naval aide behind him announced in stentorian tones, "To the American yacht *Atlantic,* owner Mr. Wilson Marshall, the first prize." The kaiser swept the 18-inch-tall, solid gold German Emperor's Cup off the dais and thrust it into Marshall's hand without further comment. The Americans were promptly ushered off-stage.

Adolph Tietjens and his son were next in line. The emperor greeted them with handshakes, a faint smile, and "Well done." "To the German yacht *Hamburg,*" announced the naval aide, "owner Club Seefahrt, the second prize." It was a lumpish porcelain vase from the Imperial Porcelain Manufactory of Berlin that did not glint or glitter. Lesser third- and fourth-place trophies were given, respectfully, to the English yacht *Valhalla* and the earl of Crawford, and the American yacht *Endymion* and George Lauder Jr.

Start to finish, the ceremony lasted only a quarter of an hour. The owners of the other seven yachts that had taken part in the great ocean race got no trophies. Each was handed a framed photograph of the kaiser, with his autograph signature.

Winning the Kaiser's Cup was, undeniably, the acme of Wilson Marshall's life. It didn't matter what Caspar Whitney thought. He and *Atlantic* had won the greatest yacht race in the world—so decisively that he and the boat were assured an honored place in yachting history. For a yachtsman and New York Yacht Club member, there was nothing higher. No one would ever ask Wilson Marshall who he was, where he was from, or what he did again. He basked in the spotlight of his achievement and determined to share as little of it as possible with Captain Barr. As soon as the Kiel Regatta ended, he sent him back to the States by first-class liner. Neither man was sad to bid farewell to the other. Barr went straight home to his wife. In his two-month absence, attended by physicians paid by New York Yacht Club members, her health had miraculously returned. She met Charlie on the front porch of their house in New London, Connecticut, pale, but standing on her own two feet.

Under command of Captain Pagel, Marshall embarked *Atlantic* on a triumphant European tour. Wherever she called, she made headlines. In London he was hosted by Sir Thomas Lipton and feted by Lord Brassey. Marshall went on to stops at Cowes, Copenhagen, Gibraltar, Nice, Monaco, Ajaccio, and Algiers, proudly exhibiting the Kaiser's Cup at each. When he finally returned to the States, he carried the cup back to the New York Yacht Club like the Holy Grail.

For the kaiser, the defeat was bittersweet. He'd lost his own race, but *Hamburg*'s showing produced an outpouring of patriotic pride in Germany's prowess on the seas and renewed public support for building his navy. Waving the flag and proclaiming that Germany's future was "on the water," he easily won approval of his Supplementary Navy Law in 1906, which basically redoubled navy appropriations. The race revealed a very deep and rich vein of nationalistic sentiment, and he put his propaganda machine to work mining it systematically. He would compel the Reichstag to fund even more staggeringly expensive Navy Laws in 1908 and 1912 to outrace Britain in building all-new Dreadnought-type battleships.

The result was nothing short of remarkable. When Wilhelm took the throne in 1889, the German navy numbered but 24 major warships, many of them obsolete. On the eve of World War I, the emperor's German Imperial Navy consisted of no fewer than 441 warships. In composition, it was a fearsome fleet. Its five battle cruisers—nearly as big as battleships (25,000 vs. 28,000 tons)—could steam at 29 knots (more than 33 miles per hour) and carried ten long-range 11-inch guns. Its 17 Dreadnought battleships, belted in 15 inches of armor plate, could make 21 knots (25 miles per hour) while firing eight 15-inch guns, each gun capable of hurling a 1,675-pound projectile a distance of 10 miles. Its 28 older, pre-Dreadnought battleships (those built from 1889 to 1905) were still formidable fleet units; each capable of 18 knots (about 21 miles per hour) and bristling with an armament that included four 11-inch guns, fourteen 6-inch guns, and twenty 3-inch guns. The fleet's 37 modern cruisers, 15 of them armored and packing twelve 8-inch guns, could steam at 26 knots (30 miles per hour). Its 22 light cruisers, while slower, had the range and the endurance to wreak havoc on commercial shipping. Amplifying the power of these units were no fewer than 178 destroyers and 134 torpedo boats, the latter capable of speeds of up to 32 knots (nearly 37 miles per hour). In a period of 25 years, Wilhelm had built a navy second to none in terms of the advanced design and quality of its warships, but still second in size and capability to its nemesis, the Royal Navy.

Amazingly—despite the fact that its signal codes had been captured by the Russians and passed to the British in 1914, enabling the Royal Navy to decipher German radio traffic—Germany came within a whisker of winning the war. Ironically, it was not the surface warships the kaiser had built at such tremendous cost that nearly achieved victory; it was the twenty-one tiny, diesel-stinking submarines he'd reluctantly consented to build. His vaunted High Seas Fleet won a narrow tactical victory over the British Grand Fleet at Jutland in 1916, but admitted strategic defeat by retiring to its anchorages and never emerging again. By contrast, in July 1917 his navy's submarines were sinking 600,000 tons of Allied shipping a *month,* enough to bring the British Isles to the brink of starvation.

But it was the very success of this unrestricted submarine warfare campaign that finally brought America—and his former fellow members of the New York Yacht Club—into the war against him. The sinking of the RMS *Lusitania* in 1915 with the loss of 1,198 passengers and crew—including 124 American citizens, billionaire New York Yacht Club member Alfred G. Vanderbilt among them—was his undoing. Former president Theodore Roosevelt called it "piracy on a vaster scale than the worst pirates of history." The fact that German authorities had published warnings in New York newspapers prior to her departure, stating that she would be attacked and advising passengers not to sail in her, wasn't enough. Neither was the fact that what the commander of the *U-20* saw through his periscope was unmistakably, according to his identification books, an armed British merchant cruiser. Nor was the fact that, as Germany claimed at the time and her manifests later revealed, she was carrying contraband small-arms ammunition, artillery fuses, and gun cotton—the detonation of which sent her to the bottom in eighteen minutes. The fact that she'd been sunk without warning—without first stopping her, inspecting her for contraband, and making provision for the safety of her passengers and crews before sinking her, as politely required by the Hague Convention of 1907—was what outraged the United States. The fact that those 124 American deaths were followed by more, inflicted in the same manner, proved too much. On April 6, 1917—following the torpedoing of the neutral American merchant ships *City of Memphis* and *Illinois*—the United States declared war on the kaiser. Though he did not realize it, the act sealed his fate.

For Wilson Marshall, the war against Germany turned the Kaiser's Cup into a fountain of tragedy. Against his objections, his only child, nineteen-year-old Wilson Marshall Jr., quit his sophomore year at Yale and enlisted in the fledgling aviation section of the U.S. Army Signal Corps. He left his fast, 40-foot schooner *Jessica,* named for his mother, at the Larchmont Yacht Club and reported for flight training at Fort Worth, Texas. He was commissioned a second lieutenant and shipped overseas with the Twenty-second Aero Squadron before the end of the year. Wilson Marshall had never been prouder.

The telegram was delivered to his seaside estate Marina in

Bridgeport, Connecticut, four months later. It arrived on April 29, 1918. Marshall had celebrated his forty-ninth birthday just ten days before. Second Lieutenant Wilson Marshall Jr. had been killed in a training flight on Salisbury Plain, England, when his aircraft crashed and burned attempting a landing in dense fog. He was not yet twenty-one.

Marshall never recovered from the shock. In the sixteen years until his death, he seldom left Marina. The only time he did publicly was shortly after his son's death. He turned the once-coveted, now hated, Kaiser's Cup over to the U.S. Red Cross. He announced he would demolish it with a sledgehammer for anyone paying $5 for the privilege to watch; the cup's gold to be sold to benefit the Red Cross. At a sold-out war rally in New York's Metropolitan Opera House—President Woodrow Wilson himself in a box—Marshall "swung the hammer in a terrific blow." The Kaiser's Cup shattered—revealing to the world that it was pewter, cheaply plated with a thin layer of gold.

CHAPTER 27

End of an Age

The army will march back home under its leaders and commanding generals in quiet and order, but not under command of Your Majesty, for it no longer supports Your Majesty.

—General Wilhelm Groner,
German Imperial Army

The Great War hit the planet like an asteroid and left a pall that changed it forever. In little more than four years, more than 8 million combatants had been killed and 20 million wounded—*twice* as many casualties as suffered in *all* the wars waged in history to that point. Put another way, during the course of the war, an average of about 550,000 men were killed or maimed *every month*. In Europe alone there were 5 million war widows, 9 million war orphans, and 10 million refugees. Four empires—Ottoman, Russian, Austro-Hungarian, and German—had disintegrated. France, Britain, and Italy, though victorious, were bled white and bankrupt. With the exception of the United States, the economies of all the participants in the war were shattered.

Over this devastation, like a kind of nuclear winter, spread the influenza pandemic of 1918–1919. In just eighteen terrifying months the virus wiped out fifty million people—double the number killed by the Black Death in Europe in the Middle Ages. It did not spare Americans. More than half a million—five times as many as had been killed in the war—perished.

The world of 1905—where nobility and wealth ruled, optimism prevailed and mankind hoped—was killed, too. What the war left alive, it left hollow. "On 11th November we marched back 15 miles to Bethencourt," wrote veteran infantry Captain Guy Chapman of the Royal Fusiliers of the day the war ended. "A blanket of fog covered the countryside. We tramped along the muddy road. The band played, but there was very little singing. We were *very* old, *very* tired and now *very* wise."

Nothing was ever the same for the participants of the Kaiser's Cup race afterward either. The winds of fate that had once blown their tall, swift, magnificent yachts across the Atlantic for the world to admire turned irretrievably against them. It cast virtually all of them upon shores they could never have fathomed.

Kaiser Wilhelm II received the news about the assassinations at Sarajevo while yachting at the Kiel Regatta in August 1914. His first reaction was to cable his ministers, asking if it was really necessary for him to terminate his vacation and return to Berlin to tend to the crisis. Told that it was, he petulantly did. But by that time the immutable mobilization schedules, which every nation in Europe counted as either its salvation or its doom—depending on how fast or how slowly its levies could be mustered—were already falling like dominoes. Whether or not the mobilization of the kaiser's precious navy accelerated this process and helped perpetrate the war is arguable. The inarguable point is that the navy he built—the navy he loved—proved to be the eventual instrument of his demise.

In the last months of 1918, despite everything she could do, the tide of the whole war had turned irrevocably against Germany. Admiral Reinhard Scheer—with the kaiser's approval—ordered the High Seas Fleet to make a do-or-die sortie against the Royal Navy. Scheer was determined to give battle and, if necessary, go down with colors flying in an attempt to snatch victory from defeat. It was suicide. The enlisted men and the petty officers in the fleet— who had suffered defeats at the hands of the Royal Navy at Heligoland, Dogger Bank, and Jutland—knew it was futile. When Scheer ordered the fleet to put to sea on November 2, 1918, the crews of six battleships at Kiel mutinied. "They would defend the coast," according to historian John Toland, "but refused to fight a useless naval battle." Their spokesman—the man who defied Admiral Scheer and the kaiser—was a simple coal stoker named Karl Artelt. On November 3, surrounded by the red flags of revolution, he addressed a crowd of twenty thousand sailors, soldiers, and dock workers, demanding an end to the war, "recognition of Soviet Russia, abolition of the salute, equality of rations for enlisted men and officers, freedom of speech, and the abdication of the kaiser."

For the kaiser, the mutiny of the High Seas Fleet was a dagger in his back. "The fact that it was in my navy," he wrote bitterly, "my proud creation, that there was the first open rebellion, cut me most deeply to the heart." The betrayal proved his end. On November 9 he abdicated the throne and, followed by Admiral Scheer, fled to exile in Holland. The All Highest was stopped at the border by a Dutch sergeant and kept waiting for hours in the cold because he did not have a passport.

Lord Brassey flintily outlived his adversary. When war was declared, he donated *Sunbeam* to the British government for use as a hospital ship. He devoted himself to war work, lived to see Germany defeated, and died—just three months after the Armistice—at age eighty-three.

Lord Crawford was spared the tragedy of the war altogether. On the sleeting afternoon in January 1913, he suffered a heart attack at a meeting of the trustees of one of his favorite organizations: the British Museum. He died the following morning.

When the United States declared war on Germany in April 1917, Allison Armour—the gentle botanist and *Utowana*'s owner—volunteered for active service. As a special aide in the Office of Naval Intelligence, he served throughout the war.

Following the death of his only son in World War I, Wilson Marshall sold *Atlantic*. For the remaining years of his life, he remained a virtual recluse in his Bridgeport mansion.

When Germany invaded Belgium in 1914, the United States still neutral, Candace Stimson and her father delivered newly developed antitetanus serum to the Belgian army. They frequently carried it in buckets to the front lines under fire. She later organized Wellesley

College canteen units, which she financed to send to France for the
Red Cross. Her father, Dr. Lewis Stimson, *Fleur de Lys*'s owner, died
at age seventy-three while walking in the Shinnecock Hills near his
Long Island summer home, five months after the United States
entered the war. After the Armistice she joined a Wellesley unit in
reconstruction work in France. She died in 1944—never married—
at age seventy-four. Her only sibling, Secretary of War Henry L.
Stimson, was at her bedside.

Ailsa's owner, Henry Redmond, died "a rocking chair commodore" on the palatial houseboat *Everglades* in Miami in 1912 at
age forty-six of heart disease. He was attended by a personal physician and two nurses. He left a wife, five-year-old son, East Fifty-fifth
Street mansion, and summer residences at Tuxedo Park and Newport. His obituary identified him as "New York Banker and Club
Man"—at his death he belonged to more than twenty, including the
New York Yacht Club, the Riding Club, the Turf and Field Club,
the Racquet and Tennis Club, the Brook Club, the Country Club,
and the Union, Tuxedo, Metropolitan, Knickerbocker, Downtown,
Mid-Day, and Philadelphia Clubs.

Paul Eve Stevenson, *Rudder*'s correspondent aboard *Ailsa,* published his account of the race in 1907. It was a commercial failure.
His marriage dissolved in 1909. He died suddenly in 1910 of unex-
plained causes at age forty-two—alone in the Belmont Hotel in
Manhattan.

In the winter of 1911, in Southampton, England, while having
breakfast with his family, Charlie Barr placed a hand on his heart,
uttered a cry of pain, and fell forward into the arms of his wife,
dead. He was forty-six. In the summer of 1910, sailing the Herreshoff-designed yacht *Westward* in European waters, he had
achieved a perfect racing record: eleven starts and eleven victories,
defeating such famous yachts as *Cicely, Susanne,* and the kaiser's
Germania, Meteor, and *Hamburg*. The yachting world went into
mourning. The *New York Times* called him "fearless, full of judgement, taciturn, studious of the wind, the sea, the psychology of his
opponents and the smallest detail that meant an inch of advantage
in a race. He took the longest chances: often he frightened his crews
almost out of their heads by the spread of canvas he ordered on."

The secretary of the New York Yacht Club, G. A. Cormack, said "Captain Barr was the greatest skipper who ever lived." C. Ledyard Blair, commodore of the New York Yacht Club, expressed great grief on learning of his death. "It will be a great shock to all the members of the club," he told the press. "No man stood higher in his profession than Captain Barr. I am sincerely sorry. It will be a great regret to everybody."

The *New York Times* headlined his obituary "Defeated Kaiser's Yacht."

Atlantic came to a sad end. After the death of his son, Wilson Marshall sold her to American millionaire James Cox Brady in 1918. Her last major race was in 1928, for the King's Cup—a transatlantic contest from Sandy Hook, New Jersey, to Santander, Spain, the first transatlantic race since the 1905 Kaiser's Cup. Her owner at the time was Gerald Lambert (who'd made his fortune marketing Listerine), and her skipper was Charles Francis Adams (secretary of the U.S. Navy and captain of the 1920 America's Cup defender *Resolute*). Conditions didn't favor her. It took her sixteen days to log the 2,939-mile course to Spain—a far cry from the twelve-plus days it took Charlie Barr to complete his 3,014-mile course to the Lizard in 1905. She finished third.

During World War II she did service on antisubmarine patrol. After the war she sat at anchor off City Island, New York. By the early 1950s, maintenance and operating costs for such large yachts had become excessive, even for millionaires. Rusting in disuse, she was stripped, sold to shipbreakers, and towed to the Delaware River to be scrapped. Her lead keel was removed, but before she was broken up a New Jersey marina operator (Ward Bright) bought her. He towed her to his marina in Wildwood, New Jersey, in hopes of recommissioning her, but couldn't come up with the money. Her steel plates eventually rusted through. She sank at her berth in 1968.

Entries: 1905 Kaiser's Cup Transatlantic Race

VESSEL	FLAG	DESIGNER	RIG	LOA LWL	BEAM	TONNAGE	LAUNCHED YARD
Valhalla	UK·RYS	W.C. Storey	Ship~ Steam Aux.	245'LOA 208'LWL	37'	648 net, registered	1892 Ramage & Ferguson: Leith, Scotland
Apache	US·NYYC	J. Reid	Bark~ Steam Aux.	198'LOA 168'LWL	28'	307 net, registered	1890 J. Reid & Co.: Glasgow, Scotland
Utowana	US·NYYC	J. Beavor Webb	3-Masted Schooner -Steam Aux.	190'LOA 155'LWL	27'6"	267 net, registered	1891 Neafie & Levy: Philadel- phia
Atlantic	US·NYYC	William Gardner	3-Masted Schooner ~Steam Aux.	184'LOA 139'LWL	30'	206 net, registered	1903 Townsend & Downey: New York
Sunbeam	UK·RYS	S. Clare Byrne	3-Masted Topsail Schooner ~Steam Aux.	170'LOA 159'LWL	27'6"	228 net, registered	1874 Bowdler & Chaffers: Seacombe, England
Hamburg	Germany HYC	G.L. Watson	2-Masted Schooner	158'LOA 116'LWL	24'	134 net, registered	1900 Henderson & Co.: Glasgow, Scotland
Thistle	US·AYC	H.C. Wintring- ham	2-Masted Schooner	150'LOA 110 LWL	28'	235 net, registered	1901 Townsend & Downey: New York

VESSEL	FLAG	DESIGNER	RIG	LOA LWL	BEAM	TONNAGE	LAUNCHED YARD
Endymion	US·IHYC	C.H. Crane	2-Masted Schooner	136'LOA 101'LWL	24'	116 net, registered	1900 Lawley & Son: Boston
Hilde-garde	US·PCYC	A.S. Chese-brough	2-Masted Schooner	134'LOA 106'LWL	26'	146 net, registered	1897 Harlan & Hollings-worth: Wilmington, Delaware
Ailsa	US·NYYC	W. Fife Jr.	Yawl	127'LOA 89'LWL	25'5"	116 net, registered	1895 A.&J. Inglis: Glasgow, Scotland
Fleur de Lys	US·NYYC	Edward Burgess	2-Masted Schooner	108'LOA 86'LWL	22'	86 net, registered	1890 Bath, Maine

RYS = Royal Yacht Squadron   AYC = Atlantic Yacht Club
NYYS = New York Yacht Club   IHYC = Indian Harbor Yacht Club
HYC = Hamburg Yacht Club   PCYC = Philadelphia Corinthian Yacht Club

Summary: 1905 Kaiser's Cup Transatlantic Race

Vessel	Finish	Greenwich Time	Elapsed	Distance Sailed (miles)	Avg. Speed (knots)	Best Day's Run (miles)
Atlantic	1st—May 29	9:16 P.M.	12d, 4h, 1m	3,013	10.32	341
Hamburg	2nd—May 30	7:22 P.M.	13d, 2h, 6m	3,093	9.84	312
Valhalla	3rd—May 31	8:08 P.M.	14d, 2h, 53m	3,223	9.51	310
Endymion	4th—May 31	9:34 P.M.	14d, 4h, 19m	3,077	9.04	291
*Hildegarde**	5th—May 31	10:08 P.M.	14d, 4h, 53m	3,009	8.82	298
Sunbeam	6th—May 31	11:40 P.M.	14d, 6h, 25m	3,093	9.03	282
*Fleur de Lys**	7th—June 1	2:48 A.M.	14d, 9h, 33m	2,996	8.67	293
Ailsa	8th—June 1	4:25 A.M.	14d, 11h, 10m	3,021	8.70	264
Utowana	9th—June 1	5:06 A.M.	14d, 11h, 51m	3,101	8.91	292
*Thistle**	10th—June 1	12:44 P.M.	14d, 19h, 29m	2,980	8.39	289
*Apache**	11th—June 5	10:28 A.M.	18d, 17h, 5m	2,972	6.61	270

*Yachts who shaped their courses by the northern Great Circle route; all others shaped courses along the southern Great Circle route.

Winning Finishes: Transatlantic Races 1866–1905

Year	Winner	Prize	Start and finish	Distance sailed (miles)	Elapsed	Avg. Speed (knots)
1866	*Henrietta*, NYYC	$90,000 (cash)	Sandy Hook to the Needles	3,057	13d, 21h, 55m	9.5
1870	*Cambria*, Royal Thames Yacht Club	$15,000 (cup)	Daunt's Rock, Ireland, to Sandy Hook	2,917	23d, 5h, 17m	5.2
1887	*Coronet*, NYYC	$20,000 (cash)	Bay Ridge, N.Y., to Queenstown, Ireland	2,949	14d, 20h 30m	8.2
1905	*Atlantic*, NYYC	$5,000 (cup)	Sandy Hook to the Lizard	3,013	12d, 4h, 1m	10.32
1905*	*Atlantic*, NYYC		Sandy Hook to the Needles	3,198	13d, 10h, 15m	9.9

* After crossing the finish line at the Lizzard, Barr continued driving *Atlantic* in all-out racing mode up the English Channel to the Needles to break the Sandy Hook-to-Needles transatlantic yacht passage record set in 1900 by *Endymion*. *Endymion* had posted an elapsed time of 13 days, 20 hours, and 36 minutes. Despite light winds, Barr shattered that record by 11½ hours.

Notes and Sources

General

Firsthand accounts of the 1905 Kaiser's Cup race, though they inevitably vary, are perhaps the surest sources for reconstructing the event and provided the foundation for *Atlantic*.

Captain Charlie Barr's handwritten logbook—a rare copy of which was graciously furnished by the Royal Yacht Squadron—is a pedestrian-looking one for a voyage that resulted in a transatlantic racing record that has yet to be broken. It cost $1.10 when it was purchased—blank—in the spring of 1905. In today's dollars that amounts to about $20, not much of an outlay. In all likelihood Charlie Barr picked it up himself at Negus's Nautical Instruments shop at 140 Water Street in New York. It would have been very much in his character. According to a close acquaintance, "He seemed perfectly content to remain aboard ship all the time, excepting for the morning marketing and getting the latest newspaper." The form-printed log answered Barr's purpose. He was, after all, not writing a book. He was recording wind, weather, courses, daily positions, noon-to-noon runs, and speed. The logbook had neatly headlined columns for listing all of these on its left-hand-facing pages, and Barr used them. There were also columns for logging currents, compass deviations, leeway, and others, which he seldom used. The right-hand-facing pages of the log—under the daily heading "Remarks"—was a broad canvas upon which to write his exploits large. He almost never filled a page; he was too busy racing.

The logs of other contestants were similarly illuminating. These include the personal logs of Kaiser Wilhelm's representative aboard *Hamburg* (also courtesy of the Royal Yacht Squadron) and Lord Brassey on *Sunbeam* (which was missing from all 1905 race accounts). Log abstracts were obtained from all but one vessel in the race (dead-last finisher *Apache*).

An estimated twelve hundred contemporary 1905 newspaper and yachting magazine accounts concerning the race—painstakingly preserved in the library of the New York Yacht Club—provided much of *Atlantic*'s substance and incalculable detail.

A vast number of secondary sources—from gifted authors on works dealing with sport, yachting, shipping, martime history, and biography—added to *Atlantic*'s scope and depth.

Land Fading in the West

The chief eyewitness source of the race is Paul Eve Stevenson's 1907 book *The Race for the Emperor's Cup* (New York: Rudder). This recollection was supported by Stevenson's log abstract of the voyage appearing in *Yachtsman* magazine (June 8, 1905) as *The Journal of the* Ailsa *in the Race for the Ocean Cup* and Captain Lemuel Miller's log abstract as published in *Rudder* magazine (vol. 16, June 1905).

Death Race

Accounts of pre-1905 transatlantic yacht races vary widely. Contemporary newspaper accounts, particularly those of the *New York Herald,* whose yacht racing coverage was perhaps the widest and most authoritative at the time, have been used. Ian Dear's *The Champagne Mumm Book of Ocean Racing* (New York: Hearst Marine Books, 1985) provides an excellent comprehensive overview. James Gordon Bennett's eccentricities were legendary: Queene Hooper Foster, a New York Yacht Club Heritage Series lecturer, was a primary source. "Bully" Samuels' recollections of his packet ship days and transatlantic yacht races are extracted from 1905 interviews that appeared in the *New York Herald, New York Times,* and *Boston Herald.* Details about packet ships were drawn from Charles Davis's *American Sailing Ships* (New York: Dover, 1984), Alexander Laing's *Seafaring America* (New York: American Heritage Publishing, 1974), and John Brinnin's *The Sway of the Grand Saloon: A Social History of the North Atlantic* (New York: Delacorte, 1971).

Third Day at Sea

Reconstructions of *Ailsa*'s days at sea were based on Paul Eve Stevenson's 1907 recollections of the race, supported by his and Captain Miller's 1905 log abstracts.

Sore Hearts and Heads

The events of the 1870 transatlantic yacht race were related in the *New York Sun* (March 19, 1905). The general source for the 1887 ocean race was Ian Dear's *The Champagne Mumm Book of Ocean Racing*, supported by retrospectives of that contest appearing in 1905 in the *New York American*, *New York Herald*, and *New York Daily Tribune*.

Fourth Day At Sea

Again drawn from Stevenson's 1905 and 1907 accounts, supplemented by Captain Miller's 1905 log abstract.

Another Kind of Race

Dizzying varieties of warship types and designs, emergent or in decline, characterize naval architecture from the 1880s to 1905, when *Dreadnought* set a standard for battleship design. Chief sources for British and German warships of the era dealt with in *Atlantic* were Lincoln Paine's *Warships of the World to 1900* (Boston: Houghton Mifflin, 2000), Anthony Preston's *Battleships* (New York: W. H. Smith/Gallery Books, 1981), *Jane's Battleships of 20th Century* (New York: HarperCollins, 1996), J. R. Hill's *Oxford History of the Royal Navy* (Oxford: Oxford University Press, 1995), Chris Marshall's *Encyclopedia of Ships* (New York: Barnes & Noble/Brown Books, 1995), *Jane's Fighting Ships of*

World War I (London: Random House, 2001), and Robert Wilkinson-Latham's *The Royal Navy* (London: Osprey, 1977). Press accounts of the time, particularly from the *Illustrated London News* and the *Times,* also were referenced.

The Man Nobody Liked

Primary biograpical sources for Wilhelm II were John Van der Kiste's *Kaiser Wilhelm II: Germany's Last Emperor* (Gloucestershire, Eng.: Sutton, 1995) and Michael Balfour's *The Kaiser and His Times* (New York: W. W. Norton, 1964). Events surrounding the Blue Ribband competition were drawn from John Brinnin's *The Sway of the Grand Saloon: A Social History of the North Atlantic* (New York: Delacorte, 1971). Wilhelm's colonial policy and aspirations at the time were based on Stephen Lee's *Imperial Germany* (London: Routledge, 1999) and Byron Farwell's comprehensive *The Great War in Africa* (New York: W. W. Norton, 1986). Wilhelm's use of yachting in his naval/empire-building campaign also was widely treated by American newspapers at the time: the *Boston Sunday Globe* (April 30, 1905) provides a particularly trenchant overview.

Fifth Day at Sea

As earlier, Stevenson's 1905 and 1907 accounts, supplemented by Captain Miller's 1905 log abstract.

Spoiled Sports

The sports of society's elite—from the sacred ball games of the Maya (losers were sacrificed) to today's guided mess on Everest—would rightfully make a book of its own. The examples given were from Jeremy Bernstein's excellent book *Ascent* (New York: Simon & Schuster, 1965), Andrew Kaufman and William Putnam's *K2: The 1939 Tragedy* (Seattle: Mountaineers, 1992), Christine Hobon's *The World of the Pharaohs* (New York: Thames & Hudson, 1987), and Peter Conolly's *The Ancient City: Life in Classical Athens and Rome* (Oxford: Oxford University Press, 1988).

Clubs and Kings

Ed Holm's *Yachting's Golden Age* (New York: Alfred A. Knopf, 1999) offers a superlative overview of this era in maritime history. The rivalries involved in what finally became the 1905 transatlantic challenge were detailed in the day's leading yachting publications, including *Rudder, Yachtsman,* and *Outing.*

Sixth Day at Sea

As earlier, Stevenson's and Miller's eyewitness accounts.

Contests of Will

The crisis Wilhelm faced in South-West Africa (and the threat it posed to his naval and imperial plans) is contained in Thomas Pakenham's authoritative work *The Scramble for Africa* (New York: Avon Books, 1991). The logistical limitations of delivering land-based military power by sea, as witnessed by Germany's attachés, are made plain in Donald Goldstein and Katherine Dillon's *The Spanish-American War* (Washington, London: Brassey's, 1998). Wilhelm's passion for martial glory and his complete lack of martial experience are detailed in John Van der Kiste's *Kaiser Wilhelm II* and Michael Balfour's *The Kaiser and His Times.* The grim details and worldwide condemnation of Germany's extermination campaign in South-West Africa can be found in an abundance of contemporary newspaper accounts. The kaiser's theft of the Tod-Lipton idea for an open, international transatlantic race was made plain in a blistering editorial by Caspar Whitney, editor of *Outing* (August 1905).

The Germans

The best source concerning Germany's sole entry in the race are the logs of Adolph Tietjens, the kaiser's representative aboard *Hamburg.* Tietjens kept two: the log of the yacht's outbound voyage from Hamburg to New York, March 30–April 29, 1905, and the log of the race itself from Sandy Hook to the Lizard, May 17–May 30, 1905 (GB 2046: Royal Yacht Squadron/1905 Ocean Race—log abstracts).

The British

General biographical sources for Lords Brassey and Crawford include *Who Was Who, Volumes I and II* (London: Adam & Charles Black, 1947), H. Davis and J. Weaver's *The Dictionary of National Biography 1912–1921* (Oxford: Oxford University Press, 1922), and Ian Dear's *The Royal Yacht Squadron 1815–1985* (London: Stanley Paul, 1985). Specifics concerning Brassey's influence on British naval modernization and construction are detailed in *Past RINA Presidents* (London: Royal Institution of Naval Architects). Lady Brassey's *A Voyage in the Sunbeam,* an account of his 1876–1877 circumnavigation of the globe, illuminates his skills as sailing master, navigator, and the British Empire's ambassador-at-large. Specifics about Crawford's contributions in wide-ranging fields are well documented by the Royal Astronomical Society, the Royal Philatelic Society, the Royal Photographic Society, and the British Museum. Both men were extensively profiled in 1905 newspapers, including the *New York Herald,* the *New York Sun,* the *New York World,* the *New York American and Journal,* the *New York Daily Tribune,* and the *Boston Globe.*

Crown Princes of Capitalism

My primary biographical source for the leading American participants in the race was the *New York Times* (individual obituaries located through the *New York Times Obituary Index*). Supporting information came from *Who Was Who in America* as well as two contemporary sources of the time: *Harper's Encyclopedia of U.S. History: 458 A.D. to 1915,* and *Prominent Men and Women of the Day.* The wealth of turn-of-the-twentieth-century American millionaires comparative to those at the turn of the twenty-first century appeared in *Forbes.* Lifestyles of America's ultrarich are detailed in Matthew Josephson's *The Robber Barons* (New York: Harcourt Brace, 1934) and John Winokur's *The Rich Are Different* (New York: Pantheon Books, 1996) as well as the gossipy "society pages" of New York newspapers of the day.

Hired Guns

The profiles of professional yacht racing skippers hired to take American boats to the finish line were obtained from contemporary 1905 newspaper accounts. Primary among these were those appearing in the *New York Herald* and the *Boston Globe,* both of which were renowned for their yachting coverage at the time.

Greatest of All Yacht Captains

Summary biographies of Charlie Barr can be found in *Who Was Who in America* and other recent sources, but the most detailed and poignant are the 1911 obituaries about him in the *New York Times, Field, Yachtsman,* and *Rudder.* Reminiscences of him— from two of the men who knew him best—are related in Nathaniel Herreshoff's *Recollections* (Bristol, Eng.: Herreshoff Marine Museum, 1998) and L. Francis Herreshoff's *Captain Nat Herreshoff: The Wizard of Bristol* (Dobbs Ferry, N.Y.: Sheridan House, 1953). Accounts of his America's Cup exploits are too numerous to list: Ranulf Rayner's *The Story of the America's Cup 1851–2000* provides an excellent, comprehensive overview. The circumstances that put him in command of *Atlantic* were reported in various April–May 1905 editions of the *New York Herald,* the *New York World,* the *New York Sun,* and the *New York Times.*

Too Many Cooks

The unhappy relationship between Marshall and Barr in the weeks before the race generated headlines in the *New York Herald,* the *New York Sun,* the *New York Times,* and the *Boston Globe.* Both the *New York Sun*'s yachting correspondent (Julius Hawthorne) and *Yachtsman*'s editor bluntly criticized *Atlantic*'s lofty, light rig and untested keel and ballast change. *Atlantic*'s belowdecks layout at the time of the race was described in the log of Frederick M. Hoyt, one of Marshall's guests (Mystic, Conn.: Mystic Seaport Museum, G. W. Blunt White Library, Log 120, Manuscripts Collection).

A World in Waiting

The best, most comprehensive source about international interest in the 1905 ocean race is the New York Yacht Club's voluminous collection (four CDs-worth) of contemporary press clippings. These invaluable, firsthand accounts provide a wealth of detail. Information about the gala *bon voyage* banquet for yacht owners at Delmonico's restaurant comes from various historical and modern-day sources. The extent of the restaurant's culinary offerings can be found in Michael Batterberry's *Dining in America: The Past,* which appeared in *Wine Spectator.*

Starting Gun

My guiding sources for reconstructing the voyages of the yachts referenced were their various owner's, captain's and guests' logs: handwritten or transcribed in full wherever obtainable, in abstract form when not. The complete logs of Charlie Barr and Frederick Hoyt *(Atlantic),* Adolph Tietjens *(Hamburg),* Lord Brassey *(Sunbeam),* and Paul Stevenson *(Ailsa)* provided start-to-finish eyewitness accounts. For all other vessels in the race I've relied on owners' and captains' log abstracts as published in *Rudder* and *Yachtsman* immediately following the race. As might be expected, log observations from owners, captains, and guests differ. Some guests, such as Stevenson aboard *Ailsa,* logged calendar day entries (reckoning May 18, the starting date of the race, as Day #1), while *Ailsa's* skipper recorded noon-to-noon entries (reckoning noon on May 19, 24 hours after the start, as Day #1). On the whole, however, once reconciled, virtually all the logs extant agree on major points.

In for a Fight

Primary sources for this chapter remain the logs—full or abstract—of the individual vessels referenced. Corroborating sources include press coverage at the time of the race and immediately thereafter. Perhaps the best general summary of the race can be found in Bill Robinson's wonderful *Legendary Yachts* (New York: David McKay, 1971).

"You Hired Me to Win"

Primary and secondary sources as listed previously include captains' original, comprehensive logs and log abstracts (condensed).

The Empty Cup

Paul Eve Stevenson's 1907 account *The Race for the Emperor's Cup* (New York: Rudder Publishing) details events after the finish at the Lizard. John Moore's *Jane's Fighting Ships of World War I* (1919; reprint, New York: Random House) provides one of the most authoritative estimates of the strength of the German navy on the eve of World War I. Accounts of the smashing of the Kaiser's Cup appeared widely in New York newspapers in the spring of 1918.

End of an Age

John Toland's masterful *No Man's Land* (Garden City, N.Y.: Doubleday, 1980) traces the mutiny of Wilhelm's navy and the subsequent end of his reign. The often heartbreaking fates of key participants in the 1905 ocean race are best found in their obituaries, primarily those in the *New York Times*.

Credits

Index

Page numbers in *italics* indicate illustrations.